Beyond the Usability

Conducting Large-scale Online User Experience Studies

Beyond the Usability Lab

Conducting Large-scale Online User Experience Studies

Bill Albert, Tom Tullis, Donna Tedesco

AMSTERDAM • BOSTON • HEIDELBERG • LONDON
NEW YORK • OXFORD • PARIS • SAN DIEGO
SAN FRANCISCO • SINGAPORE • SYDNEY • TOKYO
MORGAN KAUFMANN PUBLISHERS IS AN IMPRINT OF ELSEVIER

Morgan Kaufmann Publishers is an imprint of Elsevier.
30 Corporate Drive, Suite 400, Burlington, MA 01803, USA

This book is printed on acid-free paper.

Cover design concept by Cheryl Tullis.

Library of Congress Cataloging-in-Publication Data
Application Submitted

British Library Cataloguing-in-Publication Data
A catalogue record for this book is available from the British Library.

ISBN: 978-0-12-374892-8

For information on all Morgan Kaufmann publications,
visit our Web site at www.mkp.com or www.elsevierdirect.com

Printed and bound by CPI Group (UK) Ltd, Croydon, CR0 4YY

Transferred to digital print 2013

Working together to grow
libraries in developing countries

www.elsevier.com | www.bookaid.org | www.sabre.org

ELSEVIER   BOOK AID
            International   Sabre Foundation

Table of Contents

Usability labs are a great tool for learning how relatively small numbers of users interact with a design. But we think it's time to move beyond that. The technology now exists to cost-effectively collect user experience data from hundreds or even thousands of users. Large-scale user experience research brings together a rich set of qualitative and quantitative data about how users interact with a design and their experience. It helps you improve the usability of a design, decide how to prioritize your effort in the design process, discover which of multiple alternatives provides the best user experience, and even whether you should launch your product or go back to the drawing board. We're confident it will quickly become an indispensable tool in your user research toolkit.

We're writing this book to share our experiences with large-scale user experience studies, which we also refer to as online studies. Over the last decade we've conducted countless studies, some more successful than others. During this time, we've figured out what makes for a successful study. We learned the big things, such as how to design a study and analyze the data. We also learned many little things such as which recruiting method makes the most sense when, how to interpret verbatim comments, and how to create usability scorecards based on a variety of metrics. Not only will you avoid some of our mistakes, but you will end up saving time and money, get more out of your studies, and maybe even fewer gray hairs.

This book is not just for seasoned user experience professionals. It's also meant for those new to the user experience field, or those who simply have an interest in user experience. This technique is valuable for anyone interested in gaining a holistic perspective on the user experience, with an emphasis on obtaining reliable metrics from a large number of users. We wrote the book to be approachable for people with a wide variety of backgrounds and interests. You don't have to be an expert researcher or web developer to take full advantage of this approach. We will walk you through all the basics you need to know to run an online study. We rely heavily on examples throughout the book, and have a chapter devoted to different case studies so you can see many of the different ways this research has been used.

We're not expecting you to read this book cover to cover in one sitting, although we welcome that if you so desire! Rather, we wrote this book to be more of a reference guide throughout the course of conducting an online usability study. We're expecting you to pick up the book at various times during your study, or simply jump around the book as needed. For example, if you simply want to understand what this technique offers, we encourage you to spend some time on the Introduction and Case Studies. If you've never tried to conduct an online test, you may want to focus on the planning, designing, and launching chapters. If you have a very limited budget, you should check out the discount approaches. Above all else, we want this book to be useful, no matter what your background or situation.

We hope you have a chance to visit our website (www.BeyondTheUsabilityLab. com). Throughout the book we will be referring to our website to view or download relevant studies, demos, tools, and calculators. We will do our best to keep the website current, particularly in light of how quickly this technology changes and more research is published. Finally, if you have any questions or suggestions, we would love to hear from you.

bill@BeyondTheUsabilityLab.com
tom@BeyondTheUsabilityLab.com
donna@BeyondTheUsabilityLab.com

Acknowledgments

We'd like to thank Mary James, David Bevans, and André Cuello from Morgan Kauffmann for all of your helpful suggestions, direction, and hard work in the making of this book. We owe much gratitude to Jim Berling, Tom Brinck, Joe Dumas, Lawrence Fisher, Susan Fowler, and Caroline Jarrett for reviewing the book thoroughly, with great expertise and insight. Thank you to Cheryl Tullis for contributing your graphic design talent to the concept for our cover.

Thank you to our case study contributors: Kirsten Peters, Bob Schumacher, Michelle Cooper, Elizabeth Comstock, Charles Mauro, Allison O'Keefe-Wright, Cianna Timbers, Nate Bolt, Tony Tulathimutte, Alana Pechon, Melanie Baran, Kavita Appachu, Alex Genov, Tyson Stokes, and Heather Fox. Your practical experiences provide value and clarity to this topic.

We'd also like to thank all of our contacts at the vendor services for providing us with complimentary account access throughout this project: Carol Farnsworth and John Quirbach from Keynote Systems, Marshall Harrison and Nazia Khan from RelevantView, and Alfonso de la Nuez and Xavier Mestres from UserZoom.

Last but not least, thank you to everyone else who contributed their thoughts and experiences, and pointed us to valuable resources throughout this process: Ian Cross from Bentley University, Carol Kinas, Yardena Rand, and Fiona Tranquada from Fidelity Investments, and Jeff Miller from Burke Consulting.

Bill

First of all, I would like to thank my coauthors, Tom and Donna. Your hard work, dedication, and sense of humor made writing this book a wonderful experience. I will miss our meetings, especially at Mt. Hood. I would also like to acknowledge my sisters, Elizabeth and Laura, and my mother Sara. You bring out the best in me. Lastly, I would like to thank my family. Arjun and Devika, I am constantly inspired by your creativity, curiosity, and playful spirit. To my wife Monika, I can never thank you enough for all of your support. You always believe in me.

Tom

I'd like to thank my coauthors, Bill and Donna, but for different reasons. Bill, you've been great at keeping us focused on our goals with this book and getting it done. Donna, you've taken on some of the most in-depth material in this book and handled it very well. And you laughed at my jokes even when Bill didn't. It's been great working with both of you. I'd especially like to thank my wife, Susan, for your help in editing many of the chapters and in fighting with the style sheets and other oddities in our manuscript to get them consistent. But most important, I'd like to thank my wife for your understanding and support. And for not throwing me out of the house when I said I wanted to work on a second book.

Donna

I'd first like to thank my Mom and Dad who have always unconditionally supported me. I'm especially grateful of your encouragement throughout this process, despite my occasional whiny or panicked phone calls. Thank you to my sister Suzanne, my Grandma, and my other siblings and family members for your love and inspiration. I'd also like to thank my friends, especially Liz, who have spent many, many hours of "work parties" with me in cafes, libraries, and at kitchen tables—I couldn't have done it without you. Finally, thanks to Bill and Tom for your hard work, optimism, and tolerance of my sometimes diffuse writing style and bad jokes. Oh, and thanks to coffee.

Dedication

Bill
To Monika, Arjun, and Devika, and the memory of my father, Lee

Tom
To the memory of my parents, Frank and Virginia

Donna
To Grandma Tess

Bill Albert

Bill Albert is Director of the Design and Usability Center at Bentley University. Prior to joining Bentley, Bill was Director of User Experience at Fidelity Investments, Senior User Interface Researcher at Lycos, and Post-Doctoral Research Scientist at Nissan Cambridge Basic Research. Bill is an Adjunct Professor in Human Factors in Information Design at Bentley University and a frequent instructor at the International Usability Professional's Association Annual Conference.

Bill has published and presented his research at more than thirty national and international conferences. He recently coauthored (with Tom Tullis) the first ever book on usability metrics, *Measuring the User Experience: Collecting, Analyzing, and Presenting Usability Metrics*, published by Elsevier/Morgan Kauffman in 2008. He is on the editorial board for the Journal of Usability Studies.

Bill has been awarded prestigious fellowships through the University of California Santa Barbara and the Japanese Government for his research in human factors and spatial cognition. He received his BA and MA degrees from the University of Washington (Geographic Information Systems) and his PhD from Boston University (Spatial Cognition). He completed a post-doc at Nissan Cambridge Basic Research.

Tom Tullis

Tom Tullis is Vice President of Usability and User Insight at Fidelity Investments and Adjunct Professor at Bentley University in the Human Factors in Information Design program. He joined Fidelity in 1993 and was instrumental in the development of the company's usability department, including a state-of-the-art Usability Lab. Prior to joining Fidelity, he held positions at Canon Information Systems, McDonnell Douglas, Unisys Corporation, and Bell Laboratories. He and Fidelity's usability team have been featured in a number of publications, including *Newsweek*, *Business 2.0*, *Money*, *The Boston Globe*, *The Wall Street Journal*, and *The New York Times*.

Tom received a BA from Rice University, an MA in Experimental Psychology from New Mexico State University, and a PhD in Engineering Psychology from Rice University. During his 30 years of experience in human-computer interface studies, he has published more than 50 papers in numerous technical journals and has been an invited speaker at national and international conferences. He also holds eight U.S. patents. He is coauthor (with Bill Albert) of the book *Measuring the User Experience: Collecting, Analyzing, and Presenting Usability Metrics*.

Donna Tedesco

Donna Tedesco is a Senior Usability Specialist in the Usability and User Insight team at Fidelity Investments. Among other research methodologies, she has conducted numerous online user experience studies over the last several years. Donna received a BS in Engineering Psychology from Tufts University and an MS in Human Factors in Information Design from Bentley University. She has published and presented multiple papers at national and international conferences, including the Usability Professionals' Association (UPA) and the conference on Computer-Human Interaction (ACM SIGCHI).

CHAPTER 1
Introduction

What do we mean by "beyond the usability lab" and "large-scale online user experience studies?" The usability lab has been, and continues to be, a great resource for learning about the usability of some product based on a relatively small number of users. But Web technology now enables us to move beyond the lab and efficiently conduct user experience studies with a much larger sample of users—hundreds or even thousands. That's where the large scale comes in. Traditional lab studies with small numbers of users will usually let you detect the most obvious usability issues. Getting at the less obvious, but still significant issues, comparing multiple designs, or even getting at a user's likelihood to buy your product, takes a new method better suited to collecting data from many more users. Our shorthand name for this new method is online usability or user experience studies.

Until fairly recently, user researchers may have had to conduct multiple studies—often expensive and time-consuming—to understand the complete user experience. This may have resulted in not conducting the necessary user research, leading to bad decisions or missed opportunities, or adding significant time and costs to every project. Fortunately, in the last few years, online usability testing has emerged to meet this critical need. Through online usability testing you will be able to gain valuable insight into the entire user experience. You'll be able to understand who the users are, their intentions, actual behavior, emotional reactions, and their drivers of future behavior.

Through online usability studies you will be able to gain valuable insight into the user experience, such as:

- Is there a significant difference between two (or more) designs?
- What visual design characteristics do users prefer?
- How significant are the usability issues?
- Where are users likely to abandon a transaction?
- Is there a difference in how various user groups will use and react to the design?

Going beyond the lab also means tapping into users well beyond the geographic constraints of your lab. Online usability studies allow you to reach many users all over the world, without worrying about time zones and languages.

We're writing this book to show you the value of online usability studies and how to use them effectively. Over the years we've learned through trial and error. We want to help you avoid the pitfalls. We'll show you when to use (and not use) this method and how it complements other types of user and market research methodologies. We'll help you design and build your own online usability study or choose the best out-of-the-box solution. This book will expand your user research toolkit. We will also draw upon many examples throughout the book to illustrate key points. We hope you find this research method as useful as we do.

WHAT DO YOU NAME THIS THING?

One of the first challenges we faced in writing this book was how to refer to this user research method. Various terms have been bandied about. We've seen it called remote usability testing, unmoderated testing, automated usability, self-guided usability, asynchronous usability, and online usability. We prefer to use the term "online usability study" because we believe it best represents this method without confusing it with other approaches. "Remote usability testing" may be confusing since it can refer to any usability study where the participant and moderator are not in the same physical location. "Unmoderated usability" is technically correct, but it's a bit odd to define a method based on something it's not. Automated usability suggests that no human is part of the mix. Finally, "asynchronous usability" is technically correct in that it's not "live" with a moderator, but some use this as an umbrella term including other methods such as diary studies and simple surveys. As a result, we feel that the term online usability studies is the best available option. Not exactly catchy, but it works, at least for now.

1.1 WHAT IS AN ONLINE USABILITY STUDY?

Before we go any further, we should give you some idea of how an online usability study works from the user's perspective. Jane receives an email invitation to participate in a study, similar to many invitations to online surveys she may have received in the past. She may be intrigued by the topic, or simply enticed by the incentive she will receive, so she clicks on the link in the email to take part in the study. When she begins the study, she is shown instructions about how to complete the study and is alerted to any technical requirements. Initially, Jane is asked a few questions that ensure she is eligible to participate, thus allowing the researcher to maintain an appropriate mix of participants. She is then asked a series of background questions about her experience in using different Web sites and perhaps some questions to help narrow down the set of tasks she will perform.

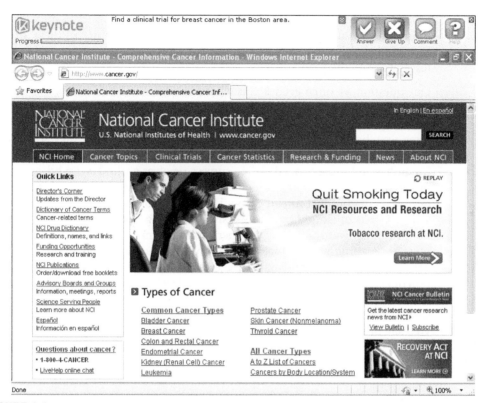

FIGURE 1.1
An example of what an online usability study looks like from the user's perspective. A small window typically sits above a Web site showing a task and controls. The participant is interacting with the Web site in the main body of the browser. Copyright © 2009 Keynote Systems, Inc. All rights reserved.

Next, Jane is asked to perform a series of tasks to evaluate a new area of a Web site. For example, she may be asked to find a breast cancer screening facility near her home. While Jane is interacting with the Web site, she is providing feedback about her experience and answering questions through a small browser window or toolbar that sits above the main browser window (see Figure 1.1). Jane's behavior on the site is being captured, such as the time it takes her to complete each task, the pages she is visiting, data she has entered, and even her mouse clicks. Once she is finished interacting with the Web site, she is asked a series of questions about her overall experience with the Web site, concluding with a few demographic questions. The final page Jane sees is a confirmation that she completed the study successfully and information about how she will receive her incentive.

As you can see, online usability studies are fairly straightforward from the participant's perspective. Depending on the tool you use, the participant may be required to download a plug-in or custom control so that clickstream data can be captured. Online usability studies are compatible with most browsers and operating systems. Participants can take part in the study anywhere they have an Internet connection. The study typically runs from 5 to 45 minutes and most involve some small incentive. The ease of participating in these studies is certainly a driving force in their popularity, from the perspective of both the researcher and the participant.

One question we often get asked is what's the difference between online usability studies and more traditional online surveys, such as the ones that pop up in annoying ways while surfing the Web? After all, we recruit participants in the same way, both techniques deal with large sample sizes, and they sometimes include some of the same questions. The key difference between online usability studies and more general online surveys revolves around *active behavior*. This means that the participant is interacting with a Web site, Web application, mobile device, or any product in some way. This interaction might be in the form of a series of tasks or simply exploring a site and giving feedback. The participant is not just looking at something, but performing some action, such as clicking on buttons, entering text, or making some type of decision. This is clearly different from most online surveys where the participant is reflecting on some past experience or conveying attitudes that have developed over time. In many market research surveys, the participant may be asked to recall some past behavior, such as whether they accomplished their last task the last time they visited the Web site or what they typically do on the Web site. While this is certainly important information to know, we don't believe this falls within the scope of online usability studies.

ARE ONLINE USABILITY STUDIES ONLY MEANT FOR WEB SITES?

Many of the examples we provide are based on Web sites. Indeed, a vast majority of online usability studies focus on Web sites. For this reason alone we refer to Web sites as the type of product or system being evaluated in an online usability study. However, we're the first to acknowledge that online usability studies go well beyond the Web. This technique can also be used to evaluate Web applications, software, mobile devices, video games, and even voice response systems. In fact, there's really no limit to the type of product or system that can be evaluated. For example, if you want to evaluate a phone-based system, an online usability study might ask the participant to make the call to the voice response system to complete the task, and once they are finished, they return to the online usability study to answer some questions about their experience. It's a fairly low-tech approach, but it's also very effective. In this example, you can still collect data about their subjective reaction to the system, task success, and even completion time. The only piece of data that would be missing is their actual navigation behavior through the system. This approach can of course be used for any interactive system. Essentially you are disconnecting the online study toolbar from the systems being evaluated.

1.2 STRENGTHS AND LIMITATIONS OF ONLINE USABILITY TESTING

So, what are the strengths and limitations of online usability studies? What can this method do for you that other research methods can't? How can online usability studies be used to improve the user experience? These are all fair questions. But to be honest, it is not so much about the unique strengths or advantages of online usability studies, but rather the combination of advantages that is at the heart of this method. Every advantage of online usability studies can be achieved through some other user research method. However, online usability studies bring together a diverse set of strengths to make it a highly versatile user research tool.

Before fully appreciating the strengths and limitations of online usability studies, it's important to consider the types of data that are collected. After all, the foundation of online usability studies lies in the data it generates. Unlike some user research methods that specialize in collecting only one type of data about the user experience, online usability studies have the potential to tap into four distinct types of data at once (see Figure 1.2). Online usability studies are well suited for collecting both *qualitative* and *quantitative* data. Because data are collected from many participants interacting with a Web site simultaneously, it's relatively easy to gather quantitative data from a large sample size in a short time period. It's common to collect quantitative data on task success, completion times, click paths, satisfaction, and user demographics, to name but a few. Online usability studies also have the advantage of collecting qualitative data about the user experience. Participants are often encouraged, and sometimes required, to provide verbatim comments about their experience. For example, a participant might be asked to explain why a task was difficult to complete or to provide specific suggestions for improvement. Unlike most online surveys that also let study participants enter verbatim comments, participants in an online usability study are providing qualitative insights during their actual experience, or reflecting on an experience that just took place.

FIGURE 1.2
Online usability studies are uniquely suited for collecting qualitative and quantitative data about attitudes and behaviors.

Online usability studies are ideal for collecting data about attitudes and behavior. This technique provides insight into not only how users think and feel about their experience, but what they actually did. For example, we might learn what they like and don't like, their overall satisfaction, what colors they prefer, their likelihood to use the Web site in the future, and other drivers of their future behavior. We can also learn about their actual behavior on the site. We can see where they went to accomplish each task (through clickstream analysis), whether they were successful in completing a task, how efficient they were in their tasks, and even what information they entered

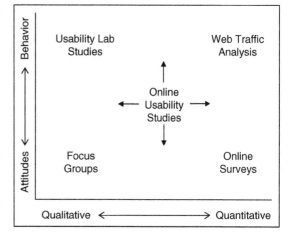

at different points along the way. You can think of virtually standing over the shoulder of a thousand participants, watching their every move, and tapping into their thoughts at the same time.

The following sections describe some distinct advantages and limitations of online usability studies or situations where they're particularly useful.

1.2.1 Comparing designs

Instead of flipping a coin to make an important design decision, we recommend letting the users decide, and preferably a lot of them. The best way to do this is through an online usability study. One of the common ways of using online usability testing is to collect data on more than one design alternative. Perhaps you think that tab-based navigation is more effective, whereas your business partner is convinced that left-side navigation links are the most effective. So, if you are able to build out two prototypes, it's easy to evaluate both design alternatives in an online usability study. It is very easy to fall into the trap of assuming you represent your users. In our experiences, we have been wrong on more than one occasion. It is hard to argue with hundreds or even thousands of users who are sending you a very clear message through data about design alternatives. We have found that online studies can enlighten us on the unanticipated implications of some of the most subtle design differences, such as a simple link label change. It's one key reason why online studies have become a regular part of our work and why we want to share these benefits with you. In some ways, online usability studies can be thought of as "a/b testing" before the product has launched.

SUBTLE DESIGN DIFFERENCES CAN MATTER

We conducted an online usability study in which the only difference between the two prototypes was the order of words on one navigation tab. Because the study is proprietary, let's just say that one version's label said "apples and oranges" while the other said "oranges and apples." Believe it or not, we found that users were statistically better at completing their task using one version than the other.

1.2.2 Measuring the user experience

Online usability studies are probably the most efficient way to collect detailed and scalable usability metrics. For example, you might be interested in identifying reliable patterns in user preferences, detecting performance differences in subtle design options, or reliably measuring the impact of task performance on satisfaction. Traditional lab usability testing is not well suited for these types of investigations because a large sample size is required to obtain reliable metrics. Achieving a larger sample size in traditional lab testing requires a significant amount of time (up to a few weeks) in the lab, adding up to significant costs and possibly project delays. An online usability study allows you to reach hundreds or even thousands of people in a short amount of time. Once the study has been created, you can usually obtain whatever sample size is needed with little or no extra effort for data collection. Of course, the cost may increase depending on your incentive, but data collection and analysis time may increase only marginally.

1.2.3 Finding the right participants

Recruiting participants who meet specific criteria can be a challenge in any user research study, especially if they are dispersed geographically. What do you do if you need to find 100 people who own ferrets, shop online for ferret food, and have never used your Web site? Online usability studies provide a solution by being able to recruit literally anyone who has access to the Internet. You don't need to worry about only finding people in your city that can come into the lab. Anyone can participate in the study when they are at home, on their lunch break at work, or even using a mobile device. You can also take advantage of very large user panels, composed of thousands of Web users throughout the world. Casting a large net for participants also means you can be picky about who participates in the study. Through the use of carefully selected screener questions and quotas, you'll be able to find the right type of participants and achieve the desired mix of demographics. We'll discuss strategies for writing effective screener questions in Chapter 3.

Online usability studies also work well when you need to evaluate your product in many countries. Running moderated studies with participants who are not fluent in the language(s) you speak may be a challenge. Fortunately, some vendor solutions allow you to translate your studies into different languages. At the very least, allowing the participant to read the questions at their own pace should help tremendously, even if it is not in their first language.

1.2.4 Focusing design improvements

An online usability study is one of the most effective ways to help product teams focus on the areas of a Web site that need the most improvement. Online usability studies help identify and prioritize areas where users are having the most difficulty in accomplishing their tasks. A quick glance at task success rates and completion times will often reveal which aspects of the design require attention and their relative priority. When a Web site is evaluated in a traditional usability lab study, you can easily identify usability issues and the underlying reasons why participants did not do well on certain tasks. However, you often don't know the magnitude of the issue. If two out of six participants experienced a particular problem, how does that translate into the larger population? Without the benefit of a much larger sample size it is problematic (at best) to predict how many will experience that issue once the design is launched. Online usability testing allows you to make much more accurate predictions of the impact of specific usability issues and helps focus your design resources.

It's easy for some to think of online usability studies as only useful in collecting a bunch of metrics. That's not true. This technique online allows you to collect a tremendous amount of qualitative feedback about the participant's experience. One type of qualitative data that we have found especially useful is verbatim comments about why certain tasks are difficult. For example, if a user gives a low score on ease of use for a specific task or abandons the task, they can be asked to provide their reasons for the low score or abandonment and possibly suggestions for improvement. Examining the verbatim comments provides guidance about the nature of the problem and potential design solutions. It may be helpful to categorize the suggestions for improvement to see what might work for the largest number of users. To be fair, the richness of qualitative feedback from online usability studies pales in comparison to more traditional usability testing where there is a direct interaction between the moderator and the participant.

1.2.5 Insight into users' real experience

In a typical lab usability study you're generally asking participants to perform a set of tasks. While this is certainly useful in identifying usability issues, it often falls short in understanding what the user's real experience might be like. For example, there might be some characteristics about a user's technical setup such as the size of their monitor, the browser they use, screen resolution, or system performance that all impact their experience. When they come into a lab setting, all that useful information is thrown out the window. Online usability studies collect data in the user's natural environment, warts and all. So, if the participant is using a lower screen resolution and the design you are testing has key information lower on the page, you're likely to see longer completion times and perhaps even lower success rates.

Even beyond the technical aspects, users are performing tasks and interacting with the Web site with all the distractions of everyday life. Most people who use the Web are doing so while doing something else or at least have something else competing for their attention. When they come into the lab, we miss this reality. Rarely does someone have the luxury of focusing exclusively on a Web site for an extended period of time. Online usability studies may be a more accurate reflection of what is happening in the real world because the study is taking place in the same context where the user normally would be interacting with the Web site.

One of the most valuable aspects of an online usability study is having users anonymously evaluate a Web site in their natural environment. When participants come into a lab setting or there is personal contact through remote evaluations, there may be a bias toward positive feedback. Essentially, participants tell us what they think we want to hear. This might happen face to face in the lab or over the phone during a remote session. This is commonly known as the social desirability response bias (McBurney, 1994). In the context of a usability test, a participant may not want to disappoint the moderator, and therefore provide more positive feedback than if that moderator were not present. Online usability studies eliminate this possibility, as data can be collected anonymously.

1.2.6 Where are users going (click paths)?

One of the most informative aspects of any online usability study is where the users go to complete a task and where they get detoured. Online usability studies can capture the navigational patterns of the users and how they're actually inter-acting with the Web site. For example, you might be interested in where users are dropping off from an important transaction. There might be a confusing question or the user might be looking for a key piece of information to continue. By look-ing at the click paths we're able to not only see where the users drop off at each stage, but also the reasons why. Qualitative feedback in real time, as they are mov-ing through a flow, often reveals the nature of the problem. This is in stark con-trast to mining the server logs, which might show general traffic patterns and click paths, but with no way to know if the users were satisfied with their experience, what their intentions were, or why they deviated from the desired behavior.

1.2.7 What users are saying about their experiences

What do users think about the look and feel of a Web site as they are using it? Why do they like or not like specific areas of the Web site as they are looking at it? Why do users have difficulty with certain tasks? What exactly are they looking for in real time? All of these questions provide insight into the users' overall expe-rience. Online usability studies provide the opportunity for participants to enter comments about their experience as they are interacting with the Web site, usu-ally in the form of a comment box. However, it's much more useful when the user receives an automated prompt asking them a very specific question. For example, if the user is taking a long time completing the task and they are continuously active on the Web site, they might be asked what they're looking for, what they're having trouble with, and how the site can be improved to match their expectations. The information gathered from what they are telling us about their experiences in real time (and not relying on memory) is highly informative and insightful.

1.2.8 Saving time and money

Online usability studies work particularly well when you need to collect different types of data under a tight budget and/or severe time constraints. For example, you might want to know what usability issues are the most serious on your Web site and compare it to the competition. But, you may also need to understand user preferences for various design alternatives or even reactions to different pricing models. When you need to gather both qualitative and quantitative data, from a behavioral and/or attitudinal perspective, online usability testing makes the most sense. Instead of run-ning two, three, or even four different studies over a period of time and running up significant costs, you can collect enough data to answer all research questions with an online usability study and save your organization a lot of money!

1.2.9 Limitations of online usability testing

Like any user research method, online usability studies are not suited for every situation. The most obvious situation where online usability studies may not make sense is when you are focused on identifying major usability issues, particularly as part of a rapid design iteration cycle. If you just need to know what the major problems are and to fix them with quick turnaround, online usability studies are probably not the best choice. In this case we recommend more traditional usability testing either in the lab or remotely, with a small sample size of four to six representative users.

Another situation in which online usability studies don't work well is when you need a deep understanding of the users and their behavior. While online studies allow for various types of open-ended responses, they're not ideal when you need to ask the users a host of complex questions or you have questions with many clarifications or nuances. There is only so much that can be gleaned from an open comment field. A much better option is running a traditional lab study if investigating the interaction of a Web site, a focus group for understanding preferences or attitudes about a design, or ethnographic field study to gain insight into your users, their environment, motivations, and unmet needs.

Another limitation of online usability studies is the amount of time you have with a participant. In most usability lab tests, whether in person or remote, you can easily run a session of 60 or 90 minutes. It is unthinkable to do that online. Most online usability studies range from 15 to 45 minutes long. If you are evaluating a Web site with many tasks, you may be required to create multiple studies or only focus on a subset of tasks. Even with a generous incentive, user's attention will start to fade at 20 or 30 minutes into the online session.

An online usability study may not be the best option if you are concerned about maintaining tight control over a prototype design. In an online study, a participant can easily take screenshots of your prototype and send them around his organization. This is not an issue when testing in the lab, but certainly could be a possibility when testing remotely or in an online usability study.

Finally, and perhaps most obviously, all participants in an online usability study need to have access to a reliable and affordable Internet connection. According to Internet World Stats (2009), only 24% of the world's population are Internet users. In fact, only 74% of the population in North America are Internet users, and only 49% of the population of Europe. If your targeted users are not Internet users, you may need to bring them into your lab or go out into the field.

1.3 COMBINING ONLINE USABILITY STUDIES WITH OTHER USER RESEARCH METHODS

Using more than one user research method during a project provides a more complete and reliable picture of the entire user experience. There are four different user research methods that are excellent complements to online usability studies: lab usability testing, expert reviews, focus groups, and Web traffic analysis. Each method can effectively be used before or after an online usability study. Table 1.1 summarizes the strengths and limitations of each of these methods.

Table 1.1	How Common User Research Methods Compare Among Key Characteristics						
Method	Sample Size	Native Environment	Task Data (success, time, etc)	Preference/ Attitudinal Data	Asking Follow-up Questions	Artifact (live Web site, prototype, etc)	Moderator Influence
Online usability study	large or small	yes	yes	more reliable	limited	any	less
In-Lab/ remote usability study	small	depends	yes	less reliable	yes	any	more
Expert review	N/A	N/A	N/A	N/A	N/A	any	none
Focus group	small	no	no	more or less reliable	yes	any	more
Web traffic	large	yes	no	not available	no	live Web site	none

1.3.1 Usability lab (or remote) testing

Usability lab testing (whether remote or in person) collects in-depth feedback on a design (usually a prototype) during the design phase. Sessions are usually 1:1 with a small number of participants (typically 10 or fewer), with a focus on how participants are using the prototype, and opportunities to improve the design. Usability lab testing is a central part of an iterative design process.

TIP
Rubin and Chisnell's "Handbook of Usability Testing" (2008) is an excellent practical guide to carrying out a traditional usability study.

Online usability testing and lab testing go very well together. In some situations we first go into the lab to identify the most egregious usability issues, refine the design, and test again. Once we feel the design is in reasonably good condition (all the big issues are solved), we turn to online usability studies. We usually run an online usability study to validate the user experience of the design. Not only do we look at basic usability metrics such as task success, completion times, and ease of use ratings, we also collect data about the future behavior, look and feel, and emotional reactions. We leverage the power of the large sample size of the online study to give us a clear picture of what will happen once we launch the product. Online usability testing essentially becomes our crystal ball. If we see some major issues, we are able to make the necessary fixes before it is launched. If all data look good, senior managers can sleep well at night!

A little less common approach, but still useful, is to kick off the project with an online usability study, followed by a traditional usability lab study. An online usability study may be used as a diagnostic tool in identifying major usability problems. For example, an online usability study might reveal a disproportionately large percentage of participants who have difficulty with a task or a particular task that takes a long time to complete. Or, a pattern in the verbatim comments is identified, but there still is not a clear idea of the real problem. If this is the case, we recommend going into the lab where you will have an opportunity to probe the participants to see why they had a particular problem. Essentially, the follow-up lab study gives you the opportunity to probe the "why" behind data from the online usability study.

1.3.2 Expert review

An expert review is a common user research method used to evaluate the user experience without getting feedback from actual users. Instead of relying on feedback from actual users, the researcher evaluates the product based on a set of heuristics or guidelines, along with an understanding of the targeted users and their goals. An expert review is useful prior to an online usability study to help identify the most egregious usability issues before the study launches. This is similar in concept to doing a lab study first in that it provides a way to fix the obvious problems and focus on the more subtle issues using a large-scale online usability study.

TIP

Jakob Nielsen's book "Usability Engineering" (1993) is a classic text on using usability heuristics to conduct an expert review.

An expert review is also useful following an online usability study. An expert review, similar to a lab study, can help better understand the nature of the issues observed in the data. An expert review might help pinpoint the underlying causes and provide insight into possible remedies. One of the advantages of an expert review is that it is relatively quick and inexpensive.

1.3.3 Focus groups

It's common to use focus groups as a way to generate new product and design ideas. Bringing a group of representative customers into the same room can be very insightful, not to mention entertaining. Listening to their issues and concerns with your product and what they like about competitive products is an excellent source of design inspiration. We often use feedback from focus groups to generate a series of design options. Once we have a handful of viable options, we turn to online usability studies to evaluate each one with quantitative and qualitative data. We might gather data about the visual appeal, how likely they are to utilize a set of features, perceived usefulness, and so on. Sometimes the design option that is most preferred in a focus group does not win out in the online usability study. While focus groups are notorious for "group think," online usability studies quickly level the playing field by removing those potential influences. In our experience, it makes more sense to run focus groups ahead of an online usability study (for reasons just mentioned) than the other way around.

1.3.4 Web traffic analysis

We've found that Web traffic analysis is useful before and after an online usability study. Web traffic analysis is often used to identify potential areas of concern, such as a large percentage of users dropping off at a particular point in a transaction. In this case, an online usability study is ideally suited as a follow-on research method. It allows you to look at clickstream data of the entire transaction, coupled with the verbatim comments at each step. These two pieces of data are essential to uncover the real reasons why users dropped off at each step in the transaction.

Web traffic analysis typically occurs after an online usability study as part of a validation phase. For example, you may have tested various design options through an online study and determined one design provided a better user experience than the others. At some point after launching the new design you may look at the resulting Web traffic and whether your business and user goals were achieved. Perhaps you are interested in driving more traffic to one area of the Web site or in converting a higher percentage of prospects. Online usability studies are ultimately only a sample of a larger user population. Follow-up Web traffic analysis provides the final piece of evidence to confirm your research assumptions.

> **TIP**
> Check out Mike Kuniavsky's book "Observing the User Experience" (2003), which includes a very helpful section on how to conduct focus groups and analyze focus group data.

> **TIP**
> Avinash Kaushik's book "Web Analytics: An Hour a Day" (2007) is a great resource on laying out an entire Web analytics strategy for an organization.

SAMPLE ONLINE STUDIES

One of the best ways to understand online usability studies is by looking at different examples. Throughout this book we will touch on a number of different sample studies that we conducted primarily for this book.

- **Comparison of two pet-supply Web sites**: This was a comparison of the Petco.com and Petsmart.com sites done using the RelevantView tool. Participants attempted the same set of four tasks using one of the two sites.
- **TerraPass.com Study**: This study was done using the UserZoom tool. It shows how online usability studies can be used for more open-ended research questions. The only task was to explore the TerraPass site to learn more about carbon offsets.

- **Online Photo Gallery Navigation Study**: This example, which was done using a home-grown tool, shows how online usability studies can be used to test subtle design differences—specifically different approaches to navigating an online photo clip-art gallery.
- **True Intent Study of MeasuringUX.com**: In this study, done using Keynote's WebEffective tool, we intercepted visitors to the MeasuringUX Web site and evaluated their experience on the site as well as opportunities for improvement.
- **Comparison of Obama and McCain Web sites**: This study was done on the eve of the 2008 U.S. presidential election to compare the sites of the two primary candidates. This was done mainly to illustrate that online studies can be done quickly, as the entire study, from planning through analysis, was done in 2 days.
- **Comparison of Apollo Space Program Web sites**: This was a comparison of two very different Web sites about the Apollo Space Program: the official NASA site and the Wikipedia site.

Additional details about each of these studies can be found on our Web site.

1.4 ORGANIZATION OF THE BOOK

This book is organized around the chronology of an online usability study. Each chapter reviews questions and issues you're likely to encounter as you carry out an online usability study, from planning through execution and analysis.

The first section of the book (Chapters 1 and 2) provides the background information needed to plan an online usability study. Chapter 2 reviews important decisions you'll need to make about setting up an online usability study. We'll discuss issues such as study types, budgets, and time frames. These high-level tactical decisions will drive a host of other study characteristics, such as sample sizes, recruiting strategy, and participant compensation.

The second section of the book (Chapters 3–6) covers everything you need to know to design, launch, and interpret results from an online usability study. Chapter 3 will help you design the study, including introducing it, writing effective screener questions, designing tasks, and choosing the right post-task questions. Once the study has been developed, Chapter 4 focuses on launching the study. This chapter includes material on piloting, singular and phased launches, and monitoring results. Chapter 5 focuses on what you need to do once all data come in. We review techniques for cleaning up data, such as detecting fraudulent participants, running consistency checks, tests of data reliability, identifying outliers, and recoding variables. Chapter 6 provides you with all the tools you will need to analyze data. We'll review how to handle verbatim responses, interpret task success and efficiency metrics, understand click path behavior, identify the most salient usability issues, and present usability data in a compelling way.

The third section of the book (Chapters 7–10) focuses on implementation. Chapter 7 provides a comprehensive review of some of the out-of-the-box technical solutions such as Keynote's WebEffective, RelevantView, UserZoom, and Loop 11. We'll look at basic elements common to each technology and unique features to consider when choosing a vendor. Chapter 8 provides a set of step-by-step directions for building your own online usability study. Chapter 9 includes a set of seven case studies. Each case study illustrates how online usability studies have been used in a wide variety of situations, including important lessons learned and impacts to the bottom line. Chapter 10 brings all the key pieces of information together in the form of 10 keys for carrying out a successful online usability study.

CHAPTER 2
Planning the Study

Adequately planning an online usability study is essential to its success. You need to make some important decisions before designing (Chapter 3) and launching (Chapter 4) the study, including determining its overall goals, budget, and timeline. Each of these will shape what type of study to conduct and will prepare you to move forward. You'll also need to determine who the target users are and decide how to recruit them. Since there will be many more participants than a typical lab study, and they will be working unobserved, it's especially important to carefully plan how to find an appropriate sample of users and how to weed out undesirable ones. This poses a unique challenge for online studies, but one that can be surmounted with a little diligence.

Based on what we described in Chapter 1, you may realize that an online usability study is the right approach for your particular project. But now what? With any usability study, online or not, it all starts with determining the goals for running the study in the first place. This includes identifying the users and their tasks, the appropriate type of online study, how to design the study, and what metrics it should produce.

2.1 TARGET USERS

The first questions to ask at the beginning of any user-centered design project are "Who are the users?" and "What are their primary goals using this product?" It seems obvious, but often this information isn't thought through or specified in detail by product stakeholders. Ultimately, if the study doesn't target the right users, it runs the risk of yielding largely irrelevant data, and all of your hard work will be for naught!

The goal is to identify all unique user groups of the product. Sometimes the answer is obvious, and the product owners will intimately know who their users are. Other times product owners think they know who's using the product but don't have any evidence to back up their assumptions. They might assume they know the users based on purchasers (who could be "procurers" but not actual users), anecdotal evidence, or dangerously out-dated information. Make sure to get to the bottom of exactly who the users are, and which of those groups should be included as part of the usability study.

TIP

The process of identifying users is discussed by many usability books, so we won't belabor it here. The classic books we defer to are Dumas and Redish (1999) and Rubin and Chisnell (2008).

If there is more than one unique user group that you want to test with, keep in mind that you need enough participants from each group to detect any differences between the groups. This is discussed more in Section 2.7.1.

DO YOU REALLY KNOW WHO YOUR USERS ARE?

In working on the redesign of a logged-in area of a large Web site recently, we asked the product owners about the ages of the most frequent users. They weren't sure, but guessed late 40s or early 50s. We went off and did some analysis of the logins over the past 6 months. (They were all existing customers who we had information about, including their year of birth.) To everyone's surprise, we found that the most frequent users were between 70 and 75!

What are the users' primary goals in using the product?

Again, this should be a simple question for the stakeholders of a product, but it may take some digging to arrive at a reliable answer. Why would users come to the Web site? What are they ultimately looking to do? Instead of taking product owners' words for it, it's best to do some up-front research if possible. Some techniques commonly used include the following.

- *Field research/contextual observations*—This type of user research involves going out to real users and watching them "in the wild" as they try to accomplish their goals in their natural environments. It's also an opportunity to interview them about their experiences and goals.
- *Task analysis*—Task analysis is the process of defining and understanding all aspects of users' tasks with a product, including every step involved in the task and the time it takes, as well as the mental and environmental factors involved. This builds upon any previous user research done, including field research and contextual observations. Using this and other existing data on users, their tasks can be mapped out extensively.
- *Persona development*—Personas are detailed profiles of specific representative users, including not only their primary goals with the product, but also other characteristics about that user, such as their level of education, computer expertise, and any qualities of their personality that may affect their interaction with the product.

- *Market research findings*—A market research group may have collected data concerning user needs and intentions. It's very likely that this will include information about the core set of tasks most users are performing.

As with any usability study, the tasks for an online usability study should be based on real data, hopefully generated from user research methods like the ones just given. If no task information is available, you might want to conduct a more open-ended study, such as intercepting Web site users in real time and asking them what their goals are and whether they accomplished them (a "true intent" study).

ADDITIONAL RESOURCES ON THESE METHODS

Knowing the users and their primary goals is critical to design and evaluation. If the methods described in this section are not that familiar to you, we recommend the following resources:

- Field research/contextual analysis: Karen Holtzblatt, Jessamyn Burns Wendell, and Shelley Wood's "Rapid Contextual Design: A How-to Guide to Key Techniques for User-Centered Design" (2004).
- Ethnographic research: David Millen's "Rapid Ethnography: Time Deepening Strategies for HCI Field Research" (2000).
- Task analysis: JoAnn Hackos and Janice C. Redish's "User and Task Analysis for Interface Design" (1998).
- Persona research and development: John Pruitt and Tamara Adlin's "The Persona Lifecycle: Keeping People in Mind Throughout Product Design" (2006).

2.2 TYPE OF STUDY

There are various types of online studies to choose from depending on the goals of the project, as well as your budget and timeline. While this is not an exhaustive list of the types of online studies, we think they provide a useful framework.

Comprehensive usability or user experience study

Like with traditional usability testing in a lab, you'll often want to just take the "usability temperature" of a site and see how it comes out. Perhaps this is because you want to identify whether it needs improvements (it usually does!) or you don't know where to begin with improvements. In either case, it's helpful to do a broad sweep of the site, with tasks touching various aspects of the design.

As noted in Chapter 1, there are some cases where an online usability study is best used to supplement other methods. If assessing overall usability is the goal, this may be one such case. Although you can obtain a rich set of subjective comments and sense of usability problems through metrics such as task completion, time, and click paths, the results observed are likely focused directly around the tasks that you created. If the tasks are too high level, too low level, or don't span the full content of the Web site, they're likely to miss some usability issues. Therefore it's difficult to obtain both depth and breadth of usability issues with one entire study (online or not). But it's even harder with online studies in the absence of real-time participant commentary and follow-up questions that may lead to detecting problems with areas of the design that weren't anticipated or targeted with tasks. Therefore, if comprehensive usability assessment is the goal, online studies are beneficial, but you may also want to run a typical lab study or multiple online studies to make sure that all aspects of the design are being exercised thoroughly.

TIP

With a comprehensive online usability test, consider also including some self-generated tasks (see Chapter 3.4.9) or first perform a true intent study to get a better sense of users' goals instead of other people's assumptions about their goals.

Usability or user experience baseline

Sometimes the goal of an online usability study is to obtain a baseline against which to benchmark future designs or releases. Online studies are especially well suited for this because of their ability to generate a rich and reliable set of metrics. And metrics are at the heart of baseline and benchmark comparisons. A baseline study is usually similar to a "comprehensive usability" study in that it may try to encompass the full product's usability in one test. But in addition to determining a full set of tasks at the correct level of granularity and breadth across the site, the key is also to determine tasks that won't change over time. They must be meaningful and representative of users' goals with the product because the same tasks will be used in a future study or studies to benchmark new designs against that baseline.

Competitive evaluation

Competitive evaluation is related to overall usability and baseline testing. This involves conducting a test or multiple tests at once using the same tasks and metrics to compare one Web site against one or more competitors' sites. Perhaps this is simply to determine how the overall user experience of one site compares with others or perhaps this is to see specifically which areas of the site fare better or worse than competitors, as well as where ideas can be borrowed from competitors. These contribute to the overall goals of creating a better user experience and enhancing the usability-challenged parts of the Web site. An online study will help to do all of this, again with the ability to do statistical comparisons with the rich data sets obtained. Just make sure to conduct the comparison in the same time frame, using the same tool, metrics, and tasks so that the comparison is clean and free of noise.

Live site vs prototype comparison

Another common comparison is between a prototype for a new design and the currently live Web site. This can be thought of as a baseline and benchmark study in one—you obtain the baseline results for the live site and then results for a new design to benchmark against it. This goal is really meant as a "do no harm" check. There is a new Web site design, but the goal is to make sure that it truly would be a net *improvement* over the current site before spending more money and time pushing forward with it. Instead or in addition to a simple proof of concept, this type of test could also give specific direction around what areas of a new design need to be improved to meet or exceed the quality of user experience at the current site.

Feature- or function-specific test

Online usability studies are especially useful when focusing on a specific feature or function. This can be a particular page of a Web site, a specific task, or even something as specific as a promotion, advertisement, or a block of text. When conducting a design comparison, it can even get as specific as focusing on changing a word or link or Web control. When focusing on a specific function or feature, you can be more certain that the tasks will likely cover most aspects of the design being tested. You are also able to cover a specific aspect of the user experience in a quick and efficient way, where maybe a conventional lab test would have been a waste of time or money to conduct for such narrow focus or not provide an adequate sample size to make a reliable decision.

One of our favorite uses of an online usability test is to compare alternative designs of a feature or function. This is where quantitative (performance) and qualitative (attitudinal) measures come together nicely. Through the online studies we've conducted, we've been amazed at how something as subtle as a link label, spacing, alignment, or a background color can affect the time taken for users to complete a task, perceptions of a design, or their overall impressions and satisfaction with a Web site. Online studies afford the ability to compare multiple versions of something very easily and with precision.

DO SWEAT THE SMALL STUFF

In one recent online study we conducted, we compared 12 versions of the same Web site. The *only* differences between the versions were two terms used. One was a term for a section of the Web site, which appeared as a link label in the left navigation. The other was a term for a subsection of that section, again appearing as a navigation link on the landing page for that section. We had three alternatives for the first term and four alternatives for the second term, resulting in 12 unique combinations. Each participant was sent to 1 of the 12 prototypes (a "between-subjects" design, as explained in the next section). Suffice it to say that amazingly we found statistically significant differences in participants' performance (task completion and time) and satisfaction in using some terms vs others, and ultimately one combination of terms came out on top. Stakeholders were quickly convinced that they were making the right decision in making this change that impacted hundreds of thousands of users.

We think this is a great example of how a minor change in wording could have a great impact—an online study is the perfect fine-tuned instrument to detect these changes.

2.3 BETWEEN-SUBJECTS VERSUS WITHIN-SUBJECTS

If the goal is to compare two or more Web sites or design alternatives, you'll face the question of whether to test these between-subjects or within-subjects. "Between-subjects" means that each participant receives one version or another during the session, but not more than one. "Within-subjects" means that each participant will receive all or some of the versions being tested during their session.

In the simplest sense, a between-subjects design is the cleanest way to test different versions of something. If each participant interacts with only one version, doing all of the same tasks, and being asked all of the same questions as participants on other versions, then any statistically significant results are attributed solely to the version difference. Participants can't possibly be biased by perceptions or prior knowledge of another version because they haven't seen any other version. But in order to conduct a between-subjects test, you have to be confident that there will be a large enough number of participants to detect these design differences. (See Section 2.7.1 for more discussion on the number of participants to test with.)

A within-subjects design is best used when you want participants to compare and contrast different versions of something. Perhaps the focus is less usability related, but more about their reaction to the branding of one design versus another or different alternatives for a new promotional campaign. Another candidate might be comparing a dynamic, highly interactive version of an online tool [sometimes called a "rich Internet application" or (RIA)] versus a straight, nondynamic HTML version of a tool. Here, usability data can be generated for both versions, but a within-subjects test can also yield some comparative commentary and ranking between versions.

When testing with a within-subjects design, it's often the case that fewer participants are required to approach statistical significance, as each participant is evaluating more than one design at a time (and thus each version is being evaluated in more instances). However, the potential factors to mitigate are the effects of ordering and the tasks being performed on each.

WHAT IS STATISTICAL SIGNIFICANCE?

A term you may have heard thrown around in connection with user research, as well as other fields such as psychology and market research, is "statistical significance." We expect that some of you know this term all too well, some vaguely understand it, and some of you have no clue what we're talking about! This is a loaded term that can result in very detailed and mundane explanations of statistics. To put it in simple terms, statistical significance means that any difference you've observed between two things being compared—two groups of people, two versions of a design, two Web sites, etc.—is *not simply due to chance*. Let's say that task completion is being compared for Web site A and Web site B. Web site A yields a higher task completion than Web site B. You can do a simple statistical test to show whether you can be 95% sure that the observed higher task completion rate for Web site A is not just due to chance. Why 95% (you can actually look at a higher or lower chance percentage), and what's the test to determine this? We'll explain more about this in Chapter 6.

Order and sequence effects

In experimental psychology, "ordering" and "sequencing" effects are terms used to refer to how seeing or interacting with one version might bias a participant's perceptions or interaction with the following versions. If all participants use super difficult Web site version A first before using mediocre version B, participants may artificially or unrealistically perceive version B as extremely usable, just by comparison. Here's another example—often referred to as a particular type of order effect called a "learning effect." Versions A and B are two alternative designs for how to order a booklet printed and bound. After going through version A, participants will all be primed (another experimental design term) in terms of the general concept or model for how to print documents, including options for stapling, finishing, laminating, and binding. Even if version B is a different design for how to execute the order, the participants will anticipate the kinds of decisions they need to make and thus will be faster, probably more successful, and may therefore perceive the second design as better.

> **TIP**
> For more information about techniques to counterbalance order, refer to any experimental design book. A common method used is called a Latin square, which is an ordering matrix for each participant.

The typical way to reduce ordering and sequencing effects is to alternate the order in which participants get the versions to interact with, known as counterbalancing.

Counterbalancing can get harder to do and more complicated when dealing with many versions and an unknown number of participants. Another way to deal with this (which we do most frequently) is simply randomizing the order in which participants get certain versions, or even what subsets of versions to receive in addition to what order. For example, there are 12 total versions but participants are to see only 3 per session.

Task effects

In addition to the order of versions being tested in a within-subjects design, another aspect of the study to think about is whether to use the same tasks on all design versions. As discussed, exposing participants to the same task and thus domain knowledge twice in a row may create a learning effect for how they think of and approach the process. If you're using the same tasks for all versions in a within-subjects test, be very careful about counterbalancing the order to make sure that each version is first in the order a number of times.

Another approach that will help mitigate these effects is to have the study tool pull subsets of tasks for each version so that the participant never performs the same task twice across all of the design versions. But again, you would have to make sure that each task is performed on each design version a sufficient number of times so that a clean statistical comparison can be made. Some vendor services can support these kinds of requests with sophisticated scripting, but it can get very complicated very quickly and may cost extra for customization.

TIP

If you want to take a between-subjects approach for the study but still obtain some comparative feedback from users, another option to consider is supplementing the online study with a lab-based within-subjects study. The lab-based study will be easier to counterbalance order as it will be a smaller, fixed number of participants.

Because of these factors, we recommend sticking with a between-subjects design whenever possible! If you have access to a large enough sample of participants, between-subjects is the cleanest and easiest approach. Of the several hundred online studies we've done where we compared alternatives, over 90% have been between-subjects.

2.4 METRICS

An online study allows for collecting both quantitative and qualitative data. And unlike traditional lab usability tests where most of what you learn comes from direct observation, online usability tests require a bit more detective work using task success data, task times, measures of efficiency, self-reported data, verbatim comments, and perhaps clickstream data.

2.4.1 Task-based data

Online usability studies involve some kind of user tasks. People are actually trying to *do something* on the site as opposed to just looking at it. What they're trying to do might be something they decided for themselves or it might be something that you asked them to do. There might be just one task or many tasks. There are several forms of task-based data.

Task success (also known as task completion)

With any tasks, perhaps the single most important piece of information is whether the participants were able to accomplish them, which can often be determined by whether they got the "right" answer or may even be self-identified by the user ("I found it"/"I didn't find it"). But in some cases, there may be shades of gray between success and failure. Even the mechanism used for collecting "end of task" data can make a difference.

Task times (also known as "time on task")

Sometimes it not only matters whether users succeed at a task but also how long it takes them. If your objective is to buy that new digital camera you were just reading about, you're much more likely to buy it on a site where you can find and purchase it in 2 minutes than one where it takes 20 minutes. Similarly, if the users of a site are the employees of a company, they would certainly prefer the online expense reporting system that allows its users to complete an average expense report in 15 minutes than one that takes 30 minutes.

There are at least two main cases where task time may be an important factor.

1. When the perception of being able to do tasks quickly is important. This is clearly the case with any time-sensitive activities, such as replying quickly to an urgent email message. (Note that because most people tend to be very poor estimators of the passage of time, in many cases it is more an issue of perception than fact.)
2. When you care about the speed or efficiency of the users. With many public Web sites, it usually doesn't matter whether some task takes 10 or 12 minutes to complete, at least to the people running the site. (In fact, most Web analytics packages make the assumption that more time spent on the site is better. They think that means the site is "stickier" or more engaging. It could just mean the users are more confused.) But if the users of a site are the employees of a company, then time translates directly to money. The longer it takes them to do a task, the more it's costing the company.

In some usability studies, you can run into a "ceiling effect" in task accuracy data, where most people were able to accomplish most of the tasks. While that's usually a good thing, it doesn't help that much when trying to compare different designs or different versions of a site. In that situation, it's helpful to have task time data as an additional comparison point. As a result, in many online usability studies we look at task times.

Efficiency

Efficiency is a way of combining task success and task times into a single measure that represents task success per unit of time. Sometimes in online usability tests you see what's called a speed/accuracy trade-off: participants going faster but making more mistakes. Combining the two measures into a single measure of efficiency is a good way of spotting these trends. The good news is that if you measure task success and time, you'll have all the data you need to calculate efficiency!

Clickstream data

Some vendor tools allow you to capture click-stream (click-path) data, which show exactly what participants clicked on, how many times, and in what order throughout a task or session. This is another way of verifying task success or can be used in conjunction with traditional task success and other metrics to help you understand more about the experience a participant had with a Web site.

TIP
If clickstream data are important to you, it is one premium piece of functionality that you may have to pay for. As of now, we don't know of any free solutions that provide clickstream data. We talk more about commercial services in Chapter 7.

Self-reported data

In many usability studies you care more about the participants' perception of how easy or difficult the tasks were than you do their actual task performance. In the real world, the users' perception of how well the site supported what they were trying to do is what they're likely to remember, which is why most online usability studies ask for some kind of subjective assessment of each task. This subjective assessment for each task is typically done using just one or two rating scales right after the participant completes the task, such as a simple rating of task difficulty or confidence attempting the task.

Task comments or verbatims

Although this may not be considered a "metric" per se, we wanted to remind you that these will be an important part of measuring the user experience. While task performance data (success and time) and self-reported data can help you identify tasks that participants had the most trouble with, the comments they provide for each task can help you understand why they had difficulty.

2.4.2 End-of-session data

After the participants in an online usability study have attempted all the tasks, they might think they're done, but a critical part of the study still remains: the final questions and rating scales. This is when they're asked to summarize their experience with the site as a whole or with various aspects of the site.

As with task-based data, there are a couple of forms of end-of-session data.

Overall self-reported data

Most online usability studies include some type of rating scales at the end of the session. These can take on many forms, with some addressing specific *features* of the Web site (e.g., navigation, search, site map) and others addressing specific characteristics of or *reactions* to the Web site (e.g., visual appeal, page load times, likelihood to return to the site).

Overall assessment tools

In addition to self-reported questions asking about specific characteristics or features of the Web site, it's relatively common to include a standard battery of rating scales designed to assess the Web site as a whole. Several standard assessment tools are available in the usability literature (e.g., SUS, QUIS, CSUQ, USE). The system usability scale (SUS) has become particularly popular because it is reliable with small numbers of participants and is relatively short (10 rating scales).

Comments or verbatims

As mentioned regarding task-based comments and verbatims, those at the session level can also be an effective tool in identifying and prioritizing positive and negative aspects of the design being tested.

WHICH METRICS SHOULD YOU USE?

If the goal of the study is comparative, such as a competitor study, a baseline or benchmark study, or looking across various design alternatives, we recommend as many quantitative metrics as possible. At the very least, we usually measure task success and task time. If your goal is more exploratory and/or focused on participants' perceptions of the experience, your metrics may be more around comments, rating scales, and perhaps self-defined task success. If you're looking for qualitative usability issue detection, you might focus on task success, comments, ratings, and clickstream data, but perhaps something like time isn't as important to your goals. As always, it's contingent upon what you're looking to get out of the study.

2.5 BUDGET AND TIMELINE

A simple online usability study can be conducted soup-to-nuts in as little as a day, while a complex one can take up to several months. It can be nearly free or at minimal cost or can range up to tens of thousands of dollars if your needs from vendors are specific and complex. We've done online studies at both of these extremes of time and budget.

2.5.1 Budget

The budget for an online usability test mainly depends on the cost of vendor tools and/or services, the method of recruiting, participant incentives, and, of course, the people time put into the study. This section discusses these factors, but because they're so variable depending on your particular situation, we're only able to give you ranges of cost.

Technology costs

Technology costs are the most variable, as the tools needed to be implemented for the study vary widely in sophistication. The study can be implemented for free or at minimal cost if a simple survey tool is used (see Chapter 8 for more information on this method) or if in-house resources are used to build a tool (at a different kind of cost). However, it also can be multiple thousands of dollars when using some of the more sophisticated vendor services that allow for things like

- Screening out or sorting participants up front
- Tracking click paths
- Branching ("skip logic") to other questions or designs based on answers to questions and tasks
- Providing messaging or questions based on specific click events
- Integrating or providing panel recruiting or importing email lists

- Custom coding other unique requirements needed, such as ordering matrices or random task assignment
- Unique data filtering based on parameters, e.g., drilling into task success for people who took a particular click path.

Recruiting costs

Recruiting may be a cost included as part of a vender service if you choose to use one. The cost to recruit also depends on who is doing the recruiting and who is being recruited. If a broad, open audience is being targeted and/or the tool is built to self-screen participants, recruiting could be of no or little cost. If there are customer lists available, it might be as simple as emailing the customers with the opportunity to participate—again at little or no cost.

However, costs escalate when a unique group of users is needed or when using a recruiting panel. A recruiting panel is a common market research resource in which a service will have all types of potential participants on file who have agreed to participate occasionally in surveys or other Web-based studies. Recruiting panels are discussed in more depth in Section 2.6.2. The costs of panels are typically per complete and can range from $2 to $20 or more per complete, depending on things such as the vendor used, the length of the study, and the recruiting criteria used. For example, if 500 completes are targeted at $2 per complete, the panel cost would be $1000 total. Because there are many players in this space who do things differently, the choices for recruiting and hosting the study are not cut and dried. For instance, instead of a panel, lists of emails could be rented. Costs are also affected by whether the vendor tool used to host the study will use its own panel members or imported lists and whether they send out invitations.

Participant incentives

The cost to provide participant incentives also varies. If you're not providing an incentive, there is obviously no cost! The incentive could also be as small as $50–100 won in a prize drawing to up to thousands of dollars if each participant is given a small token, such as a $10 gift certificate. We talk more about choices for incentives and when to use them in Section 2.8. Some of the vendor services and panel services also provide incentives as part of the cost for their services.

People time

"People" time is another cost component that also varies from study to study. Although the actual study execution itself is automated (no lab time!), this variable comes in with planning, piloting, and analysis. After doing this for a while, we most commonly conduct a quick online usability study from start to finish within two person weeks or less (the two person weeks equates to 80 person hours and are likely spread out over 3 or 4 "real" weeks while balancing other projects). Some studies can be turned around with fewer hours, whereas others range up to a person month (160 hours) or more if they're more complex and require more planning and resources. One factor to consider is the numbers and types of key stakeholders and the management of meetings with them to discuss the goals of the study, tasks, approach, and so on. Potential stakeholders and their roles include:

- Design team members: Producing any designs and/or prototypes being tested
- Business team members (program and project managers, product managers, business analysts, etc.): Driving goals for the design and testing
- Technical team members (prototypers, developers, database specialists, QA engineers, etc.): Creating the prototype or providing test accounts and production environments for live sites, informing the technical aspects of designs being tested
- Marketing and market research teams: Representing marketing goals for design and test, coordinating research efforts
- Corporate communication/email management teams: Managing communications and guidelines for communications with external participants
- Legal and compliance teams: Reviewing content from designs, usability study, and outgoing communications to be seen by external participants
- Customer or client relationship management teams: Working with particular segments of users to participate in the study while maintaining guidelines for the relationship
- Vendor contacts: Collaborating in building and hosting the study, recruiting, and billing

In a large-scale study for a large corporation, you may work with individuals from most of these groups to plan the study or perhaps there will only be a core team planning the study, with results eventually communicated to larger groups of stakeholders. Maybe even it's just you conducting a study in hopes to inform a project or best practices for an organization. We've had 1 person total on a study, all the way up to 30 or so very involved stakeholders (this is not recommended!) for more complex and high-profile projects. Obviously, the more stakeholders and processes to work through, the more time it will take to schedule and conduct meetings and to manage the communication of details.

Other factors to consider include

- Whether a wireframe or prototype is used versus a live site and whether person time is included for developing the prototype
- How much time is being dedicated to technology support (e.g., coding a homegrown tool vs using an external tool or outsourcing to a vendor) and time required for study setup in the tool.
- Number of pilot tests and level of attention paid to pilot results and reiteration on study design
- Number and spread of study launches, if multiphased
- How easily data can be downloaded and prepared for analysis or if a vendor is doing analysis as part of their service

- Amount of data to analyze, including all conditions tested, user segments, metrics captured, and whether there is qualitative data (e.g. comments) to analyze
- Detail of the report and debrief

Most typically in our experience, the time required for planning meetings, analysis, and reporting is like that of any lab-based usability test. Getting a prototype ready for the test is also a typical cost associated with usability testing. There are a couple of main differences with online testing: the possibility of producing multiple prototypes for comparative purposes and the use of a special automated tool to implement the study. If the study requires some complicated technological abilities, a tool may need to be coded or customized in-house at a significant person-hours cost. Alternatively, that person-hours cost can be saved but traded for the external cost of using one of the high-end vendor services. If the study is simpler—let's say just requiring task time and success, and some rating scales—a simple survey tool can be used for dirt cheap. We go into more detail on these options in Chapter 8.

Of course, the price of conducting the study should be proportional to the magnitude of the potential positive impact of the results. As with any research study, it's a matter of speculating on the return on investment (ROI). That ROI really depends on what is being tested and what you're trying to accomplish.

2.5.2 Timeline

In addition to "how much," it's no surprise that the next question we're often asked is "how long?" We know that it would be easiest for all if we just said "2 days" or "2 weeks," but as the usability joke goes, we have to say that, again, "it depends!" The variable factors listed in the last section not only impact budget, but they also impact timeline. It also depends on how many people are working on the study at once. What we can do is give you a few different example studies based on past projects to give you an idea of timing of different kinds of projects. For the consistency of all examples, we set the timeline starting in January 2010.

Study A

> **What:** Test of two alternative designs for a wizard-like interface on part of a Web site, using prototypes. Between-subjects design.
>
> **Who:** Internal company employees recruited via a company-wide message posted.
>
> **Technology:** Internal, homegrown tool that was already built and established before the study.
>
> **Metrics:** Task time, task success, post-task and post-study ratings and comments
>
> **Stakeholders:** Core set of design and business partners (about four people total)
>
> **User experience researchers:** One lead, second resource helping on analysis.
>
> **Time frame:** 2.5 weeks

Study A is probably our most common timeframe for a study. The project on which study A is based was a medium-to-high priority project, but only

ID	Task Name	Start	Finish	Duration	Jan 3 2010						Jan 10 2010							Jan 17 2010					
					4	5	6	7	8	9	10	11	12	13	14	15	16	17	18	19	20	21	22
1	Plan Goals and Structure of Study	01/04/2010	01/06/2010	3d	▓	▓																	
2	Build Prototypes (2 Wizard Flows, with Slight Difference)	01/05/2010	01/11/2010	5d		▓	▓	▓	▓	▓	▓												
3	Build Tasks and Questions into Existing Online Study Tool	01/07/2010	01/11/2010	3d				▓	▓	▓	▓												
4	Pilot and Test Tool (2 Iterations)	01/11/2010	01/13/2010	3d								▓	▓	▓									
5	Launch Study	01/14/2010	01/15/2010	2d											▓	▓							
6	Analysis	01/18/2010	01/19/2010	2d															▓	▓			
7	Present Results	01/20/2010	01/20/2010	1d																	▓		

FIGURE 2.1
Gantt chart showing the timeline for study A.

involved vetting the study through a core set of four stakeholders. End to end, this project took about 2.5 weeks, with all parties working on other projects simultaneously. If dedicated solely to this project, it could have happened in a week's time. Figure 2.1 shows the timeline for this example study.

Study B

What: Test of three options for labels for a set of form fields on a financial calculation widget. Between-subjects design.
Who: Internal company employees recruited via email
Technology: Internal, homegrown tool already built and established before study
Metrics: Task time, task success, post-task and post-study ratings and comments
Stakeholders: Core set of design and business partners (two people)
User experience researchers: One lead
Time frame: 1 day

Study B is a shortest-case scenario. It is based on a situation where there was discussion among team members in a morning design meeting about the best label to use for a set of form fields. Differing opinions on the issue made it a perfect candidate to take to a quick online test. Again using an existing online study tool, the study was practically designed, launched, and analyzed same day. Figure 2.2 shows the timeline for this example study.

ID	Task Name	Start	Finish	Duration	Mon Jan 4							
					8	9	10	11	12	1	2	3
1	Point Online Study Tool to Prototypes and Create Tasks and Questions	01/04/2010	01/04/2010	1h	▓							
2	Pilot with Team Members and Iterate	01/04/2010	01/04/2010	1h		▓						
3	Launch Study Internally	01/04/2010	01/04/2010	2h				▓	▓			
4	Analyze and Report Back Results	01/04/2010	01/04/2010	2h							▓	▓

FIGURE 2.2
Gantt chart showing the timeline for study B.

Study C

What: Large-scale study comparing multiple Web site navigational structures. Targeted three distinct user groups and three different prototypes per user group (nine unique prototypes). Between-subjects design.

Who: External participants who were existing customers. Recruited using customer lists. Email invitations sent out by the company's email management team.

Technology: External Vendor Tool

Metrics: Task success, subjective ratings, clickstream data

Stakeholders: Multiple (20–30 people total)

Business team: Three core people with many more consulted

Design team: Five core people, including designers, visual designers, and a prototyper

Legal and compliance team: One core person with five more consulted

Email team: One core person with four consulted

Client relationship managers: One core person with more consulted

Vendor: One core person

User experience researchers: One lead, second resource helping with managerial work such as vendor funding and coordinating with client relationship managers

Time frame: 3 months

ID	Task Name	Start	Finish	Duration	Jan 2010				Feb 2010				Mar 2010			
					1/3 · 1/10	1/17	1/24	1/31	2/7	2/14	2/21	2/28	3/7	3/14	3/21	3/28
1	Plan Goals, Structure of Study, Design Alternatives to Test, Recruit Criteria, Recruiting Method	01/04/2010	01/14/2010	1.8w												
2	Conversations with Client Relationship Managers About Recruiting Methods and Restrictions	01/11/2010	01/15/2010	1w												
3	Designs Wireframed, Reviewed, Visually Designed	01/18/2010	02/05/2010	3w												
4	Discussions with Email Team to Plan Study Invitations (Timeline, Capabilities, etc.)	01/18/2010	03/08/2010	7.2w												
5	Study Design and Visual Designs Finalized and Approved by Stakeholders	02/05/2010	02/08/2010	.4w												
6	Designs Prototyped	02/08/2010	02/22/2010	2.2w												
7	Desined Screens Reviewed by Legal and Compliance Group (Round 1)	02/08/2010	02/12/2010	1w												
8	Study Tasks and Questions Built in Commercial Tool, Iterated, Finalized	02/08/2010	02/22/2010	2.2w												
9	Online Study Content Reviewed by Legal and Compliance Group (Round 2)	02/15/2010	02/22/2010	1.2w												
10	Technical Piloting	02/23/2010	03/01/2010	1w												
11	Participant Piloting	03/01/2010	03/05/2010	1w												
12	Study Launch Phase 1	03/08/2010	03/11/2010	.8w												
13	Study Launch Phase 2	03/11/2010	03/15/2010	.6w												
14	Analysis	03/15/2010	03/26/2010	2w												
15	Present Results	03/29/2010	03/29/2010	.2w												

FIGURE 2.3
Gantt chart showing the timeline for study C.

Study C is likely to be a longest case scenario, lasting 3 months. The project on which this study is based was high priority and very complex. Because the target participant groups were existing customer segments, the content and management of the study, prototypes, and invitation emails needed to be handled with great care and vetted through multiple internal groups and stakeholders. Specifically, meetings were required with:

- Client relationship managers to handle rules and restrictions of targeting one type of user group.
- The internal email team to discuss how the customer lists would be used and invitation emails generated consistently with other communications and campaigns.
- The legal and compliance team needed to review all outgoing material.
- The study vendor to have custom coding done, such as appropriately routing participants, ordering, and randomizing various prototypes and sections, as well as providing participants with random subsets of tasks.

Figure 2.3 shows the timeline for this example study.

Study D

What: Study comparing alternatives for placement and visual treatment of content promoting a new Web feature. Two different areas for placement used, with three different visual treatments, resulting in six unique prototypes. Mixed-subjects design (both between and within).

Who: External participants who were not existing customers, recruited using a panel service

Technology: Free survey tool tweaked to work as an online study (see Chapter 8)

Metrics: Task success, task time, subjective ratings

Stakeholders: Core set of design and business partners (six people); panel service (one core person)

User experience researchers: One lead

Time frame: 1.5 weeks

This study involved using a free survey tool to create the online study and a panel service to recruit participants. All panel services are different, and each individual study is different depending on how strict the recruiting criteria is, but in this case users could be recruited from panels and the study conducted in as little as 3 days. Figure 2.4 shows the timeline for this example study.

As you can see from these examples, many factors can determine the timeline of a study. The size, structure, and political culture of the organization can add complexity to a timeline, as well as the extent to which a panel and/or online study vendor service is involved. The timeline also varies depending on whether the product being tested has already been designed and prototyped. If it's a live Web site being tested, for example, there will obviously be

ID	Task Name	Start	Finish	Duration	Jan 3 2010						Jan 10 2010							
					4	5	6	7	8	9	10	11	12	13	14	15	16	17
1	Plan Goals, Structure of Study, Design Alternatives to Test, Recruit Criteria, Recruiting Method	01/04/2010	01/05/2010	2d														
2	Prototype 12 Design Variations	01/05/2010	01/08/2010	4d														
3	Work with Panel Service on Costs, Recruiting Criteria, Timeline, etc.	01/06/2010	01/11/2010	4d														
4	Build Study Tasks and Questions with Tool	01/08/2010	01/08/2010	1d														
5	Pilot Study with Internal Employees	01/11/2010	01/11/2010	1d														
6	Launch Study Through Panel Service	01/12/2010	01/13/2010	2d														
7	Analysis and Send Out Results	01/14/2010	01/15/2010	2d														

FIGURE 2.4
Gantt chart showing the timeline for sample study D.

no prototyping time needed; however, the planning phases may take longer in this case because the tasks have to be constructed carefully so that they're not triggering real transactions and so that they are resistant to possible real-time changes to the live site.

2.6 PARTICIPANT RECRUITING

There are many ways to recruit participants for an online study, some more costly than others. Participants can be recruited while they are in the process of finding some information on a Web site, known as a "true intent intercept" study. They can be recruited via an existing database they opted into, known as a user panel, or they can be recruited directly through a variety of other means.

2.6.1 True intent intercept

A true intent study is one in which actual users of a Web site are intercepted in real time while they are on the site. This can happen at various points in the user session:

- When the user has first entered or logged into the site
- While the user is interacting with the site, such as upon entering a particular page, feature, or other click event
- When the user closes or logs out of the site

A true intent study therefore targets existing users of a product so there is no question as to whether it's an appropriate user group. True intent studies are meant to ask users just that—their actual intentions for using the site, including what they came to do or look for (and how well they found it, if it's asking on exit). However, actual users can be intercepted to participate in any task-based study as well. An algorithm can be used to decide which users to target for the study. The most commonly used algorithm is the simple "Nth" visitor technique. For instance, every 10th, 50th, or 100th user would get a message inviting them to participate in the study.

There are a few things to keep in mind when using intercepts to recruit:

- The response rate tends to be very low, especially when intercepting at the beginning of or during the session. Users are typically coming to a site with a specific goal to accomplish and, unless they're just browsing, are likely to dismiss any tangential information or messages that are not relevant to their goal. If routing users off to another Web site for a task-based study, it's best to intercept them upon exit of the Web site so that they are not taken away from their task.
- If the intercept is implemented as a pop-up window using Javascript, it's likely to be blocked by current browsers that have pop-up blockers in place. Some vendor tools are working toward alternative solutions, such as using DHTML, Flex, or Flash layers. Others use pop-unders, where the window is in place behind the current Web site so that it is seen later.
- If the goal is to simply intercept a user at the beginning or end of their session or on a particular page of a Web site, this can be done simply by inserting some code in the Web site. Some vendors facilitate true intent studies as well. This is useful for more complex goals such as intercepting a user upon a click event or series of click events. Another useful thing some vendor services can do is take feedback from one point in the session and "pipe" it to a later question. For example, a user can be intercepted upon entering a car Web site and asked what they are looking to do. The user enters or selects "find an accessory for my car." Then again upon exit of the site, the user can get another intercept that says, "You stated that you were here to 'find an accessory for my car.' How was that experience?"

2.6.2 Panels

A user or customer panel is a database of contact information for people who have previously agreed to participate in upcoming surveys or studies. A particular organization can create its own panels from customer lists or a proprietary customer panel can be used.

> **TIP**
> Some commonly used companies for panels at the time this book was written include eRewards, Greenfield, Harris Interactive, ORC (Opinion Research Corporation), Synovate, and TNS/Research International.

How they work

Most panels allow anyone to join, but some are by invitation only so that they can avoid users who aspire to professional survey-taking for money. To join a panel, a user typically has to complete a profile with various details about themselves. This can range from the basics such as name, date of birth, gender, age, income level, and education level to more detailed questions such as computer and Internet connection type, shopping habits, brand names used, travel experience, and interests and activities. Then, depending on criteria necessary to participate, eligible participants are contacted from the panel service every so often to participate in surveys or studies. Panels are usually set up to incent panelists for their participation.

Panelist incentives

Incentives can be paid out either by the organization sponsoring the study or, more commonly, by the panel company itself and be included in costs for the panel.

- Many panels are set up with point reward systems, where users' participation will grant them an allotment of points to accumulate and spend on various rewards over time.
- In addition to point systems, panel companies sometimes also hold periodic sweepstakes for grand prizes as large as $10,000.
- Many will use individual incentives, such as Amazon.com rewards, gift certificates, or just cash.
- For more affluent user groups (e.g., doctors or high-level executives), panel companies will often facilitate donations to charities as the incentive.

If using a panel company's incentive program but hosting elsewhere, there may be some technical coding work that needs to be done on your end in order to appropriately assign unique ID numbers to participants, as well as confirmation of their completed sessions, and pass that information back to the panel provider so that they could confirm participation and provide incentives to users. They may also require that you code the study so that participants are passed or logged into the panel Web site at the end of the study.

Integrated services

Many of the panel vendors provide full-service market research solutions such as hosting a study, consulting with you to build a research study, or even designing and/or building the study for you. However, at this time, most of these services are targeted toward traditional market research surveys. Some of the large online usability study vendors such as Keynote WebEffective, RelevantView, and UserZoom, however, do provide panel services and/or support for panel integration.

If using an existing list of customers or rented email lists, market research companies can also be hired simply to send study invitations out to lists of people provided to them and/or allow you to create your own panel. Why would you use a market research service if you don't need them to actually find participants for you? There are a couple of reasons you may want to do this.

- There are situations where it might be beneficial to have the study invitations sent out by a third party. This may be because it's a competitive study and therefore the sponsor shouldn't be disclosed or perhaps a particular organization has many rules and regulations around how and when they contact and compensate their own customers or prospective customers.
- It saves time and money to have another organization manage tens, hundreds, or thousands of contacts. The organization you're working for may not have the infrastructure to support large-scale emailing and management of study participation. It's easier in some cases to outsource to professionals who specialize in this business.

Cost

Cost is extremely variable with panel services, especially since the providers sometimes integrate with other services for the study. The most common approach for panel invoicing is charging per "complete" (completed session).

> **TIP**
> In survey and market research, the cost per complete is often referred to as CPI, or "cost per interview."

Although panel companies usually do have flexible tier structures for their costs per complete, they provide quotes that are unique to each study. A very basic, short study with minimal criteria can cost as little as $2 per complete. Higher costs are determined by things such as lower anticipated drop-off rates (e.g., the study is especially complex, long, and/or has many questions or a low incentive), and most commonly by stricter recruiting criteria. For instance, if a study involves finding panelists who are turning 18 in the month of June, have a pet rabbit, and are interested in becoming acrobats, the panel company is likely to either tell you to get lost or charge an extremely high fee. Joking aside, you can see how panel costs can become increasingly high for unique requirements. This is often referred to as "incidence," and the incidence level affects cost. We've heard of charges upward of $30 per complete for recruiting very unique, low-incidence user groups. If using the panel company to also build and/or host the study, the per-complete rate may increase to upward of $100 per complete depending on the complexity of their involvement.

Depending on the agreement you have established with a panel service, they may either cap the study at a predefined number of completes you specify (e.g., 500) or have no cap and charge for however many completes came through. Some companies will lower the cost per complete as larger numbers of participants complete the study. For example, a contract may specify that you will be charged $10 per complete up to 200, $8 per complete up to 300, $6 per complete up to 400, and so on. There is also the possibility of setting up a master contract with some panel companies for a lower cost structure if their services are needed frequently.

Quality of panelists

An obvious concern of user panels is the integrity of the participants and their data. As online surveys have become more popular, various Web sites and forums have appeared where people share information about how to get the most incentives for the least effort. In fact, it seems as though some people are making survey-taking a full time job. Users of these sites point each other to surveys and give tips on how much they can make in a week or month. If you look at these forums you'll find that people also trade tips on how to skip through surveys without trying or putting in a good faith effort. These participants are often referred to as "mental cheaters." They'll engage in activities such as "flat lining," where they enter the same number for every rating scale just to get it done as quickly as possible.

> **TIP**
> Mental cheaters are also referred to as "satisficers," a combination of the words "satisfy" and "suffice." Jon Krosnick (1991) developed a theory of the satisficing behavior of survey respondents.

Studies show that the quality of panelists' data differs from panel to panel. Burke R&D's Quality Panel Research (2008) had participants from various user panels participate in a survey in order to measure the incidence of fraudulence across them. One of their measures was the percentage of participants who claimed they had heard of a brand name that didn't actually exist. The results are illustrated in Figure 2.5. Across 24 different panels, there was a range of between 2 and 11% of participants who claimed they had heard of a nonexistent brand.

It's clear that some panels are more riddled with fraudulent participants than others. Market research companies are aware of this and the best ones are making strides toward preventing these types of panelists from participating in studies. Some of the methods they use include:

- Work by invitation only based on purchases users have made or organizations they're affiliated with
- Use point systems: because a panelist has to complete many studies over time to accumulate enough points for valuable rewards, they are more likely to put forth good-faith effort in each study so as not to be excluded from the panel altogether
- Limit participation in studies to a certain number per time period (e.g., twice per month) so that panelists don't become "professional survey takers," at least within that panel
- Verify the participants' identity and profile data by doing a check of their IP address, zip code, and street address against public record
- Remove or blacklist participants after they are recognized as fraudulent from a particular study, e.g., complete surveys too quickly to have put forth good effort

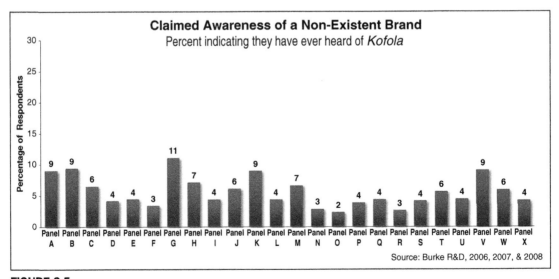

FIGURE 2.5
A graph from Burke R&D's Quality Research Panel in 2008 showing the incidence of participants in various panels who claimed they knew about a brand name that didn't exist.

- Maintain and refresh databases of participants to make sure they're based on recent profile data, etc.
- Devise and run algorithms against data to detect any cheating behavior such as flat lining
- Help with screener and survey design to create "speed traps," also known as "red herring" questions. We discuss more about these methods in Chapter 3.
- Find the necessary participants directly without asking panelists to hand off or forward the study to the appropriate person

Although the potential for some participants who misrepresent themselves and mental cheaters may make it tempting to give up and avoid any kind of online study, we still feel that you can overcome this bias. If using a panel, work with them to determine what they do to eliminate these types of participants. In your own study design, it starts with screening out participants who misrepresent themselves (see Chapter 3.2.2), as well as putting into place some speed traps in the study (see Chapter 3.8.3). Finally, there are some methods you can use to weed out the bad seeds from your data set after the study, as described in Chapter 5.

2.6.3 Direct and targeted recruiting

The third way to recruit is in a direct and targeted way. That is, rather than intercepting users or going through a panel to recruit them, you're soliciting them directly. There are a few ways of going about this.

Emailing

If you have a predefined list of potential participants, you can email invitations to them directly. This may be a customer list you have or perhaps an email list that you rented from a market research company. Just be careful about a few things. First, some email list brokers are not very careful about the quality of their participants. Participation rate can also be lower than usual if people did not know that they were explicitly being added to a list. As with panels, do your homework about how the email addresses were obtained and how any user profiling data were collected and are being maintained.

Second, if using customer lists, there may be some rules in an organization with regard to how you are communicating with them and what you say. Make sure to check into this first before proceeding.

Third, if you're planning on sending out hundreds or thousands of invitations from a particular email address, think about the implications of doing so. For instance, the host server may not be built to support such "stress" at once and could crash or cause other issues as a result. Many people also use automated responses such as "Out of Office" messages, which can fill up an inbox quickly. If the invitation is coming directly from one person instead of an entity such as a generic company messaging system, it may cause participants to respond with inquiries or requests to be taken off a mailing list. Our first suggestion is to try to use a system that is built to send out mass email at once. There may be a group that manages this inside the organization or you can pay a third-party hosting service to handle communications (often the same market research companies that rent out lists and offer panelists). If doing so is not possible or too costly, we recommend doing the following:

- Stagger or phase launches with email groups. Essentially, send invitations to one small group, wait a day or two, send invitations to another small group, and so on. This can also have positive side effects, as discussed in Chapter 4.2.2.
- Send out invitations from a generic inbox. This doesn't mean one of those nonsensical email addresses that are detected or perceived as spam! This means that rather than having one particular person's inbox take the ownership and technical backlash of being the inviter, there could be one inbox that is set up solely to handle it. If you have the luxury of naming a new address, try to keep it something legitimate sounding, such as usabilitystudies@abccorp.com. If you plan to monitor the inbox, consider putting into place some filters to sort different types of email coming in. For example, anything that says "Out of Office" in the header is likely a Microsoft Outlook "Out of Office" message and can be sent directly to another folder or deleted.
- Work with technical partners to ensure that email servers are able to handle mass outbound and inbound messages. The servers might need to be "stress tested" first.

TIPS FOR NOT GETTING CAUGHT BY SPAM FILTERS

After you've gone to all the trouble of designing and building your online study, you don't want your messages recruiting potential participants to get caught by spam filters. Although spam filters are constantly evolving to do the best they can to detect true spam, there are some guidelines that should help you prevent your messages from getting lumped in with spam. Here are some of the more important guidelines.

- Make sure that your message is structured correctly from a technical perspective, with proper headers, including a valid "from" address and associated user name, and from a valid domain. Include a short but descriptive subject line.
- Avoid using words or phrases that seem particularly "spammy," including "free," "click here," "prize," "money," or "opportunity of a lifetime." Obviously you should also avoid specific product names that have come to be associated with spam. (You probably don't want to use a drawing for a Rolex watch as your incentive!) Make sure there are no misspellings, which often are hints of spam. Also avoid the use of ALL CAPS and extra punctuation marks!!!!

- If you are using HTML email, make sure you include a reasonable amount of content in the message relative to any images. (A message that's composed primarily of images is often treated as spam.) Don't use invisible text. Make sure your HTML is clean and simple, free of extraneous markup. Include a plain text section in the message as well.
- Avoid sending your message to multiple recipients within the same company at the same time. Their firewall might interpret it as a spam attack.
- Test your message by sending it to multiple email accounts you've set up, including Gmail, Yahoo, HotMail, and as many others as you can.

Posting on the Internet

The Internet is a big place and there are many opportunities to post on Web sites, including blogs, forums, newsletters, and even through search engine marketing. One commonly used Web site is www.craigslist.org. If you post on the Internet, consider building in some careful screening criteria to weed out inappropriate or fraudulent participants. Random posting rather than targeted emailing has a higher chance of eliciting people who may not be right for the study or may just be in it for the incentive.

Posting in paper ads

It is possible to recruit for an online study in a physical medium, such as a newspaper classified ad. It can be useful in certain situations—for instance, posting to a business or financial journal to elicit high-level executives and financially savvy individuals. However, it also adds a layer of complexity; because readers must remember or keep the email address or URL provided in the ad, the response rate may not be as high as in email. It also opens up some possibilities for individuals who are not that computer savvy to participate, which may or may not be appropriate for the targeted population. If you are using this route, consider supplementing it with another recruiting method for both of these reasons.

Friends, family, and co-workers

We'll talk about something called "convenience sampling" in Section 2.7, and recruiting friends, family, or coworkers is the ultimate type of convenience sampling. We only use this method in an act of desperation because there is a lot of bias that comes into play with these groups. Co-workers can be too close to the content or too familiar with the principles of Web design and usability. Friends and family might be part of a targeted population for a Web site, but their knowledge of you and your work, and perhaps their intrinsic motivation to please you or approach the product with particularly positive or negative perceptions, can all bias the results of data. As a result, we don't typically recommend using this method unless you're recruiting *friends of* friends, family, or co-workers who are at least a step removed. Another option is to use these types of people for some slice of the pilot testing.

2.7 PARTICIPANT SAMPLING

One of the most important decisions in conducting an online study is how to obtain a sample of participants. The first goal is to identify the number of participants needed to complete the study. Then you'll want to determine the appropriate sampling method needed to obtain the participants.

This section touches on some complex topics, including statistical effects, significance, and sampling techniques. These are typically not a focus in lab-based usability testing, as it involves such a small number of participants. But because online studies involve large numbers of participants, these are useful concepts to become familiar with. You may not internalize them in one sitting, but they will at least provide a sense of things to look for and think about when recruiting participants.

2.7.1 Number of participants

The appropriate number of users is a question we often hear regarding online usability studies, and it's also a question that is frequently debated. Statistical purists might argue that you need several hundred participants in order to see anything meaningful in the data. There are formulas on the Internet and in stats books that determine those lofty numbers of participants that are needed. Although the more participants the better, based on our practical experience, hundreds are not necessarily a requirement. Let's say that you're looking across two alternative designs and want to see whether there is a difference in task success. You have 15 participants in each group, 30 total. Whether or not you'll see a difference depends on the following.

- *Magnitude of the effect.* If it's obvious and anticipated at a glance that Web site A will perform much worse than Web site B, it won't take many data points to approach a significant difference.
- *Significance level.* You may have heard people throwing around terms such as "alpha level," "power," "confidence level," and "probability level" and cite numbers such as "$p < 0.01$," "$p < 0.05$," or "$p < 0.10$." This is the degree to which any differences seen may be due to chance. It's basically how much error you're willing to allow to sneak into your data as noise. An alpha level of 0.01 is being *extremely* conservative and leaving very little (1%) up to chance, and an alpha level of 0.10 is allowing a little more (up to 10%) up to chance. The less conservative you're willing to be (and higher 'p' level), the more likely you'll see statistical differences, but keep in mind that there is some level of "noise" in the data.
- *Repeated measures/pairing.* If you're conducting a within-subjects test where all participants see all versions, the statistical test you do will take into account that the *same person* worked with all versions and therefore calculate data on one version relative to the others. "Repeated" or "paired" measures are stronger, which is why this design requires fewer participants to see an effect.

- *Expected variation of the sample.* This one is often hard to detect, but one way of looking at it is basically how differently you expect the participants to behave or respond to things. If there is a wide variety of user types and characteristics, there is likely to be a larger variance and therefore more participants will be needed. However, let's say that the targeted user group is customer service associates who were all trained to interact with their tools in a certain way. Perhaps there's a chance of a smaller variance with this group in terms of how they'll perform on tasks. Smaller variance in data will lend itself better to seeing any statistical differences between versions of a design.

We've successfully seen results with as few as 30 participants. But we recommend at least 50 to 100 participants at a minimum (per distinct user segment), depending on some of the things discussed earlier. Think about what is being tested, the user groups being tested, and what it is that's being measured. It also helps to look at pilot data to see how the results are coming in prior to the planned study launch. If there is a wide variation in pilot results, you might want to play it safe with a larger sample size.

TIP

Remember to pad the number of participants a little more to account for participants who mentally cheat. As discussed in Chapter 5.3, you'll be able to clean up data to remove any of these types of respondents.

2.7.2 Sampling techniques

There are two main types of samples: probability and nonprobability samples. Nonprobability samples are cases where you do not know of every unique member of the population in question (i.e., the entire user group in our case). Another way to describe it is when every member of the population *does not* have an equal chance of being invited to participate. Probability samples are when you do know of every unique member of the population and therefore each has a probabilistic chance of being invited for the sample (e.g., 100 users of a product, each has a 1/100 chance of being invited). Here's a taste of a couple of common nonprobability sampling techniques.

- *Convenience sampling.* This is the most common nonprobability sample. You might send invitations to people in your company, students from a school you're affiliated with, the city you live in, and so on. It's referred to as "convenience" sampling because unless the targeted user group is truly limited to those people, it is likely introducing some bias to recruit just a particular slice of the population.
- *Snowball sampling.* This is a type of convenience sampling in which those participants invited invite other participants and so on to create a pyramid effect.

With probability sampling, you can choose a more scientific way to sample because you know the number and characteristics of the true population.

For instance, a particular product has a small contingent of users. Some of the common techniques include the following.

- *Simple random sampling.* This is a known population of users from which you take a random sample via some means, such as a program or application, an Excel formula, or a simple "pick out of a hat" lottery.
- *Stratified sampling.* You assign everyone in the population to a specific (but meaningful) group and then take another probability sample within each category. The users are therefore chosen randomly, but there is a representation from each "strata." Note that the nonprobability sampling method that correlates to stratified sampling is called quota sampling. It means that despite not knowing the true population, you divide the users you know about into groups and still try to get some representation from that group (usually via convenience sampling).
- *Systematic random sampling (also known as just systematic sampling).* The idea here is that you list all of the users in no particular order (in fact, it should not be in any logical order) and then pick every Nth user. You define what N is; for instance, if there are 1000 users total and the goal is to invite 500 to participate, you'd simply take every second person from the list and invite them.
- *Multistage sampling.* This takes different samples in different ways to eliminate bias. For example, you may do a random sample, then stratified, and so on.

Chances are that the number and characteristics of users for a product you're testing may not be entirely known, especially for Web sites, and still further for Web sites that don't require users to register or create an account (and thus can't be tracked). If using a generic participant panel, it's likely a convenience sample and is not necessary to worry about probability sampling techniques. However, in cases where you're providing a recruiting service with part of a customer or user list from which to invite people, you may want to use one of the probability sampling techniques discussed. For example, if there are 10,000 customers on a customer list and it needs to be whittled down to a 1000 person sample for study invitations, you might use a simple random or stratified sampling method to get a representative sample of customers.

If recruiting by posting on the Web via message boards, forums, or in newspaper ads, rather than using email invitations, it's likely a snowball sample as people might forward on the information to others that they know. Just be aware that this comes with a self-selection bias. This type of bias is where the participants who choose to participate may have certain outstanding and overrepresentative characteristics, such as being the ones who particularly love and/or hate the Web site enough to participate. One way to minimize this bias is to use a phased launching strategy (breaking up the study launch into multiple groups).

TIP

Check out http://stattrek.com/Reading/Sampling.aspx for references to some good books on sampling methods and the biases associated with them.

2.8 PARTICIPANT INCENTIVES

Whether to offer participant incentives, and how much, can be hotly debated among usability and market research professionals. Not surprisingly, offering an incentive increases response rates and the likelihood that participants will finish a survey once they've started it. One study by Survey Sampling International (cited in Miller, 2006) found that a survey response was 50% greater when offering a $5 incentive as opposed to no incentive at all.

However, other research also conducted by Survey Sampling International (2007) showed that sometimes incentives eclipse some participants' intrinsic motivation. They recommend focusing on boosting this motivation while minimizing monetary incentives. They suggest wording that engenders a sense of autonomy ("thanks for *choosing* to complete…") and competency ("we appreciate that this study *took some effort…*") in participants, as well as a sense of value of participation ("the results of this study *will help us…*"). We discuss more about motivation in Chapter 3.1.1.

It's also no surprise that with a monetary incentive comes its ugly stepsibling, bogus participants and data. There are no clear answers as to whether providing an incentive does more damage than the good of increased participation, but there are some things that can be done to curtail bogus data. It doesn't hurt to use phrases that indicate genuine thanks and that promote intrinsic motivation. It's also helpful to keep the incentive modest for the targeted user group and to put other strategies into place to prevent tainted data, such as speed traps and data cleansing techniques described in Chapter 3.8.3 and in Chapter 5.

WHAT SHOULD YOU CONSIDER WHEN DECIDING INCENTIVES?

If you're using a panel for recruiting participants, there are typically incentives and/or incentive guidelines already in place through the panel service, which makes your job easy. But what if you're on your own?

If you decide to provide a material incentive, keep in mind that online usability studies can mean very large numbers of participants, so it's typical to keep the per-participant incentive down to a small token, such as $5 or $10.

Another option is to enter the participants into a drawing for a larger prize, such as a company product or a gift certificate. There is disagreement about whether individual incentives, drawings, or a combination of the two work best. From what we've seen, all methods work fairly well. Make sure, however, that you're aware of the laws governing your state and country. Some states and countries characterize a prize drawing as a lottery, and it may not be legal in some cases.

Appropriate incentives vary widely depending on the user types, company policies, and the time involved. For example, if dealing with doctors or lawyers and the study takes away much of their money-making time, the incentive will need to be considerably higher than average (or donations to charities on their behalf as some panel services do). If using employees within an organization or even customers, you may face a corporate gift policy and need to give some small, nonmonetary incentive such as a movie pass or gift card. Some companies even consider movie passes and gift cards monetary equivalents, in which case you might have to provide "nominal" gifts, such as promotional merchandise (t-shirts, mouse pads, etc.).

The incentive should also be something universally alluring so as not to attract a particular group of people who may bias the results of the study. For example, if you're studying a Web site that sells sporting goods, and the incentive is a baseball signed by a famous baseball player, the incentive may only draw baseball fans who are likely to use the sporting goods Web site differently than other prospective customers and users.

Finally, if you're unsure about the best way to provide incentives, conduct a miniresearch study in your pilot test with a smaller number of people by giving one group one incentive, another group another incentive, and comparing the response rates for both. Then proceed with the method that wins!

2.9 SUMMARY

This chapter discussed various aspects of planning your study, from high-level study goals to budget, timeline, and recruiting. We hope you take away the following points from this chapter.

- Make sure to first identify who the target users of the product are and what their main tasks and goals are, using reliable data sources and methods such as contextual inquiry and task analyses.
- Determine exactly what it is you want to test—from a specific label, feature, or function to a full-scale site-wide usability evaluation—and whether you want to compare a design against competitors, alternative designs, or past or future designs.
- Think about whether it's appropriate to run a between-subjects or within-subjects test. This will partially be determined by how many participants you expect to get and whether you want participants to rank or rate versions against each other.

- Determine which metrics are appropriate for the study; will it be sufficient to measure task success only or will you want additional clues such as click paths, task times, and questions around the broader user experience?
- Keep in mind that the budget and timeline can vary widely, depending on what tools you're using and what stakeholders are involved in the study. A study can range from as little as a day to as much as 3 or more months.
- Decide whether you want to use a panel for recruiting, but keep in mind some of the risks of data quality that come with it and do your research about panel companies. There are many ways to recruit without a panel, but know some of the risks associated with them.
- Try to target at least 50–100 completes for each unique user group, but more is always better if you can afford it. The number of participants needed to see a statistically significant difference is dependent on various factors, some of which you can "guesstimate" up front.
- Be aware of the various participant sampling techniques available to you. Although it's likely that you may use a form of convenience sampling, you may, in some cases, be able to use a form of probability sampling if you have a discrete user list to draw from.
- Although it's often debated, we feel that it's useful to provide some small incentive for participants such as a prize drawing or gift certificates. If you offer an incentive, make sure to have measures in place to keep fraudulent participants from participating and to prevent mental cheating during the study.

CHAPTER 3
Designing the Study

This chapter walks you through the steps in designing an online usability study. We cover all the major sections of a study in the order a participant would likely encounter them: introductory content, screening and starter questions, tasks, follow-up questions, and wrap-up. The end of the chapter includes a discussion of some special topics, including progress indicators and speed traps.

With online testing it's especially important to put thought into the study design since you can't change it on the fly. When creating questions and tasks, it's important to anticipate how you may want to structure the study results and tie them back to your business goals. The last thing you'll want is to have clients or business partners asking for data that you didn't collect.

We also want to emphasize that all studies and user groups are different. Just as a seasoned designer never gets a *design* right the first time, don't expect that you'll get the *study design* right the first time either, so be prepared to pilot test (pretest) the study, which is discussed more extensively in Chapter 4.

3.1 INTRODUCING THE STUDY

When creating an online usability study, you should consider how to set expectations for the participants so that they are not likely to leave the study early—often referred to as bailing or "drop-off." Especially these days when there are tons of spam, it's hard for people to know when to trust something that asks for their time and clicks.

To set these expectations, you should start with one or two concise introductory pages that address the

- Purpose of the study
- Sponsor/contact information
- Time estimate
- Incentive
- Technical requirements
- Legal information/consent
- Instructions

TIP

Some good sources of how to write plainly and concisely include Ginny Redish's book, "Letting Go of the Words: Writing Web Content that Works," Caroline Jarrett's Web site www. editingthatworks.com, and U.S. Government site www. plainlanguage.gov.

Ideally, you want to limit the text as much as possible and format it to enhance scanning. Using bullet points instead of dense paragraphs is a good way to do this.

3.1.1 Purpose, sponsor information, motivation, and incentive

First, you should briefly describe the purpose of the study, without giving away any information that may bias the behavior of the participants. For example, if the focus of the study is on the effectiveness of ads, you may want to be more general up front if you suspect that they may look at the ads unnaturally throughout the test. Tell them something less specific, such as you are studying how users interact with different types of Web pages. However, with any research it's ethically important to disclose the purpose of the study at the end of the study if you were being more general toward the beginning.

Try to use this introduction to engage the participants' interest so that they are not tempted to fly through the study incentive hungry and with little care. Emphasize that the purpose of the study is to gain their valuable feedback so that the product can be better for them. Make them feel they have a stake in the quality of the product. When people feel as though they're not just another number, they will take it seriously and the incentive will become secondary.

Just as it's important to make people feel engaged enough to participate in the study, it's equally important to gain their trust. Establishing trust will help get participants to take part in the study and also produce more reliable data. In the introduction, you should establish the legitimacy of the study so that participants aren't concerned that the study is a façade for a virus that will eat away at their computer or that you're secretly trying to sell something or fundraise (often referred to as "sugging" and "frugging," respectively). One way to establish trust is to make it clear who's sponsoring the study and who to contact with questions. If you're conducting a competitive study and don't want to reveal the sponsoring organization's name, still give contact information for a third party, including a name, phone number, and email address.

TIP

Research shows that if people have a preexisting relationship with or positive perception of an organization, it will make them feel more secure and likely to participate. Also providing a phone number has been shown to build trust (Fogg, 2002).

If you're using an existing customer base or user panel or have conducted surveys with the same population in the past, it's not as important to emphasize the sponsorship. However, it's always a good idea to provide contact information, even if the participant is just having technical trouble or needs some assistance. It all goes back to establishing trust with the participant.

As with establishing trust, it's important to elicit intrinsic motivation at the outset of the study, as most drop-offs occur during the first half of a survey or study (Brazil et al., 2008). You may want to appeal to their sense of belonging in a group of special users, who can make a difference for others, and in a way that will also benefit them. Make them feel as though they are contributing to their fellow customers, co-workers, their profession, or society in general.

As discussed in Chapter 2.8, you may want to provide an incentive to participants. If so, make sure to emphasize it in the introduction (without sounding gimmicky and cliché) and again at the end of the study, including how and when participants will receive it.

3.1.2 Time estimate

Providing the participants with a time estimate is especially important in setting expectations. We recommend that you express the time estimate as a range, such as "5– 10" minutes or "15–20 minutes" or you can use descriptors such as "about" or "approximately" to describe the time required to complete the study, such as "this study will take about 10 minutes to complete." It's critical to be realistic in the estimate and, if possible, to base it on pilot testing. If you underestimate, the drop-off rate will be much higher, as participants may realize that it's starting to take longer than they wanted to spend. If you overestimate, the number of participants willing to take the study may be lower.

Several factors influence how long people are likely to spend with an online usability study, but they generally boil down to one overriding factor: motivation. The more motivated the participants are, the more time they'll devote. We've conducted online usability studies that participants completed in only 5–10 minutes and others that took close to an hour. Of course, the other general rule is the shorter the study, the more participants you're likely to get. Obviously, getting someone to devote 5–10 minutes doesn't take much motivation and, from what we've seen, may increase the participation rate significantly if you're able to keep it that short and sweet. But getting someone to devote an hour does take some serious motivation.

An interesting trend we've seen is that there seems to be a threshold in many peoples' minds around 15–20 minutes. If a study is expected to take less than 15 minutes, many people seem more willing to just go ahead and do it. However, if a study is expected to take more than 20 minutes, many people seem to view this as a more serious time commitment.

A STUDY WITHIN A STUDY

In one online usability study we conducted, it ran for 2 days and an email message was sent to all the potential participants each morning. On the first day, our email message and the introductory page of the study gave an estimate of about 20 minutes to complete the study, which was our best estimate at the time. After we looked at data from the first day, we saw that the average time was actually between 10 and 15 minutes. As a result, we revised the time estimate to 10–15 minutes for the second day. The participation rate improved significantly.

Similarly, Hogg and Miller (2003) found that the drop-off rate for a survey increased significantly when a survey took more than 15 minutes to complete. What's more, the participants who dropped off from the longer surveys were shown to have less intrinsic motivation (inherent interest) in the concept of the survey. Although there may be something lost in translation from an online survey to an online usability study, it is not a stretch to assume that the same thing may apply here; not only will a longer study produce more drop-off, it may lead to a type of self-selection bias, where those who are left completing the survey may be more interested or knowledgeable about the concept being tested.

FIGURE 3.1
Introduction screen for an online usability study of the National Cancer Institute Web site.

Figure 3.1 shows a simple example of displaying the purpose and time estimate from an online usability study of the National Cancer Institute Web site. Because time on task is collected as part of this study, note that the participants are asked to plan for participating when they'll be least interrupted.

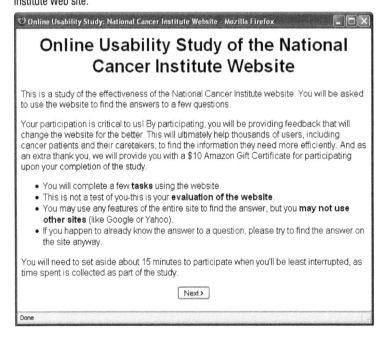

3.1.3 Technical requirements

Ideally you'd want the study to work with any operating system, Web browser, and screen resolution, but sometimes that may not be the case. Regardless, you should still let participants know up front what the technical requirements are, as in the examples shown in Figures 3.2 and 3.3. If you're using a commercial service to administer the test, this information may be built into their tool or instructions already.

Most commercial tools offer the option to ask the participant to download a browser companion

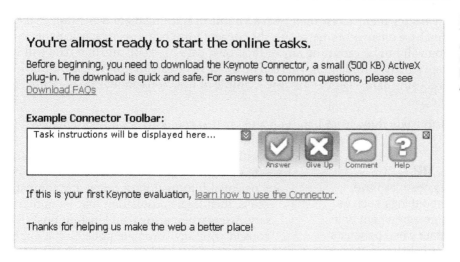

or scripting component in order to track URLs, clickstreams, task times, etc. If you have any control over the instructional text, again be sure to explain in plain terms what the user will be download-ing and whether it's of any risk to their computer or to the protection of their personal information.

3.1.4 Legal information and consent

Depending on the subject matter of the study, you may need to consider creating a legal disclaimer or nondisclosure clause. For example, you may be showing an external audience some proprietary information or new designs that you want kept confi-dential. In some cases you may require the participants to

> **TIP**
> If using a commercial service, check with your vendor to see what participants will have to download to use it. Some tools are built to uninstall any downloaded components upon completion of the study.

acknowledge that they will not share the information they see with anyone else. This is especially important because anyone can easily take a picture or screen capture of something they're looking at and email it out to others.

Some type of informed consent agreement is quite common in usability studies and is the ethical responsibility of the researcher to administer. It's more often used for face-to-face usability testing so that you get the participant's permission to record video of them and to explain their rights as a participant in the study. In any user research, though, you want to assure them that their data are strictly confidential and that their personal information will not be used. If you are having them access their own accounts or tracking them while they make a purchase on an ecommerce site, the consent form helps assure participants that you will not be capturing any of their own data or, if you are, that data will be kept strictly confidential. This can be tricky so be careful how you are capturing and using data. Figure 3.4 is one example of how consent may be presented to the user.

Before you throw your hands up and say that you don't want to be entangled in consultations with lawyers, please note that we're erring on the conservative side to raise awareness of potential risks. If you're doing a simple study that doesn't involve any personal information or reveal any company secrets, then legal consultation may be unnecessary. Assess your personal and institutional risk, consult with any corporate policies that apply, and decide if this is important enough to pursue. We do, however, think it's always your responsibility to inform participants that their data will be treated confidentially, regardless of whether the text is vetted formally through a lawyer.

TIP

Some services may have already covered things such as a nondisclosure agreement and treatment of data when panelists registered to participate in studies through them. Check with your vendor, if you're using one.

FIGURE 3.4
A Sample Statement of Informed Consent and Non-Disclosure Agreement as part of a scrolling text box.

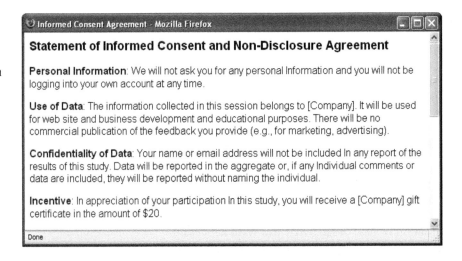

Informed Consent Agreement - Mozilla Firefox

Statement of Informed Consent and Non-Disclosure Agreement

Personal Information: We will not ask you for any personal Information and you will not be logging into your own account at any time.

Use of Data: The information collected in this session belongs to [Company]. It will be used for web site and business development and educational purposes. There will be no commercial publication of the feedback you provide (e.g., for marketing, advertising).

Confidentiality of Data: Your name or email address will not be included In any report of the results of this study. Data will be reported in the aggregate or, if any Individual comments or data are included, they will be reported without naming the individual.

Incentive: In appreciation of your participation In this study, you will receive a [Company] gift certificate in the amount of $20.

Done

3.1.5 Instructions

Instructions are an important part of beginning any study. They need to be clear and concise. Some of the points you may need to cover include the following.

- An assurance that the study is an evaluation of the Web site, not of the user, and that they just need to put forth their best effort.
- If you're giving participants tasks to do, ask them to try to find the answer regardless of whether they already know it.
- Ask them to respond naturally, as if they were using the Web site on their own.
- Special instructions on how to advance through and answer the tasks, access help/instructions, pause, or quit the study at any time.

If you find that you're covering a great deal of information from the preceding sections in one screen or window, consider presenting instructions on a subsequent screen so that users won't be overwhelmed. Figure 3.5 provides one example of how instructions might be presented to the participant.

We know that users can't always rely on their short-term memory nor do they find it fruitful to try to learn instructions. If the instructions page feels fairly lengthy, consider adding a way for participants to access the page again at any time during the study. Some commercial services allow you to do this.

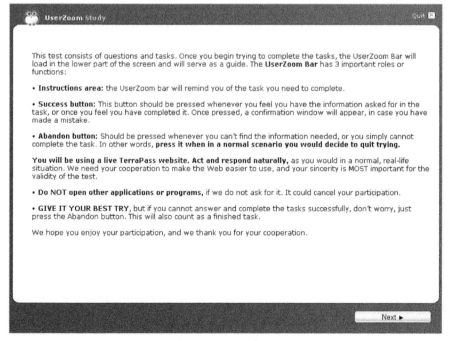

FIGURE 3.5
An instructions screen customized using UserZoom.

3.2 SCREENING QUESTIONS

In any kind of online usability study, you may include some questions at the beginning to automatically screen out participants who don't meet basic criteria for the study. The idea is that if someone doesn't answer the screening questions in a desired way, they are not asked to participate in the study. It's simply a way to ensure that you are only reaching the intended audience.

3.2.1 Types of screening questions

The types of screening questions to use will differ depending on the Web site you're testing. In general, however, consider whether to screen out at least two groups of people:

- People who clearly do not make up the target user groups. For example, if you're testing a teenage girl's fashion Web site, it's pretty safe to say that men over 50 are not a viable user group. Similarly, if you're testing a Web site that allows people to rent jet planes for everyday personal use, you will probably only be targeting participants at a very high income level or net worth.
- People who may bias the results of the study. The most common example of this is to screen out participants who have higher technical expertise on average, such as developers or Web designers. Unless the Web site is targeted to that user group, these types of professionals are more likely to think like the designers did and "get" what average users may not have.

When constructing screening questions, the first thing you want to do is identify all of your criteria for participating in the study. Then look at the criteria and do a sensitivity check. Are you screening by sensitive information, such as race, nationality, age, gender, or income? If so, make sure you have a valid reason to do so (e.g, high net worth individuals for the jet-renting example). Be aware that asking these kinds of questions may make participants suspicious and therefore unlikely to participate.

Note that you should also try to make a distinction between what criteria should *screen out* participants versus *sort* them. If you're unsure or skeptical about whether to exclude certain groups of people, sorting them will allow you to still get representation from them without biasing targeted user group data, as they're being categorized separately. The decision of whether to screen out or sort also has implications for the automated screener. For example, you may want about half males and half females. If you have a quota, such as a 500-person cap for each gender, the screener tool should include functionality to keep track of how many males and how many females participate and to screen out one gender once the quota is filled. Many vendor tools allow you to do this.

FIGURE 3.6
Familiarity of the subject of the Web site is an example of a screening question.

How familiar are you with carbon offsets?

- ○ Very familiar
- ○ Somewhat familiar
- ○ Not at all familiar

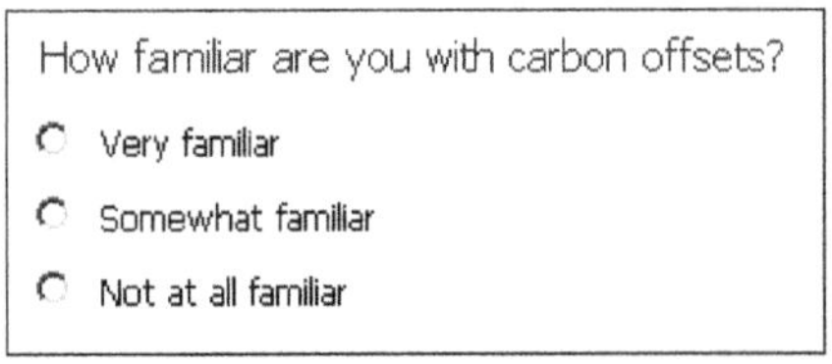

One common example of a screening question might be to see how familiar users are with a particular topic or Web site. A very simple example is illustrated in Figure 3.6 using the TerraPass Web site example. Participants are simply asked how familiar they are with carbon offsets. If the designers were targeting groups of people who are newer to the concept and may come to the site to learn more, they might want to screen out participants who are already very familiar with the concept.

We make an intentional distinction between *screening questions* and *starter questions* (Section 3.3), as the purpose of each is different. A screening question is meant to include, exclude, or sort a participant based on their answers to a question, whereas a starter question is meant to provide background information about participants that will be helpful in slicing, dicing, and informing the data analysis.

3.2.2 Misrepresentation checks

There may be some people trying to participate in studies just for an incentive. Your responsibility to mitigate this problem therefore starts by making sure that people *are who they say they are* in their screening questions, which we refer to here as "misrepresentation checks." The exact checks will depend on the subject matter you're dealing with. The goal is to devise sets of questions where certain combinations of answers are either impossible or statistically very unlikely. An example of this comes from Burke R&D's Quality Panel Research (2008). They had participants from various user panels participate in a survey in order to measure the incidence of misrepresentation across them. Panelists were asked at the beginning of a survey whether they were left-handed, right-handed, or ambidextrous ("uses both hands equally"). See Figure 3.7. Whereas the percentage of the

> **TIP**
> Figure 3.7 shows that there is some misrepresentation attempted out there, but also that it varies by user panel. Make sure to look into some of the measures that panel companies take against misrepresentation and fraudulent participation.

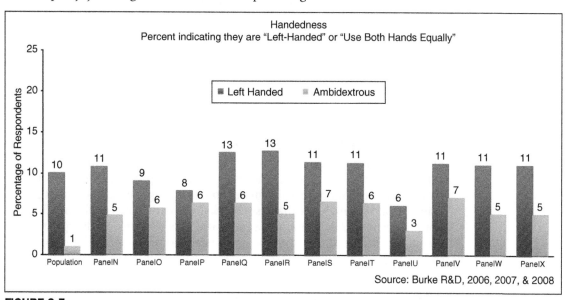

FIGURE 3.7
Chart from Burke, Inc. (2008) showing the percentage of respondents from various panels who claimed that they were left-handed and ambidextrous, as compared with the general population.

population who are ambidextrous is only about 1%, respondents in five different panels claimed that they were ambidextrous 5 or 6% of the time. If a participant answered "ambidextrous," it is likely that they were just trying to answer anything to qualify for the survey.

Asking handedness doesn't quite translate to a related screening question for an online user experience study, but perhaps you can devise a set of questions in the context of the Web site domain that can achieve the same goal. The example in which the Burke Institute asked respondents whether they had heard of a nonexistent brand is one type of question you may ask. In our example study of pet Web sites (PETCO and PetSmart), one might ask participants which brands of pet food they buy and then add some brands in the list that don't exist. If someone claims that they have pets and buy pet food and then choose made-up brand names, they may be misrepresenting themselves.

3.2.3 Exit strategy

It's important to be graceful when screening out a participant. Just because participants are dealing with a computer, it doesn't give you license to give people a "so long, loser!" message if they don't meet screening criteria. This is placing the blame on the user and potentially damaging your reputation with them in the future. Therefore it's important to inform the users gently when they do not meet screening criteria.

It is also important to try not to reveal why the user was screened out of the study. This is another measure against misrepresentation; if a user has just checked off that he is a male and is immediately terminated thereafter, he may be tempted to go back and check off "female" to become eligible to participate and get the incentive. For this reason, it's helpful to group screening questions together. This prevents users from immediately understanding what screened them out.

An example of a generic but gentle exit message might be, "We're sorry, but we have filled our quota for people with your background. Thank you for your interest, and we appreciate your time."

3.3 STARTER QUESTIONS

Along with screening questions, you may want to collect some data about what type of experience or expectation users have with the product or how much technical experience they have. This can help provide insight when looking at performance data. You might see that less experienced participants perform differently from the experts. Also, you may want to use how they answer the questions to customize the study. For example, you may want to use branching logic and choose to give only certain tasks to specific participants based on their interest or experience.

Although we want to focus this chapter more on task construction than question construction, we didn't want to leave you without at least a few high-level tips to keep in mind when writing screening and starter questions.

- Closed questions (providing participants with answer choices) are easier than open-ended questions to categorize and analyze. The only time you may want to use open-ended questions (e.g. free-form text boxes) is when you think there will be answers you didn't anticipate, you feel that providing participants with answers may bias their responses, or you are looking for a general opinion, which shouldn't be the case for screening questions, but perhaps you may incorporate it as a starter question.
- Avoid "double-barreled" questions that combine two questions in one, as participants may not know which question to answer. For example, "To what extent is this Web site easy to use and important to you?"
- Avoid asking yes/no questions as they can sometimes lead or bias a participant into an extreme statement. For example, asking "Do you use this Web site all the time?" can mean different things to different people and may feel somewhat bullying into that position. A better question would be using a multiple-choice question or rating scale offering different intervals for frequency of use.
- Be specific where possible; participants will interpret "daily," "weekly," and so on more easily and consistently than "always," "sometimes," and so on.
- Avoid asking hypothetical questions. For example, "Would you use this Web site every day for your job if we added a way to buy office supplies?" Participants are not great at knowing how they'll behave in a situation and sometimes confuse fantasy with reality when faced with hypothetical questions.
- As always, try to stay neutral. Avoid using language that will lead, bias, or clue the participant in to your feelings or motivations as the researcher. This also means avoiding, "presupposition" questions, i.e., assuming something about the participant that may not necessarily be true. For example, asking "What is the most fun part of the Web site?" presupposes that the participant finds any part of the Web site "fun," which may not be the case.

> **TIP**
> A number of survey design books discuss proper question construction, a couple of good ones being Floyd Fowler's "Improving Survey Questions: Design and Evaluation" (1995) and Don D. Dillman, Jolene D. Smyth, and Leah Melani Christian's, "Internet, Mail and Mixed-Mode Surveys: The Tailored Design Method" (3rd Edition, 2008).

3.3.1 Product, computer, and Web experience

Perhaps the most important starter questions you'll want to ask are those involving participants' usage and experience with the product. These factors are likely to correlate with performance metrics during the study.

The trick with these types of questions is to keep them clear and focused. Don't assume that the amount of time someone has *had* a product, *been* a customer, or has been *registered* on a Web site equals how long they've been *using* the product or Web site. You can ask those questions, but make sure you ask separate questions about their usage. Also don't assume that just because someone uses something all the time that they think it's great. Some people have to use something because it's their job, they can't afford competitor products, it's all they know

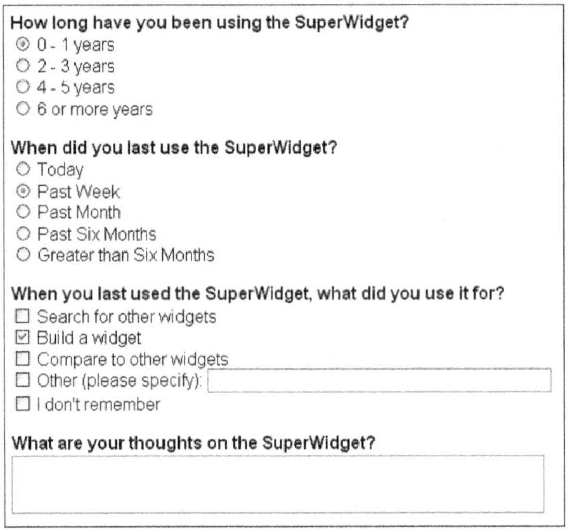

How long have you been using the SuperWidget?
- ⊙ 0 - 1 years
- ○ 2 - 3 years
- ○ 4 - 5 years
- ○ 6 or more years

When did you last use the SuperWidget?
- ○ Today
- ⊙ Past Week
- ○ Past Month
- ○ Past Six Months
- ○ Greater than Six Months

When you last used the SuperWidget, what did you use it for?
- ☐ Search for other widgets
- ☑ Build a widget
- ☐ Compare to other widgets
- ☐ Other (please specify): _____
- ☐ I don't remember

What are your thoughts on the SuperWidget?

[_____]

FIGURE 3.8
Example starter questions about past experience with a product.

how to use, or for some other reason. If you want to know something about usage or experience with a product, ask it directly so that you're not making inferences!

Figure 3.8 shows some examples of past experience questions. Note that rather than asking in general what people use the SuperWidget for, we ask the last time they used it and what they used it for in that instance. Giving a concrete instance to think about helps ground people so that they're not taxing their memory or going "checkbox crazy" assuming they've used the SuperWidget for everything under the sun at some point.

Commonly, we also ask for participants' familiarity with the Web site. Note, however, that although familiarity may be a useful measure to provide insight into the analysis, it does not imply frequency of use (again, no inferences!).

Figure 3.9 is an example using PetSmart and PETCO in which we asked users how many pets they have.

In this study, this question was used for branching purposes (logic built in that routes respondents to different questions based on their answers). If a participant entered "0," they went on to start the study. If a participant entered "1" through "4 or more" they were brought to another question, as seen in Figure 3.10.

How computer and Web savvy a participant is can also impact their success in using the product. One thing to note is that Web *experience* may not be the same thing as Web *expertise*. Chadwick-Dias, Tedesco, and Tullis (2004) found that Web expertise is not always correlated to how much someone has used the Web, but is strongly correlated with opportunities for learning collaboratively when watching or working with others (family members, co-workers, classmates) on computers. You can ask the standard questions around how long and frequently people use the Web and computers, but be aware that this may not make up the entire picture. You may also want to ask them some more questions about what they do on the Web and computers, how they learned it, and in what locations they most often use it.

FIGURE 3.9
Example starter question that branches based on response (created in RelevantView).

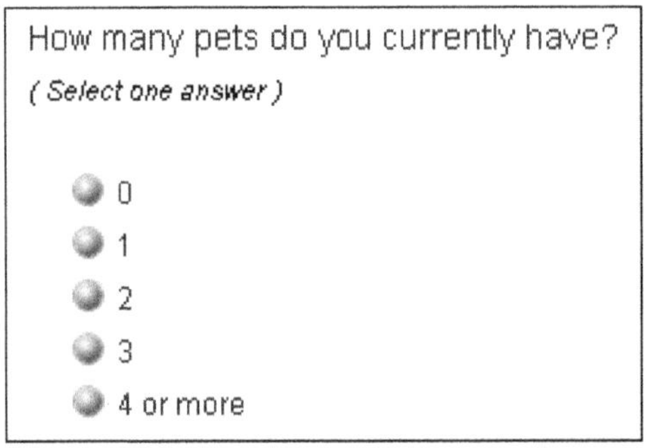

How many pets do you currently have?

(Select one answer)

- ○ 0
- ○ 1
- ○ 2
- ○ 3
- ○ 4 or more

3.3.2 Expectations

One metric that you may want to use in the study is a measure of how well the product actually meets the participants' expectations. Sometimes you'll find that certain tasks are difficult for participants, but if they *expected* it to be difficult that may not be something to worry as much about as the case where they expected it to be easy.

Albert and Dixon (2003) used a methodology where, before the study or task itself, participants would rate how easy or difficult they *expected* each of the tasks to be on a rating scale. Then participants were asked after each task to rate how easy or difficult it *actually was* on the same scale. Users don't necessarily require prior experience on the Web site to develop an expectation; they use their prior experience with similar types of tasks on the Web or just their assessment of the complexity of the task to help guide their expectation rating. One may naturally expect some tasks to be more difficult than others. For example, it should be easy to get a stock quote on Google, but it would probably be difficult to rebalance your entire portfolio to match a new projected retirement date.

By doing this, Albert and Dixon were able to take participants' data and identify areas needing great improvement (expected to be easy, but wound up difficult), as well as other areas that posed an opportunity (expected to be difficult, was difficult).

Expectations can also be gauged on a broader level. For example, you could ask users how easy or difficult they expect the site to be in general and measure the discrepancy with post-study questions on the same topic.

FIGURE 3.10
Question given to participants if they indicated that they had one or more pets (created in RelevantView).

3.3.3 Reducing bias later in the study

As with the introductory text, it's important in both screening and starter questions not to "show your cards" or reveal too much information to the participant up front. This is a principle common to any kind of user experience study or market research survey. For example, let's say that you're planning to do a competitive study for Alpha Corp comparing three different products—Alpha Corp's Web site, Beta Corp's Web site, and Gamma Corp's Web site. It's probably not a good idea to ask all of the questions solely about the usage of Alpha Corp's Web site, even if that's the scope of the screening criteria, or later analysis. Instead, you may want to ask about the participants' usage of all three products or Web sites so that they can't guess who the sponsor is. Brand recognition can have a large impact on people's reactions to products.

Another example may be that you plan to target a particular part of a Web site. Let's say that you want to test how people use the Alpha Corp store locator, which is one small piece of the whole Web site, but you don't want to lead the user to think unnaturally or excessively about the store locator before they begin the test. So you may want to add some "distractor" questions about other parts of the site. Distractor questions are questions that may not necessarily provide value, but make it harder for participants to guess the purpose or focus of the study up front and result in more accurate data for the central task.

ASKING SENSITIVE QUESTIONS

As with screening questions, you should do your best to avoid any starter questions that are sensitive in nature. Starter questions are usually focused on experience, expectations, or about a Web site so it's not likely you'll need to ask anything too sensitive, unless the product you're testing is particularly sensitive in nature. For example, let's say that one of the prior experience questions is whether someone has used a site regarding defaulted loans, consolidating debt, or dealing with bankruptcy or unemployment. If it's important to gather that variable to filter data by, you may consider including that kind of question at the end of the study along with demographic questions. That way you'd still be able to collect it, but by putting it at the end of the study you're less likely to scare people off.

3.4 CONSTRUCTING TASKS

Task construction is a vital part of an online study. The automated, self-service nature of the study means that there is no room for misinterpretation. You won't be there to clarify tasks or interpret user intentions. The tasks need to be able to reliably speak for themselves.

The following sections outline some points to keep in mind when constructing tasks. Note a couple of things to consider when reading them.

TIP
Unless you're really comfortable with your commercial service's functionality for analyzing click paths, we still recommend having some form of answer-based task completion collected—in case you find that there was a technical glitch with collecting clickstream data or that data are cumbersome to analyze, both of which we've definitely encountered before.

- In these sections we assume that you want to provide a set of specific, targeted tasks to get the user to interact with specific areas of the site and record their task success, among other measures. For this reason, much of the discussion doesn't apply to true intent and open Web studies, which tend to elicit less about empirical behavior and more about the user experience with a task or Web site in general.
- We also assume here that participants are giving some kind of *answer* to each task, whether it is a specific piece of information or data, a specific page identifier, or their own "self-reported" task success. For this reason, much of this discussion does not apply to studies where you're using clickstream data as the only task completion metric.

3.4.1 Making the task easy to understand

It's important to balance the need for specific tasks with the amount of mental effort required for participants. For example, if you're testing a company directory's search capability and the task is to "find a man with the last name

SELECTING AND CONSTRUCTING TASKS FOR ANY USABILITY STUDY

Our primary goal for this chapter is to focus on aspects of study design specific to online studies, but if you're new to constructing tasks for usability testing, here's the 40,000-foot view of guidelines that apply to *either* online or lab studies:

- Most typical usability studies include tasks representative of the most frequent and/or important real-world tasks that users may do on the site. But this is not always the case—sometimes you'll want to construct a less-frequent or less-important task in order to get participants to interact with new functionality that needs to be tested. You may also construct tasks around areas that you and other stakeholders anticipate to be a potential usability issue.
- Sometimes a great source for tasks is the output of a task analysis or of other methods such as ethnographic research or persona work.
- Tasks should be fairly short, explicit, and easy for anyone in the target user group to understand.
- Tasks should be realistic, unless you're constructing a task as a proxy to get people to explore a particular area (we'll discuss more about this in the following sections).
- Tasks should always be worded in a way that doesn't lead the participant. For example, if the area you want them to get to is called "Caribbean Vacation Destinations," don't use that exact phrase in the task. Instead ask them to look for information on going away to Jamaica. The only times you might break this rule is if something has no other practical name, such as "print" functionality on a Web page. It would be way too awkward to ask participants to "make it so that this comes out on paper!"

of Flovegneiren whose office is on the third floor of the Park Street building, works in finance, and whose first name starts with a B," the task begins to sound like a college entrance exam question rather than a task. (We know from experience, as one of our earlier online studies included tasks like this!) The result of this is time wasted interpreting a question, and potentially taxing the participant's working memory, both of which can take a toll on task completion times, as well as the quality of results.

The *end goal* of the task should be clear as well. Using our Apollo program example, a task might be to "find out in what time period the Apollo program was started." Here, the term "time period" is not clear enough. Some users may look for a specific year, whereas others may look for a decade or a presidential administration. A better task would be specific and pointed—perhaps to find the year of the first manned Apollo spacecraft launch.

Don't mistake the term "easy to understand" for "easy to guess." The task should not be so easy that a participant is likely to know it offhand without looking. If the task is one of common knowledge, for example, "Who won the 2008 U.S. presidential election," then users will likely take shortcuts and pick the answer they know rather than find it on the site. In cases like this we recommend using some proxy question that still evaluates the same area of the design. For example, in the pets study, one of the tasks was to find the weight of a bag of a particular brand of ferret food that starts with a "Z." This is likely not to be a common task; a small percentage of users would be looking to buy ferret food, let alone finding out the weight of the bags available. However, if we were to ask participants questions about a common cat or dog food brand, it's very possible that users would already know some of these things. So here the ferret food example is just being used as a proxy task to have users navigate to a product page.

3.4.2 Writing tasks with task completion rates in mind

Assuming that task completion is one of the primary metrics for the study, you'll need to know whether participants accomplished the task successfully. This is unlike a typical moderated study, where you may note someone's *degree* of success. With online usability studies, there generally isn't a concept of "partial" success. It's usually a binary situation: the task was successful or unsuccessful for the participant. There may be different types of task success or failure, but there's usually not an in-between category (i.e., there is no easy way to score something as "successful with minor problems" or "75% successful," as with moderated usability testing where you're watching them in person and able to make a subjective judgment). Depending on how you implement the study, this has implications for how you formulate and word the tasks.

Let's use an example where you're testing navigation on a bookseller Web site. If you want a task to be "Find the book by John Smith on bicycles," you need to be able to confirm that the participant actually found the answer. Let's assume that your goal is focused on users' experience navigating to a book on the site when having just an author's name (John Smith) and topic (bicycles). There are a few ways to approach this problem.

> **Option 1:** The easiest way is to reword the task so that there can be a discrete answer. For example, "What is the ISBN number of the book by John Smith on bicycles?" That way, the user can either input the number or select it from a drop-down list of choices. In this case, finding the ISBN number in particular isn't that important to you; it's just the means by which participants can indicate their answer discretely. This option is very direct and our most commonly used method, but is sometimes not easy to construct when dealing with changing content on a live Web site (e.g., such as stock quotes) or a wizard-like task where there is no clear "answer" to find (e.g., opening an account).

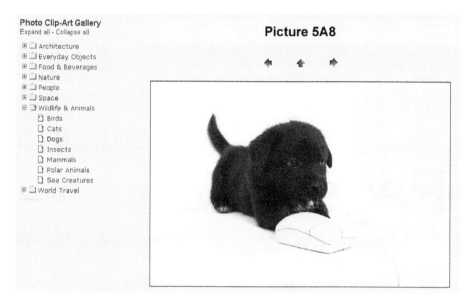

FIGURE 3.11
Each page and piece
of clip art is given a
code, which will then be
selected as the answer
from a drop-down list.

Option 2: If you're using a prototype of the Web site, you may have the ability to tag pages. For example, you could put a code or a letter of the alphabet on a variety of pages throughout the site and then have the user input the code of the page with the answer (see Figure 3.11). This option requires a little more work on the prototyping side, but frees you up to be more natural with the task wording, e.g., "Find the page that shows…" or "Find the photo that shows…" rather than asking for a discrete piece of information.

Similarly, rather than tagging pages of the Web site, you can create a "dummy" page that users may get when clicking on the appropriate link in a prototype (Figure 3.12).

These techniques can work well, but be careful; you'll want to include a code on almost every page or at least every plausible page for a task so that participants don't make educated guesses based on which pages have codes and which don't. The codes should also be random, i.e., if you're using the alphabet, the first task should not correspond to an answer page that is labeled "A," the second task answer "B," and so on.

Option 3: Similar to Option 2, if collecting clickstream data only, you may be able to word the task instructing the user to find a particular page as opposed to finding a specific piece of information. For example, instead of saying "Find out how much it costs for ground (regular) shipping of a gift card" and collecting the price as the answer, you might ask, "Find the page that tells you how much it costs for shipping gift cards." In the latter case, you're just using clickstream data to determine success rather than an answer that the participant gives or chooses.

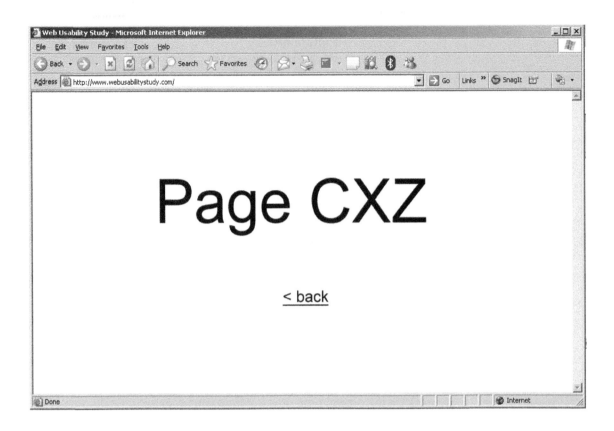

FIGURE 3.12
Two different ways of approaching "dummy" pages. (Top) The page clicked to contains only the code. (Bottom) The link clicked brings up a pop-up with description and code.

Option 4: Rather than relying on clickstream data as in Option 3, another option is to have participants enter the URL or page title itself as the answer to a task. But make sure before you pursue this option that each URL or page title is a unique identifier. Some Web sites that use frames or make use of Rich Internet Application platforms such as AJAX or DHTML tend to yield a static URL that doesn't change when users click to new pages or components.

"FIND AN ANSWER" OR "FIND A PAGE"?

Whether a task directs people to find a discrete answer or a particular page depends on what you're looking to discover and the nature of the design. The "find a page" method is often used to test the navigational path in getting to a page, usually when the page itself isn't that complex or important to test. The "find an answer" method is typically geared toward testing more interactive pages, where simply finding the page wouldn't capture the entire experience. Here, participants need to go an extra step further to interact with the information on the page in order to answer the task.

3.4.3 Anticipating various paths to an answer

An important consideration with online usability studies is being aware of the various paths a participant can take to an end point. In our bookseller example, let's say that your goal is to compare two designs of the primary navigation bar to one another. In this case, you might want to force the participant to use the site navigation rather than a search box. This is simply a way to minimize "noise" in data so that everyone is approaching the tasks the same way and you're comparing "apples to apples" when looking across the data comparing the two designs. There are a few options for how to do this.

Option 1: If you're using a prototype, you can take away the search box altogether for both designs. This was what we did with our photo clip-art study in which we compared different variations of an expand/collapse menu structure. Some comments showed that users were unsatisfied with the lack of a search field, which most likely led them to rate the experience lower (with self-reported subjective ratings), but this sentiment was rated *equally low* across both designs. This is okay if your only goal is to compare both designs' navigation bars, as we did. In other words, only *differences* in ratings across designs matter rather than absolute ratings of any one design. As a result, if ratings for one design are significantly higher than the other, you can attribute that difference solely to the difference in the design of the navigation. If some used the search box (and especially more so on one design than the other, for whatever reason), it could have potentially muddied the results of the comparison.

FIGURE 3.13
Event-based messaging as a result of clicking the "Search" button.

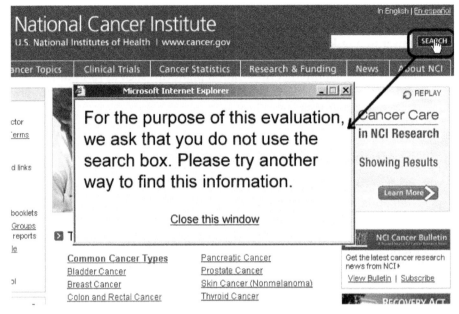

Option 2: Disable the search box and instruct users at the beginning of the study not to try and use it. However, if participants don't read the instructions (we know this is a likely scenario!) they may become frustrated that it's not working. A similar technique is to provide a search input field, but always display a placeholder page or pop-up explaining that the search is not working in this prototype. Some commercial services allow the ability to show a message to a participant if he or she has done something specific, such as clicking the "Go" button next to the search box (see Figure 3.13). This can be a good option if you don't have a prototype and are using a live Web site.

Option 3: Another option when testing a prototype is to set it up so that the user will arrive at different answers or unique pages depending on whether he or she searches or navigates. For the bookstore example, you can offer one ISBN number for participants whose path is through the search field and another ISBN number for participants whose path is through the site's navigation. Alternatively, if you're labeling pages with codes, you may label those two end pages with different codes. Either way, you actually may be able to determine during the analysis phase what percentage of participants used the search versus the navigation while attempting the task based on their answers (and then do your comparisons within the navigation-user groups). Of course, keep in mind that this may involve some fancy prototyping footwork to accomplish.

Option 4: You can word the tasks so that the participants would not be likely to use the search box for every task. Using our pets study example, one task was "You remember the ferret food you like to buy starts with a 'Z'.

Find out the weights of the two bags of this food available for purchase."
If the task were to specify that the food is called "Zupreem," it is a likely
item for users to search because it's so unique. Creating the "starts with
a Z" scenario may not be the most realistic or representative scenario for
this user group, but it's not a stretch either. The point we want to emphasize is that it serves as a proxy task to get users to *navigate* to a specific
area without using the search. The experience with the actual task is not
your goal in this case, but rather the navigational journey of getting to a
product page.

One thing to note here is that you want to make sure there aren't other answers
that satisfy the same task wording. We were comfortable using "ferret food that
starts with a 'Z'" because we knew there weren't other products on the site that
satisfied that criterion. Be sure to do your homework first! And if you miss
something, don't worry—you should catch any odd result patterns in the pilot
testing!

A small interjection here: we're not implying that if you're testing a Web site with
a search engine you shouldn't let participants use it. In the example of the bookseller, we were assuming a scenario in which you're comparing two navigational
designs. But let's say that instead you were just assessing the general usability of
one design and know that the most common scenarios are users coming to the
site with a particular title and/or author in mind rather than a vague sense of
what they're looking for. In that case, you want participants to get to the answers
fast, no matter how they do it. You'll get more realistic and useful information
by letting users get to the answer any way they choose.

3.4.4 Multiple-choice answers

As mentioned previously, you might be able to use clickstream data to determine whether the participant was successful in the task. In most cases, however,
it's easier to ask participants to find a page or a specific answer and enter it
once they've found it. This can be a code, an actual piece of data, or something
such as a page title or URL. Whenever possible, you should provide multiple-
choice answers (via a drop-down list or radio buttons). Why? Well, a free-form
text input box might pose unique analysis challenges. Consider the following
examples.

- Different interpretations of answers: If you're asking a dollar amount,
  one participant may enter "$11" whereas others may enter "Eleven,"
  "11 dollars," or "11.00."
- Misspelling: An author's first name might be "Alison" but some people
  will probably spell it "Allison" (especially if they are unable to view the site
  simultaneously while they're answering the question).
- Mistyping: Many people are not trained in typing and will look at the
  keyboard while typing rather than at the word itself. Others may type so
  fast that they switch letters around. You may wind up with common typing
  mistakes like "hte Doors."

These problems are more common than you may think! It could be an analysis nightmare because there is no automatic way to score task success if you have a spreadsheet of data in all different, unanticipated formats. Therefore, you might have to look tediously through many entries to manually code a task as successful or not. Drop-down lists or radio buttons, however, have predetermined values that are returned with the same spelling and format for each participant, which simplifies the analysis greatly.

Ideally, participants would see the Web site, task, and a way to answer the task simultaneously, which is in fact how most of the vendor tools are built. But a few tools have constraints on their setup so that participants are asked to interact with the Web site first and then to answer the task on a subsequent page. Therefore, predefined answer choices make it much easier for participants because they are using recognition of the answers instead of having to recall them.

When using multiple-choice answers, you should be mindful of the number and types of choices you include in the list. Let's say you're trying to decide between using 5 or 10 choices. Obviously, offering 10 choices rather than 5 will decrease the chance of someone choosing the right answer randomly. It also decreases the likelihood that someone might use deduction to figure out the answer. But it depends on what the choices are. Consider the example shown in Figure 3.14 from the Apollo Program usability study.

In this example, the choices each contain two astronaut names. It might take a second for the participant to read through the choices. If there were 10 choices like this, it would take more mental effort on the part of the participant to review the choices and discern the differences. But let's hypothetically say that the task was to pick *one* astronaut from a list. Then, having only 4 or 5 to choose from may be too easy to guess. In this case, you may want to increase the number of choices.

This example also points out some desirable features of the "distractor" options, that is, incorrect answers. In this case, the answer is Cernan and Schmitt, the Apollo 17 astronauts who walked on the moon. But all of the distractors are also the names of astronauts who walked on the moon, so they all have a "ring of authenticity" to them. Including options such as "Laurel and Hardy" might have been fun, but very easy for participants to eliminate.

FIGURE 3.14
Task from the Apollo usability study.

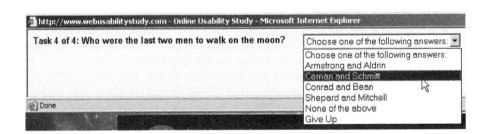

Not only should the answers *sound* legitimate, but they should actually be plausible. For example, the participant's task is to find the page of an ecommerce site where she can update her billing address—using the example of page letters, let's say this is page H. You may be tempted to throw in random letters as the other choices in the answer dropdown—P, J, and R. But what if the billing address page looks *exactly* like the shipping address page, which is page Q? People may get to page Q, decide that it's the answer, and find that it's not in the list, so keep looking. The results of the study now have a slight bias toward success for that task where people otherwise might have gotten it wrong. Including plausibly wrong answers will give you additional insights when analyzing data, as it may confirm suspicions of possible usability issues you anticipated.

If you're using a code for an answer such as a page number or letter of the alphabet, be careful of too few choices there as well. If the site or scope of the design is small, the participant could easily identify where all the choices are and decide which one is most correct. Here it's recommended to use more choices, as shown in Figure 3.15.

3.4.5 Including a "none of the above" option

The example in Figure 3.15 also illustrates why it's a good idea to include a "None of the Above" option. Including such an option is another way to discourage participants from answering by deduction. For this reason, you may not have to worry about including many answer choices if you include a "None of the Above" option. Take note, however, that some participants may use "None of the Above" as a way to give up on the task. Therefore we also recommend including this option in addition to a "Don't Know" or "Give Up" option, which is discussed in the next section. Having both will allow you to differentiate between participants who were unable to find an answer and participants who found one that was not listed in the answer choices.

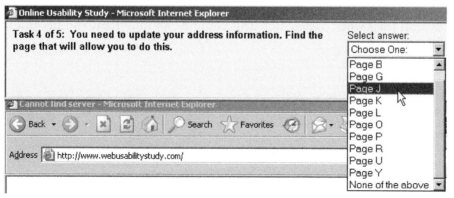

FIGURE 3.15
Task from a usability study using page letters as answers.

IS "NONE OF THE ABOVE" AN INVITATION FOR MENTAL CHEATERS?

There is discussion in the market research world about whether including "None of the Above" as an answer for a survey question encourages mental cheaters to choose that option. There are arguments and study results on both sides of that discussion. Our answer to that debate is simply to include task times as one of the metrics in the study. That way, you can weed out data from anyone who spends less time answering a task than is possible for that task. Many commercial services also allow you to do this automatically by specifying a time threshold. We talk about this and other data cleanup techniques in Chapter 5.

3.4.6 Including a "don't know" or "give up" option

In most online usability studies we conduct, we include a "Don't Know" or "Give Up" option. One example is shown in Figure 3.14, where "Give Up" is an option in the drop-down list. Some commercial services also provide ways to give up on a task, such as WebEffective, which offers a "Give Up" option next to it (Figure 3.16). Many of the tools also allow you to change the labels of these buttons if you want to use different verbiage.

There are different schools of thought around a Give Up option. Some may argue that providing this option prompts participants to put in less effort when going through the study. However, not providing the option will force people to guess an answer when they haven't found one, which could introduce more noise in data and more frustration for the participant.

Our recommendation is to include the Give Up option. First, it will acknowledge to the participants that it's okay to give up on a task and will encourage them to move on with the study rather than exiting altogether. Second, it will allow you to make a distinction between the percentages of tasks that failed as a result of *giving up* compared to participants *thinking they're in the right place* when they're not. This could be an important and insightful distinction.

FIGURE 3.16
Keynote's WebEffective provides a "Give Up" option for every task. Copyright © 2009 Keynote Systems, Inc. All rights reserved.

The tool may also allow you to branch off where a person chooses the "Give Up" option. For example, if someone clicks "Give Up" you can interject an open-ended question asking why they gave up or perhaps some questions probing more pointed questions about their experience with the task. Be careful not to make the user feel like a failure when doing this. Instead of "Why did you give up?" ask something like, "What prompted you to move on from this task?"

ARE PARTICIPANTS RELUCTANT TO ADMIT THAT THEY'RE GIVING UP?

One thing we've wondered is whether participants shy away from the idea of "giving up" on a task. As much as we remind them that the study is their evaluation of a Web site, some users inevitably feel as though it's a challenge or test of some sort. Thus, giving up can give the perception of failure to participants. Although we don't have data on it either way, we encourage you to try other phrases such as "Unable to find" or "Stop looking" and see if and how that impacts your data and the study participants' perceptions.

3.4.7 Randomizing task order and answer choices

As with traditional usability testing, it's frequently beneficial to randomize the order of tasks to minimize the learning effects on any one task. The first task that a participant receives in an online usability study almost always takes a performance "hit," especially in terms of task time. Randomizing the task order spreads this effect across all tasks. The exception is when some tasks are dependent on other tasks to be completed first or have a natural progression. Let's use the example of buying a book on a bookstore Web site. Assume that one task is to locate a particular book, another task is to add it to the shopping cart, and another task is to check out. Obviously the participant can't check out without finding and adding a book to the cart first, so there is a natural progression to the order of tasks. Randomizing these tasks would not only be confusing, but it wouldn't be possible in this situation. Perhaps a less obvious example would be the TerraPass example study. TerraPass is a Web site that allows users to search for information about and purchase carbon offsets. Because the concept of "carbon offsets" is not readily understandable to many participants, it doesn't make sense to have them jump directly into buying them. A couple of initial tasks would be appropriate, e.g., asking participants to find out more about carbon offsets, how TerraPass works, and what it costs. This would be more representative of an actual flow of information seeking.

TIP
If you're testing with an international audience, be aware of the cultural implications of giving up. Whereas Americans generally may not be shy about admitting that they can't find something, some other cultures may be less prone to do so. As always, do your research first!

TIP
Many of the commercial services available offer the ability to randomize blocks/sections, as well as some or all of the tasks and/or task answers. (A "block" is a specific grouping you can create of questions or tasks.) If randomizing is important to the study, make sure that the tool you plan to use supports this capability before you commit to it.

If using an answer list, you may also consider randomizing or rotating answer choices within the list itself. This eliminates order effects you may not be anticipating. It also makes it easy not to think about where in the list to place the "correct" answer for each task so that users don't detect a pattern. However, if the choices are part of a naturally ordered list, such as letters of the alphabet or numbers, it makes sense to keep them in order to facilitate scanning.

3.4.8 Using a subset of tasks

In some cases you might want to give each participant a smaller number of tasks selected from a larger list. This can be useful if you want to cover many aspects of the Web site without making the study too time-consuming for each participant. For example, assume you have eight tasks total but each participant is only given four of them. One participant may get Tasks 2, 5, 6, and 7, whereas another participant may get Tasks 3, 4, 5, and 8. If your tool is smart it will keep track of all the tasks and automatically balance the distribution across all participants. Otherwise, simple random chance will likely give you an acceptable distribution across a relatively large number of participants.

However, be sure that you anticipate getting enough participants performing each task or the results may not have enough statistical power. If each of the participants is only getting half of the tasks, you'll need twice as many participants as you would if they were getting all of the tasks. Also take into consideration any major segmentation you may want to do on data, for example, looking at the results by novices versus experts, age groups, and so on. Tasks would need to be attempted fairly equally across each noteworthy group of participants.

3.4.9 Self-generated and self-selected tasks

As in a typical moderated usability study, you may want to have the participant self-generate a couple of tasks to perform along with the predefined tasks. This is useful because it allows participants to share with you what they're looking to do with the Web site and perhaps identify something that you've overlooked.

If you use this technique, you should have participants generate their tasks at the beginning of the study before they see the Web site. If you let participants see or explore the site first, they will often click to a specific place first and *then* decide that the information they've found is the task they are interested in. Don't allow them to put the cart before the horse!

Self-generated tasks are also at the heart of true intent studies. In a true intent study, a real user is going on a live Web site for a real purpose and is intercepted.

Users should be intercepted upon entering the site, upon exiting the site, or both. This essentially results in a contextual, live-site online usability study. Participants can be asked at the beginning what they're trying to accomplish, and their reactions and self-reported success or failure are asked at the end of the interaction. Clickstream data can help supplement the story of their journey.

TIP

If you plan to intercept participants while they're on a live site, make sure it doesn't happen when they're about to conduct or finish a transaction, such as submitting an address change or checking out of a shopping cart!

One way to capture a self-generated task is to have participants enter a task in a text box and then have the tool store that information and present it as one of the tasks during the study. The process of asking for input and saving it for later tasks and questions is referred to as "piping."

There is usually no systematic way to score self-generated tasks as successful or not. Even if you were to have users provide answers to their own questions or if you capture clickstream data, most tasks are probably too specific to provide meaningful data across participants. However, you could ask participants an open-ended question afterward about how the task went for them or have them self-report whether they were successful. It may still be a useful piece of information to know what users are wanting or trying to do and whether they were satisfied with their experience. It also may just become a vehicle to get people using and thinking about the site in ways you didn't anticipate. The end goal is the same—understanding how the site could be made easier and more understandable, as well as just a better user experience all around.

A related technique is to let participants self-select their tasks. This means having them choose the tasks appropriate for them from a list shown at the beginning of the study. This is another take on using subsets of a task list in which the participants choose the subset rather than the system choosing it for them.

If you use this method, be sure to include some guidance rather than just telling users to "choose the task you want to do." In fact, it's best to form it as a screening or starting question so that users don't even know it's a setup for tasks. Otherwise, you may wind up with some type of bias as a result of what tasks are chosen. Users may choose something that they know how to do already, do most of the time, think would be most easy, or even most challenging.

An example of such a technique might be to have participants choose activities they think are most important or interesting to them or that they do most frequently. If they've never been on the site before, perhaps it may be what they'd expect other users to do most often. There are several ways to implement this. Rather than just selecting a task, participants could rate the importance and/or frequency of doing that task and then they're given the tasks that score in the top-2 box of that scale. Alternatively, you could have them rank order the tasks by some criteria. Figures 3.17 and 3.18 are some examples of this, using a digital video recorder (DVR) as the focus.

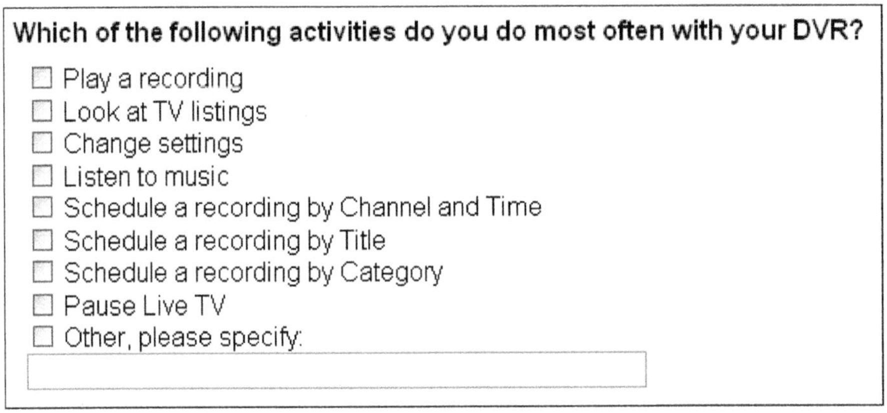

FIGURE 3.17
Self-selected tasks for
an online usability study
of DVR software.

Which of the following activities do you do most often with your DVR?

☐ Play a recording
☐ Look at TV listings
☐ Change settings
☐ Listen to music
☐ Schedule a recording by Channel and Time
☐ Schedule a recording by Title
☐ Schedule a recording by Category
☐ Pause Live TV
☐ Other, please specify:
_____

Be mindful about how you are using these criteria for participants to self-select tasks. For example, if you are using frequency to determine the tasks, this can bias participants to high task success if they are already very familiar with the areas of the Web site you're testing. However, there are instances where it makes sense to have only frequent users test the product, particularly when

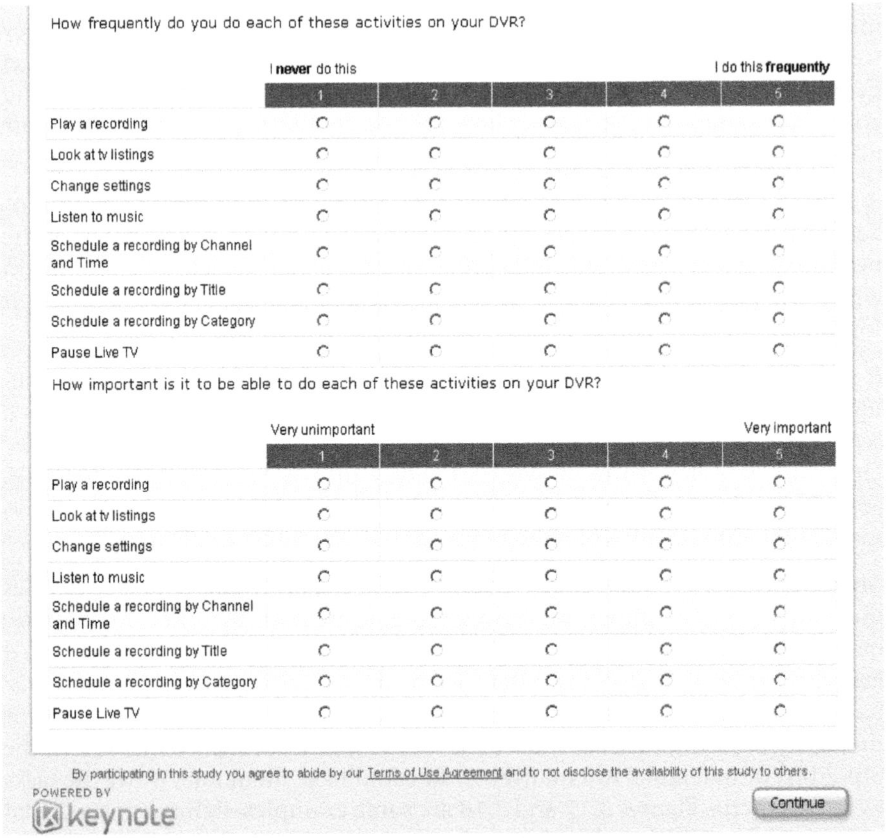

FIGURE 3.18
Example of asking
frequency and importance
as a way to generate
tasks automatically
(created in WebEffective).
Copyright © 2009
Keynote Systems, Inc.
All rights reserved.

How frequently do you do each of these activities on your DVR?

	I never do this				I do this frequently
	1	2	3	4	5
Play a recording	○	○	○	○	○
Look at tv listings	○	○	○	○	○
Change settings	○	○	○	○	○
Listen to music	○	○	○	○	○
Schedule a recording by Channel and Time	○	○	○	○	○
Schedule a recording by Title	○	○	○	○	○
Schedule a recording by Category	○	○	○	○	○
Pause Live TV	○	○	○	○	○

How important is it to be able to do each of these activities on your DVR?

	Very unimportant				Very important
	1	2	3	4	5
Play a recording	○	○	○	○	○
Look at tv listings	○	○	○	○	○
Change settings	○	○	○	○	○
Listen to music	○	○	○	○	○
Schedule a recording by Channel and Time	○	○	○	○	○
Schedule a recording by Title	○	○	○	○	○
Schedule a recording by Category	○	○	○	○	○
Pause Live TV	○	○	○	○	○

By participating in this study you agree to abide by our Terms of Use Agreement and to not disclose the availability of this study to others.

POWERED BY
keynote

Continue

it's a realistic case that the user is very familiar with the functionality or has knowledge of a special domain that's not easily understood by just any audience. As always this depends on the goals of the study and the nature of the product.

3.4.10 Self-reported task completion

Self-generated tasks are usually scored using self-reported task completion. Because the task and/or answer may be open or subjective rather than predefined, you let the participants decide for themselves whether they were successful with each of their tasks.

Figures 3.19 and 3.20 show some methods of collecting self-reported answers.

Self-reported task completion can be used in any study and with any set of tasks, self-generated or not. Aside from self-generated tasks, other cases for using this technique include the following.

- **When answers to questions or tasks may be changing**. This can be the case any time dynamic data are involved. Data may be changing moment to moment (e.g., the price of a share of stock) or more slowly (e.g., the price of a new bestseller). Sometimes you can get around this problem by providing ranges for predefined answers or by allowing a range of acceptable answers for free-form input (which, again, is a nightmare to analyze!)
- **When the important thing is that the users believe they were successful.** Self-reported task completion is a bit more controversial than other methods of collecting task completion, as in this case you may be using it to

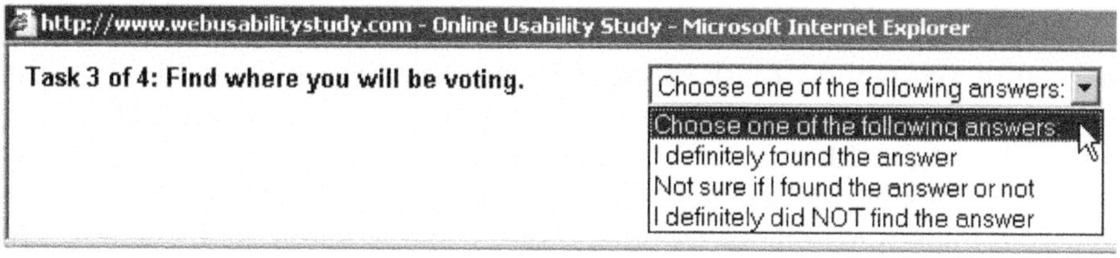

FIGURE 3.19
Example of self-reported answer choices.

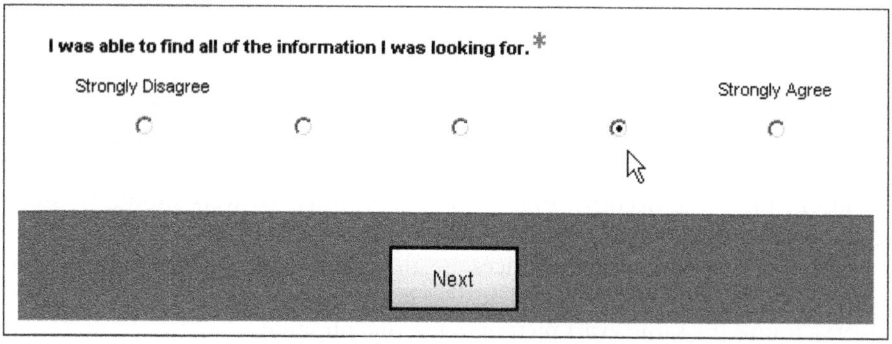

FIGURE 3.20
One form of self-reported task success as a rating scale (created in SurveyGizmo).

determine what areas of the site have usability problems or whether a competitive Web site or alternative design is better or worse. We've seen from typical usability testing that participants often think they have found the correct answer when they did not, or vice versa. Despite this, is the user's perception itself enough of a metric to judge the success of a Web site's user experience? It depends on the goals of your testing. In some cases, it's not as important that the users get an exact correct answer as it is that they feel like they have found what they were looking for. Good examples may be any reasonably complex problem or issue (e.g., the solutions to global warming), where there's usually not a simple right or wrong answer.

An example of the latter is provided by the example study comparing the Web sites of the two major U.S. presidential candidates in the 2008 election: Barack Obama and John McCain. In this study, participants were asked to do four tasks on one of the two sites (e.g., find the candidate's position on Social Security). A politician's position on something as complex as Social Security (a U.S. government-funded program to provide some degree of financial support during retirement) is never going to be as simple as "Yes, I'm for it" or "No, I'm against it." The goal of the task is really to see if participants can learn enough about the candidate's position on Social Security to feel like they have a basic understanding of their views on the subject. In cases like this, you may want to provide a scale for participants to indicate their confidence that they accomplished the task. In the Obama/McCain Web sites study, we provided three options for responding to each task:

1. I definitely found the answer
2. Not sure if I found the answer or not
3. I definitely did NOT find the answer

Of course, self-report of task success can also introduce potential bias. In the Obama/McCain study, for example, participants were assigned randomly to one site or the other, without regard for their individual political leanings. It doesn't take much of a leap to see that someone who was pro-Obama might be more generous in deciding that he had found the answer to a task on the Obama site than on the McCain site. One way to account for that bias might have been to ask participants a starter question about their political affiliation and/or preference for a candidate and either sort participants into quotas so that participation was equal across groups or segment the analysis by those groups.

If your goal is to thoroughly evaluate the usability of specific areas, first think about the content and tasks you want to use. If users are able to know whether they've found an answer, such as in the case of the presidential candidates' positions on Social Security, then using self-reported answers should be sufficient. Likewise, the example study using photo clip-art asks users to find an exact picture. Although the answer choices are all picture titles, this could have been implemented with a self-reported answer set. Users are likely to know whether they've found the same exact picture as the one presented.

It is *not* a good idea to use self-reported answers if the subject matter is more complicated and more likely to cause users to have false impressions of success. Let's take the example of one of the pets study task:

"Find the street of a PetSmart store that is in or nearest to Marietta, Georgia and offers grooming."

This task is targeted at testing the store locator on the Web site. See Figure 3.21 as an example of this.

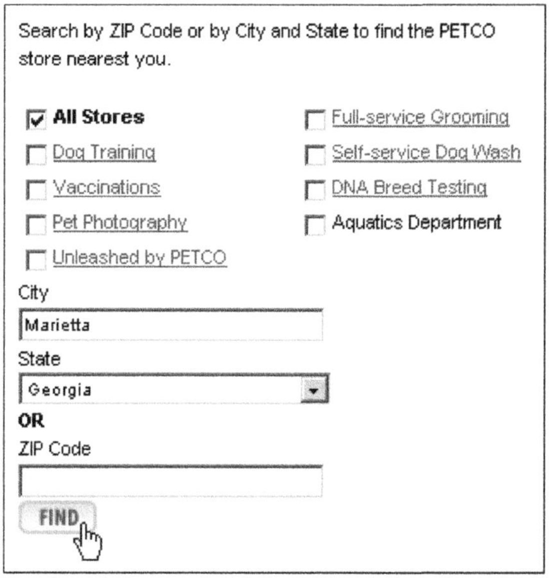

If the user fails to check off "full-service grooming" or doesn't at least look for a store with grooming on the search results page, the task is incorrect. However, the participant may still feel as though he or she accomplished the task successfully. This is a case where self-reported success does not work, and it would be better to provide specific answers so that you can detect if users noticed and used all areas of the search functionality correctly.

FIGURE 3.21
PETCO store locator.

Keep in mind some vendor tools commonly provide just the option to use two buttons, the most common being "success" or "abandon" (see Figure 3.22).

Sometimes these button names can be changed, but restricting the user to two choices may result in noisier data. If a user were to select "abandon," there is no distinction between abandoning something because they are giving up or because they were unable to find the answer. Another way may be to either provide a drop-down list of multiple answers immediately available or change the "Success" button to something like "Answer" or "Done with Task" and then give them an answer list on the next page (see Figures 3.23 and 3.24). This example does not use an abandon button, but instead gives users an answer option to say "Give Up/Not Sure."

FIGURE 3.22
"Abandon Task" and "Task Complete" buttons used in Loop11.

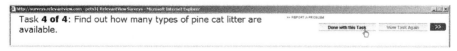

FIGURE 3.23
The user clicks "Done with this Task" when they think they've found the answer (created in RelevantView).

FIGURE 3.24
After clicking "Done," participants then get an answer choices page, which allows them to return to the task or answer and move on (created in RelevantView).

Self-reported answers are perfect for more general online studies in which you're less concerned with specific usability issues and are trying to assess the broader user experience of the site, its functionality, the brand, etc. In these true intent or open Web studies, the tasks can be even more general, such as "explore this Web site and decide when you have an understanding of what it's about." Some open Web studies can even give users a directed task, but lets them start at a search engine to find the answer anywhere they wish. The point here is that answers are not as important as the user's experience when doing the task and their own assessment of how it went. In all of these cases, the study only uses one or a few general tasks as a way to get people to interact with the Web or a Web site. Then, participants can be asked a variety of questions about their experience using the site after the study.

3.5 POST-TASK QUESTIONS AND METRICS

It's common in online usability studies to include a few questions after each task. Understanding what a user thinks about how a task went can provide insight into what specific areas of the product are working well or need attention. This section includes a discussion of some of the types of post-task ratings to collect, as well as other strategies to keep in mind when designing the study.

3.5.1 Self-reported data

There are several different types of post-task rating scales used in the field today, a few of which are covered here briefly. For a more detailed description of any of these ratings, refer to Tullis and Albert (2008).

- **Ease of use:** This is the simplest form of a rating scale asking participants how easy or difficult the task was to complete. It can be asked as a Likert scale, where a user strongly agrees or disagrees with a statement, such as:

  I found this task to be very easy:

  Strongly Disagree ○ ○ ○ ○ ○ Strongly Agree

or it can be asked as a semantic differential where you have anchor labels, such as:

This task was:

"Very Difficult" ○ ○ ○ ○ ○ "Very Easy"

Figure 3.25 shows an example of this method.

- **After-scenario questionnaire (ASQ):** This method, developed by Jim Lewis (1991), asks a few questions after each task, each with a seven-point scale of agreement:
  "I am satisfied with the ease of completing the tasks in this scenario."
  "I am satisfied with the amount of time it took to complete the tasks in this scenario."
  "I am satisfied with the support information (online help, messages, documentation) when completing the tasks."

Figure 3.26 shows an example of the ASQ, as implemented in a UzerZoom study.

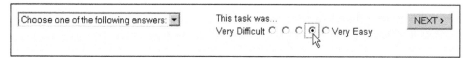

FIGURE 3.25
This study uses a simple semantic differential scale as a post-task rating, asking "This task was…"

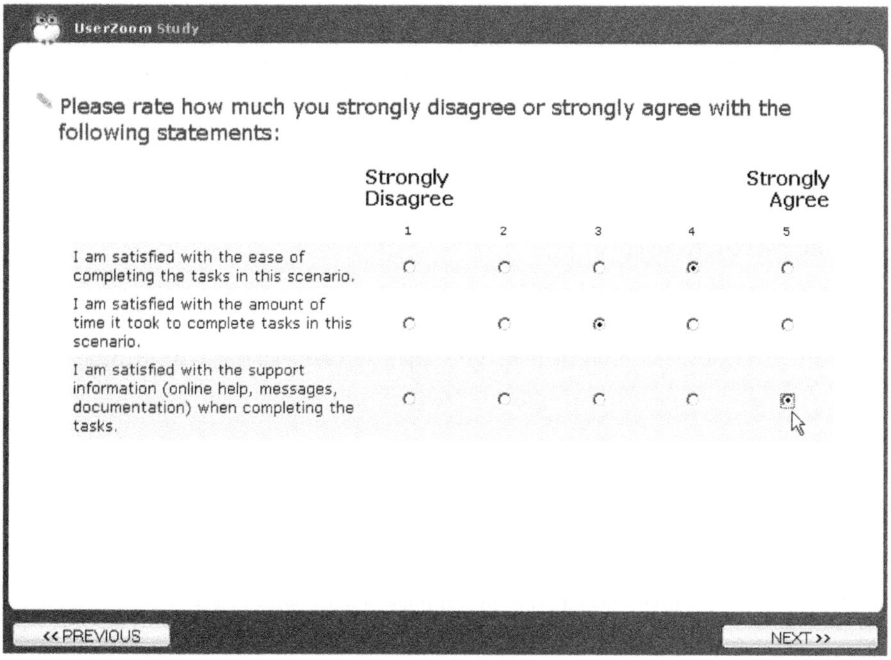

FIGURE 3.26
The ASQ consists of three questions with Likert scales (created in UserZoom).

- **Expectation measures:** As described earlier in this chapter, Albert and Dixon (2003) asked users to rate how easy/difficult they expected tasks to be before attempting them, and then again how easy/difficult they were after attempting tasks. This uses a seven-point scale, where 1 was "Very Difficult" and 7 was "Very Easy." Plotting expectations against actual ease of use response gives insights of where to focus attention and opportunities for exceeding users' expectations.

Each of these methods can be implemented in online usability studies. Expectation measures can be implemented by giving the participant a survey of expectations at the beginning of the study and then their ease of use rating again after each task. Finally, simple ease of use and ASQ questions can be implemented easily after each task.

We've found that although the ASQ and expectation ratings can provide insightful results, using the simple ease of use question does the trick just as well, if not better (Tedesco and Tullis, 2006).

You may want to ask users more specific rating scale questions about their experience for each task, such as how it was navigating through the interface. Just remember to keep it short, especially if you have a lot of tasks and questions to get through.

3.5.2 Open-ended responses

Although open-ended responses can be challenging to analyze, gathering participants' feedback is essential. Because the study is unmoderated, you are left only to interpret data without any observational notes to guide you. Eliciting general feedback after each task can be as simple as allowing a user to enter comments or asking about their experience with a specific task. These general comments that are always available should be optional because people don't always have feedback to give, and being forced to after every task or question can be frustrating and result in drop-off.

Figure 3.27 is an example of an open-ended response interface offered by Keynote's WebEffective.

Another option for open-ended responses is to prompt participants to give feedback based on a certain event, such as when they find a task particularly difficult or choose to abandon or give up the task. Using conditional logic,

FIGURE 3.27
WebEffective displays a button for "Comment" at any time during the study. Copyright © 2009 Keynote Systems, Inc. All rights reserved.

participants who rate a task as difficult can be assigned to answer an open-ended post-task question. Figure 3.28 is an example of this. Participants were given this question if they chose one of the bottom two box ratings of an ease-of-use scale elicited after the task.

The same conditional logic could be applied to unsuccessful task completion, but be careful about when to do this; participants should not be able to detect a pattern regarding when they have gotten a task "wrong."

What did you find to be difficult about this task?

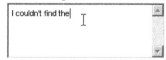

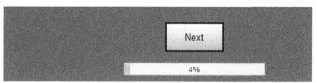

FIGURE 3.28
Open-ended response box set up in SurveyGizmo as a result of rating a task as difficult.

Finally, when providing the opportunity to enter post-task comments, take task times into account. If the tool you're using includes open-ended response time as part of the time on task, this may increase task times significantly. It depends on other factors; if you offer open-ended questions equally across tasks and designs, task times would equally be affected and therefore it may not be an issue. However, if you are only allowing comments for select tasks, designs, or based on select ratings or performance, task times may be increased unevenly and can skew data.

TIP
To mitigate risks of open-ended comments messing with the task times, look for a tool or commercial service that will support constructing tasks so that users first find the answer and click a button, which *then* stops the time before bringing them to a post-task comment question.

3.6 POST-SESSION QUESTIONS AND METRICS

Post-session (or "post-study") responses and metrics are usually collected at the end of the study, after all the tasks, in an effort to summarize the overall usability and/or user experience of the product. We've used them most successfully to compare one design alternative against others or one design against its competitors.

3.6.1 Overall rating scales

Some simple questions can be used just to sum up the user experience for participants. Similar to asking overall ease of use just after a task, you can ask overall ease of use regarding the entire experience on the Web site or section of the Web site. Figure 3.29 shows an example of this.

Of course, you are not getting the internal reliability of a full questionnaire on the topic, but this is a useful, simple barometer for how the experience went.

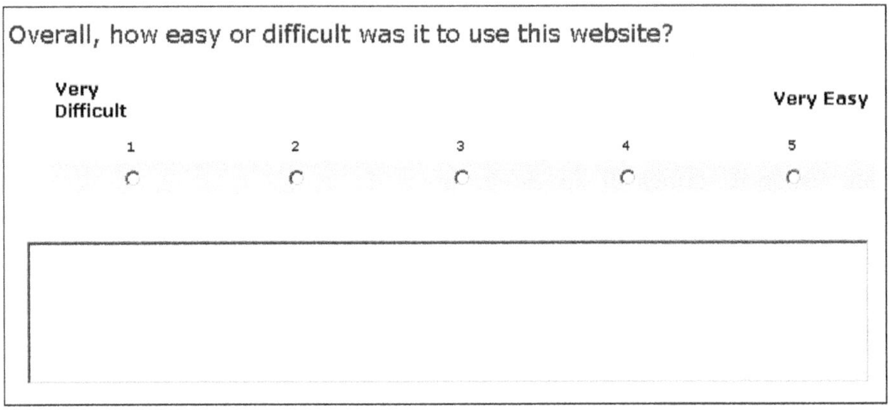

FIGURE 3.29
Overall ease of use
question post-session.

Overall, how easy or difficult was it to use this website?

Very
Difficult   Very Easy

| 1 | 2 | 3 | 4 | 5 |

In addition to ease of use, there are other more detailed aspects of the user experience that you may want to collect data on, such as navigation, visual appeal, organization, and terminology. You can also get a feel for participants' experiences with the site by asking questions such as whether they would return to the Web site or recommend it to a friend. These specific examples may be useful depending on the domain you're testing and what your goals are. This is where you can get creative with those broader user experience questions. Perhaps you want to know if participants' perception of the brand has changed after using the site or simply whether a new design is an improvement over an old one. If testing a Web site about food products, maybe you'll want to ask questions about how looking at pictures of food makes them want to taste or buy it. Rating scale questions on these topics is a nice way to collect attitudinal and emotional reactions quantifiably, especially if you plan to use it for benchmarking or comparative purposes. A couple of examples of these broader user experience questions are shown in Figures 3.30 and 3.31.

TIP
You can get creative with broader user experience questions, but remember to stick to good question construction, keep it neutrally worded, and use it as only one piece of the greater puzzle, along with results from task completion, task times, open-ended comments, etc.

FIGURE 3.30
Question asking how much a user is inspired by a Web site (created in WebEffective).

I am inspired by this website.

O Strongly Disagree
O
O
O
O Strongly Agree

POWERED BY
keynote
©1998-2009 Keynote Systems, Inc. | Contact | Privacy Policy

Continue

Final Questions:	I think that I would like to use this site again in the future.
#3 of 13:	

‹ Previous   **Strongly Disagree** ○ ○ ○ ○ ○ **Strongly Agree**   Next ›

FIGURE 3.31
Likelihood of using the
Web site in the future.

3.6.2 Overall assessment tools

In addition to rating scales asking about specific characteristics or features of the Web site, it's relatively common to include a standard set of rating scales designed to assess the Web site as a whole. Several post-session questionnaires are available for free or as part of a service. Some of these include:

- System Usability Scale (SUS): 10 questions on a five-point Likert scale
- Computer System Usability Questionnaire (CSUQ): 19 questions on a seven-point Likert scale
- Questionnaire for User Interface Satisfaction (QUIS): 27 questions in the form of semantic differential questions with 10-point intervals
- Usefulness, Satisfaction, and Ease of Use Questionnaire (Lund, 2001): 30 questions on a seven-point Likert scale
- Web site Analysis and Measurement Inventory (WAMMI): 20 questions on a five-point Likert scale
- Net Promoter Score® (NPS) created by Satmetrix Systems (2008): A single question ("How likely is it that you would recommend [site or company name] to a friend or colleague?") rated on an 11-point semantic differential scale from "Not at All Likely" to "Extremely Likely." Just keep in mind that users' perception of the company or brand could affect this likelihood rating.

> **TIP**
> Some post-session questionnaires are available online already, hosted by either paid services or free, publicly available tools. For example, Gary Perlman created a Web interface that allows you to administer QUIS, ASQ, or CSUQ and have results sent directly to your email address (http://www.acm.org/perlman/question.html).

Why would you want to include one of these standard questionnaires? Mainly because they were designed by experts in the field and, in some cases, there may be benchmark data available that you can compare the site's results to (such as the WAMMI service). While all of these questionnaires can be useful, the SUS questionnaire has become quite popular for several reasons:

- It's relatively short and simple (10 rating scales).
- It has been made freely available for commercial and noncommercial use as long as the source is credited.
- It has been demonstrated that it yields reliable results even with relatively small numbers of participants (Tullis and Stetson, 2004).

The SUS asks 10 questions all targeted at the same concept, and the polarity of the scale is flipped for every other question. For more information on analyzing SUS ratings, see Chapter 6.

Figure 3.32 shows an example of using SUS as part of a post-session questionnaire.

FIGURE 3.32
The SUS given in the form of a matrix question (created in UserZoom).

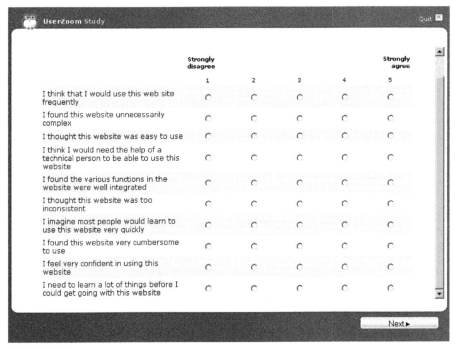

3.6.3 Open-ended questions

Finally, it is always useful to finish the session with a few open-ended questions about the experience. Instead of asking just an open-ended question on overall thoughts, participants will be more articulate with their thoughts if you ask more specific questions. Most online usability studies include one or more open-ended questions at the end of the study, such as the following.

- Were there any aspects of the Web site that you found particularly challenging or frustrating? If so, please describe.
- Were there any aspects of the Web site that you thought were particularly effective or intuitive? If so, please describe.
- Please describe anything you would do to improve this Web site.

Similar to the verbatim comments at the task level, these comments at the end of a study can be an incredibly rich source of insight into how to improve the Web site. We've found that generally about 60–80% of the participants who complete the tasks of a study provide at least some responses to the open-ended questions, particularly those asking about challenging aspects of the site or suggestions for improvement.

Another method commonly used in studies is to ask participants for their top likes and then a separate question for their top dislikes. Asking for the top few requires participants to think carefully about the experience enough to provide more than one, and internally prioritize thoughts so as not to provide too many. Breaking likes and dislikes up into two questions also forces them to think about the two separately rather than just focusing on the more negative aspects of the experience.

If you plan to use "like" and "dislike" questions, be prepared to obtain feedback on *all* aspects of the Web site, including colors, look, and feel. These questions give participants free rein to comment. If you're looking for more specific usability and behavioral feedback, using questions about challenging/frustrating and effective/intuitive experiences will yield more pointed results.

3.7 DEMOGRAPHIC QUESTIONS AND WRAP-UP

At the end of a session, it is common to finish with demographic questions. Then to wrap up, participants are brought to a thank-you page with some final information for them about their incentive and where they can go next.

3.7.1 Demographic questions

We typically ask demographic questions, such as age, gender, level of education, employment, and income, when there is a need to segment data and compare the sample of participants to either the general population or the targeted user population of the product. Although you may have worked with a panel that has this information on file, it's a good idea to ask the questions again just to make sure that data are accurate and current.

We typically place demographic questions at the end of a survey or usability study. By the time participants have arrived at the demographic questions toward the end of the study, they are usually less apprehensive and have already invested a lot of time into the study. The only times we tend to place demographic questions at the beginning of the study are when they are needed for screening or branching purposes.

We recommend keeping the questions basic and trying to avoid questions of a sensitive nature if possible. Although age and gender are typical questions, many people consider them a bit sensitive so we recommend that they're made optional. Having users type in their actual age often feels intrusive and personal to them, as can asking for a date of birth. The best method in this case is to allow people to select an age range. The appropriate age ranges might depend on market segments or other factors. If the study is being sent to the general public, try to provide as wide of a set of age ranges as possible. For example, don't make the assumption that people over 65 are not using the Web. Likewise, if you feel that you can lump all people into one market segmentation category for the product of 55+, still make an effort to break down that 55+ category in the demographic question. Otherwise, some people may feel offended in taking the study if their category isn't given equal "decomposition."

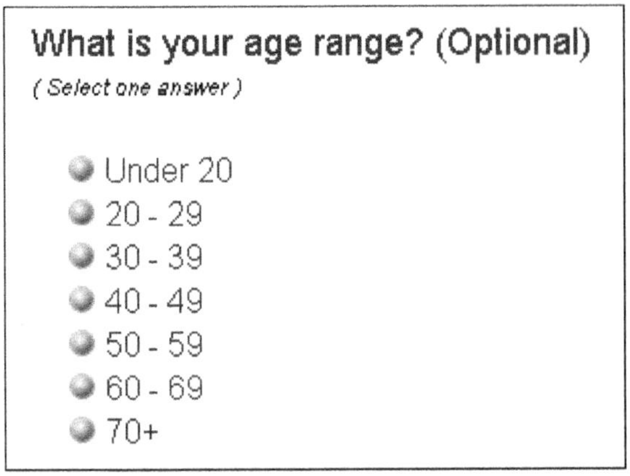

What is your age range? (Optional)

(Select one answer)

- Under 20
- 20 - 29
- 30 - 39
- 40 - 49
- 50 - 59
- 60 - 69
- 70+

FIGURE 3.33
Example age range
(created in RelevantView).

An example of an age range question is shown in Figure 3.33.

Level of education, employment status, and individual or household income are other questions used commonly in surveys for segmentation purposes. Again, these types of questions are sensitive and should be made optional. As with age, income level should be presented in groups from which to choose.

Other especially sensitive questions are sometimes used in survey research, such as religious affiliation, race, or ethnicity. These should be avoided if possible. Once again, it's not likely that these factors would impact behavioral research unless it's related directly to the domain and usage of the product.

3.7.2 Wrap-up

When the study is complete and users submit answers to their demographic questions, it is customary to end with a "thank-you" page. It could be as simple as just thanking participants for their time, but it's often useful to provide a little more information. This may include:

- Assurance that their data have been submitted
- Disclosure of the purpose of the study, if it was intentially avoided at the beginning of the study (so as not to bias participants)
- Information about the incentive, such as when and how they will receive it, when a drawing will take place, and how they will be contacted in the event that they win
- Opportunity to enter their email and/or other contact information, either for incentive purposes (if not already collected) or to receive a summary of the results of the study
- A reminder of contact information if they have any questions or problems
- A link to close the window or redirect to another Web site (e.g., the currently available version of the Web site just tested)
- Ability to print the page, especially if there is contact information and drawing information

As always, be sure to use an appreciative tone with users and leave them feeling confident and hopefully even like they had fun!

Figure 3.34 is an example of a "Thank You" page.

3.8 SPECIAL TOPICS

This section provides a few additional topics related to constructing an online usability study, including progress indicators, pausing, and speed traps.

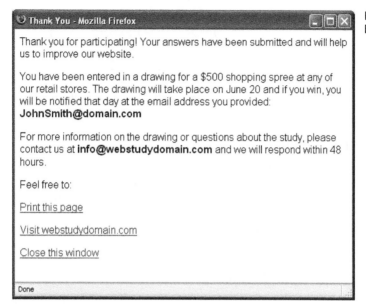

FIGURE 3.34
Example Thank You page.

3.8.1 Progress indicators

Progress indicators give participants a sense of how far along they are within a session and the rate at which they're going. They are helpful to include, especially if there are many pages to the study. If the study is only one or two pages, as with a true intent or open Web study, it is not necessary to give indication of progress.

One common type of progress indicator implemented is a bar or graphic with incrementally more of it filled for each page complete, as in Figure 3.35. Sometimes these bars are accompanied by percentage values. If the study is 20 pages long, but each page is a quick task or question, seeing the visual indicator build up quickly assures participants that they are moving quickly through the study and allows them to gauge when they'll be finished.

Another way of indicating is to number questions and tasks, "1 of X" where X is the total number of questions or tasks. This also sets the users' expectations of how long they will need to dedicate to the study.

Make sure that the tool used is showing progress for natural "chunks" of the study. For example, if the tool can only count each individual "element" as a question, but a single task is made up of four "elements"—task, answer, post-task rating, and post-task open-ended question—it will count as four questions. Therefore, if you have 10 tasks, it will be counted as 40 questions. Participants seeing "Question 3 of 40" can be turned off easily, when in reality it's just 10 natural chunks to complete. In these cases, check if your tool has the ability to customize it so that you can instead say "Task X of 10" for each set of elements. If this isn't possible, attend to this issue carefully during the pilot test and perhaps compare drop-off rates for progress bars turned both on and off.

FIGURE 3.35
Example progress indicator offered in WebEffective. Copyright © 2009 Keynote Systems, Inc. All rights reserved.

3.8.2 Pausing

If possible, you may also want to provide the ability for users to pause the session if they're unexpectedly interrupted. Not only will this allow participants to feel like they don't have to rush or put their life on hold, but it will help the sample sizes and analysis. As shown in Chapter 5, because we usually filter data for excessively long task times, providing this ability may save otherwise legitimate data from being discarded.

3.8.3 Speed traps

Burke's Panel Quality R&D (2008) has continuously monitored how "undesirable" respondents have impacted data as part of their panel quality research. They categorize undesirables by participants who misrepresent themselves in the screening process and "mental cheaters" who tend to race through surveys with little thought and effort. When looking at how undesirables' data compared with "true" respondents on a set of survey data, they found that various attributes rated for a product were much different for undesirable participants than ratings for true participants.

In addition to putting measures in place during the screening process, it can be important to catch mental cheaters during the study using speed traps. Speed traps are ways of determining whether users are putting in a good-faith effort during the study. One tactic used by Burke and others in the field includes simply asking users to do or enter something very simple. For example, as part of the SUS questionnaire, participants might be asked to select the middle option of one of the rating scales. Speed traps work best when they are part of a group of answers or questions. An example is shown in Figure 3.36.

In one study we conducted, roughly 10% of the participants actually chose a radio button other than the middle choice! This rate differs from study to study

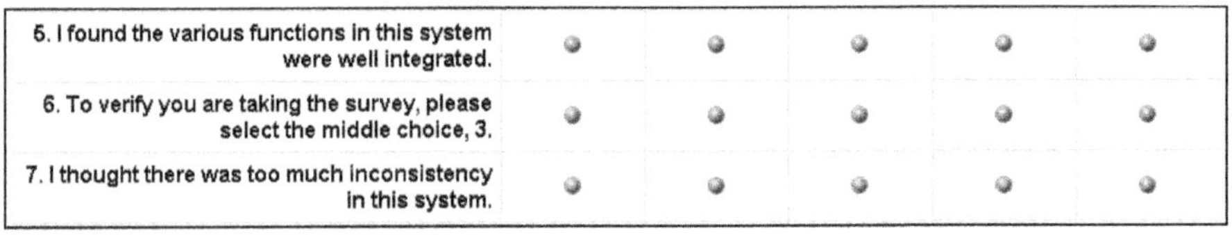

6. I found the various functions in this system were well integrated.	○	○	○	○	○
6. To verify you are taking the survey, please select the middle choice, 3.	○	○	○	○	○
7. I thought there was too much inconsistency in this system.	○	○	○	○	○

FIGURE 3.36
Example speed trap. In the pets study, question number 6 asks users to verify their place in the survey by selecting the middle choice.

as well as where speed traps are placed in the study, but nevertheless they're still important to include.

Another speed trap is to ask the same question twice, with one worded positively and one worded negatively, for example, "This Web site was easy to use" and "This Web site was not easy to use." These two questions should provide opposite ratings.

3.9 SUMMARY

The key to getting quality results in an online usability study is designing every-thing attentively—from instructions, screening and starter questions, to tasks, and follow-up questions. Remember the following points.

- The introduction should include things such as the purpose and sponsor and contact information to engage their trust, a realistic time estimate, an incentive and any other information to increase motivation, any techni-cal requirements in clear terms, necessary informed consent and/or legal language, and straightforward instructions.
- Any screening questions should be included at the beginning of the study and asked in groups or all at once so as not to clue people into what parameters might screen them in or out. Consider including questions (or combinations of questions) designed to weed out those who are trying to misrepresent themselves. Finally, be graceful in the exit strategy so that people still feel appreciated and are likely to participate again.
- In any starter questions, such as Web site experience, Web savvy, or expec-tation ratings, stick to the principles of survey design. Make sure that the questions are interpreted as you intended. Try to avoid biasing participants by using distractor tasks rather than calling out any areas that you plan to study exclusively.
- Choose tasks that will cover a good cross section of the Web site or the area of the Web site you're studying. Make tasks easy to interpret and understand. If collecting task success, use multiple-choice answers to make your analy-sis easier. Unless self-reported task completion suits the Web site and goals, provide a list of plausible answers that cannot be combed by process of elim-ination and that may even provide insight into wrong answers. Consider including a "Don't Know/Give Up" option and a "None of the Above" option. When possible, randomize tasks to counteract ordering effects. Also consider when it's appropriate to use self-selected and self-generated tasks.
- For more subjective data, include some self-reported post-task ratings or questions, perhaps with logic built in to ask open-ended questions in the event that a participant struggled with or didn't like attempting a task. Consider using a post-session questionnaire, the most commonly used being the SUS. For more insight, provide a few open-ended questions, for example, those touching on intuitiveness, frustration, and/or likes, dislikes, and suggestions for improvement.
- Demographic questions are usually asked at the end, the most common of which being age group and gender. Be careful about when and how

you ask more sensitive questions such as employment, income level, and especially religion, race, and ethnicity.

- State wrap-up points kindly and appreciatively. Thank participants for their time, give them any necessary details about incentives, restate contact information, and collect their info if you want or need to contact them for study results or incentive purposes.
- Consider including some other aspects to the study, such as speed traps to eliminate mental cheaters, progress indicators, and a pausing feature if you're collecting task times.

CHAPTER 4

Piloting and Launching the Study

After designing the study, it's time to build, pilot, and launch it. We discuss more about your options for building the study in Chapter 7, which gives an overview of various commercial services, as well as in Chapter 8, which explains how to put together a discount online study. Regardless of which implementation method you've chosen, this chapter focuses on how to prepare the study to be piloted and launched. We first discuss the various aspects of the study to validate through piloting, including technical checks, usability checks, and data checks. We then discuss factors around timing and phasing the study launch and monitoring the results.

4.1 PILOT DATA

Regardless of how small or large the study, we think it's important to do a small pilot test first. Believe us when we say that no matter how confident you are that the study is perfect, there will likely be some issue—whether it's people misinterpreting a task or question, a drop-down list not working properly on a particular browser or platform, or data being returned to the database in some unexpected format. These kinds of issues are bound to come up, and it's important to catch them before launching the full study. Just as having an unusable Web site can affect the perception of a company or institution negatively, so can administering a faulty online study. A study that is broken or confusing may also undermine users' trust in a Web site or a company's brand.

Piloting is especially important for online studies. Because there's no one moderating the study in person, it's possible to wind up with poor quality results if the study is not pretested. But this doesn't mean the whole test will take longer than if you conducted it in a lab. From our experience, the end-to-end time spent is about equal or less for online studies.

So how long are we talking? It varies. We've done pilot tests for online studies by sending out a link to a few people and were done running and analyzing it an hour, whereas for other tests we've done iterative piloting with different groups over a few days. It also depends on how quickly the pilot participants complete the test. You may be waiting on results from people for up to a week's time. We've also found that the more online tests we've conducted, the better we've gotten at constructing studies, the more focused we've been in piloting, and thus the faster the entire pilot process (not to mention full study time) has become.

PRESSURE FROM CLIENTS AND BUSINESS PARTNERS

We know that most corporate environments are fast-paced, especially in projects these days using agile methodologies. Although there may be pressure from clients and business partners to launch immediately, it's a matter of planning your time appropriately. Set expectations with the stakeholders that the pilot phase is important and worth some time. In fact, it's great to even involve them as pilot participants so that they see that importance first-hand and feel more ownership for the study.

This section outlines three types of piloting.

- **Technical checks:** Is the study working properly? This requires the least number of people and least amount of time. It may not even be necessary at all if you're using a reliable commercial service or tool.
- **Usability checks:** Is the study easy to understand, navigate, and testing what it's meant to test? This is essentially a mini–usability test of the study design itself and can be done with two or three people over the course of a couple of hours.

> **TIP**
> The three types of pilot tests can happen all at once, or sequentially. Generally we'll do technical checks and usability checks at the same time, fix anything that needs to be fixed, and then do the full pilot with data checks.

- **Full pilot with data checks:** This will be more participants, preferably real target users. The number of pilot participants depends, as it should be proportional to the participation you anticipate for a full-scale test. The goal is to have a final technical and usability check, but also to get a sense of results in the aggregate to make sure nothing questionable is happening with data.

4.1.1 Technical checks

We like to think of technical checks as a mini–quality assurance evaluation of the study. Essentially, you're trying to break it. You want to make sure everything is working properly and collecting all necessary data.

For this type of pilot study, the goal is to have two or three people each go through the study a few times quickly. It doesn't have to be anything formal; you can just run through it yourself and elicit the help of a couple of friends or colleagues. You don't have to do the study and tasks for real or with careful thought (that comes in the full pilot phase with data checks discussed in Section 4.1.3); just enter data in the fields, choose answers to every question, and proceed through the study in its entirety. This is also a good time to test the study in different environments (operating systems, screen resolutions, browsers, connection speeds, etc.). But if you don't have the time or resources to do this, the full pilot with data checks will be an opportunity to test it in those environments.

TIP

Many of the checkpoints listed may not be applicable if you're using a commercial service or tool that has already been tested and monitored by a third party. But we still recommend running through a technical check, perhaps to a lesser extent, to make sure everything's working correctly.

The following things should be looked at when doing technical checks. We liken it to the type of checklist a quality assurance engineer might use to simulate edge cases when testing a product.

- Are you unable to load a page or submit a form?
- Do you have any problems at a particular screen resolution or on a particular operating system, browser, or at certain connection speeds that make the study render oddly or be unable to complete?
- Are data showing up as something *impossible* (this is different from *improbable*, which is covered in Section 4.1.3), e.g., zero seconds for a task time or clickstream data showing one page logged for a multipage process?
- Are correct values being passed from page to page, e.g., passing an ID number that is entered on the first page of the study?
- Are correct values returned to the database? If rating scales are coded to return values of one to seven, there is an error if it's returning a zero or eight. Performing a frequency analysis on all data (counting how many times each value appears) can help check this.
- Even more granular, did what you entered return correctly? If you selected the third radio button while going through the study, did it return the corresponding value to the database? Check each value.
- Are error messages (e.g., for required fields) appearing at the appropriate times and displaying the correct messages?
- Is the study branching off to the appropriate questions based on the appropriate responses?
- Can comments fields handle large amounts of text and different types of characters?

Depending on how the study is designed, there may be more technical checks to look out for. Across all stages of piloting, there should be enough usage scenarios that you'll catch glaring issues before launching. Don't wait until a full-scale launch to find out technical problems with the study! We've learned this the hard way. When launch day has come, you'll want to sit back and monitor the results rather than race to fix technical issues affecting hundreds of people and attempting to salvage data!

TESTING WITH VARIOUS OPERATING SYSTEMS, BROWSERS, AND RESOLUTIONS

It's important to test with at least the most common operating systems, Web browsers, and screen resolutions. If you want up to date information on how much these components are being used, a good reference is http://www.w3counter.com/globalstats.php.

- Web browsers: At the time this book was written, the most common Web browsers were Microsoft Internet Explorer, Mozilla Firefox, Apple's Safari, and Google Chrome.
- Operating systems: It is no surprise that the two major players here are Windows operating systems (including Vista and XP) and Macintosh (various versions of OS X), although a small but vocal part of the population also uses the Open Source operating system Linux.
- Screen resolutions: At the time this was written, about a third of the population was using 1024 × 768, so it is important to accommodate for at least that. Screen resolutions being used are changing quickly, as widescreen laptops and monitors become more popular. So make sure to try the study out on a couple of different widescreen resolutions as well.

If the tool being used has the ability to capture participants' browsers, operating systems, and screen resolutions, it will also help give a better idea of what to consider or test for in future studies.

Finally, although it's not the primary focus of this book, mobile computing is becoming more ubiquitous. There are a host of new considerations for mobile platforms and some useful books available that cover designing for mobile Web sites and applications. Also see the case study regarding online usability testing for mobile applications in Chapter 9.

JOYS OF A TIME STAMP

Even with piloting, we've found it important to append a date and time stamp to data when submitted. This was another one of our painful lessons learned! Sometimes the study contains a technical or usability issue that needs to be fixed midlaunch or the content on a live site changes in a way that affects the tasks. When doing data analysis, you'll need to know what responses were submitted *before* the change and what data were submitted *after*. This can be tricky to investigate if there's no discrete point in time around which to work. Many of the commercial services do provide dates and times for each participant's data, but check before committing!

4.1.2 Usability checks

It's important to "practice what you preach" when it comes to usability testing. One purpose of piloting is essentially to usability test the *study itself*. This stage of the pilot is best performed by sitting with two or three people and having them think aloud as they're completing the study. Sound familiar? If possible, try to find some people who closely fit the profile of the participants being targeted. If that can't be arranged easily, we've discovered great feedback from just sitting down with co-workers, friends, or even family members. Keep in mind that the product design itself is not being tested yet, just the framework with which the study is being administered. So unless the nature of the tasks is extremely specialized, having only "real" users participate is not critical.

TIP
One instance in which it's important to get "real" users to do the usability checks is when testing with participants in other countries and cultures. Make sure to test with people who speak the native language of the study to test that the translation is appropriate.

The purpose of this stage of the pilot is to find out more about:

- The introduction, including instructions
- Screener and background questions asked
- Questions and tasks
- Web controls and pages participants need to interact with
- The overall flow and time spent on the study
- Their overall satisfaction with the study experience

Specifically, make sure that participants understand what they're being asked to do and how to step through the study to completion. Do participants understand how they need to provide an answer to a task? Are the questions asking or measuring what they're supposed to ask or are they being misinterpreted? Are they trying to type 300 characters into a comments field when there is a maximum of 255? Do they trust the information being asked for in the background questions or within the Web site itself? Do they understand that they're working with a prototype or with a live Web site? Basically you're looking for feedback on anything that might cause bias in study data, add noise, increase abandonment, or just plain frustrate participants.

TIP
Feeling like you might miss something? Check out our Web site for a consolidated checklist of things to look for when pilot testing.

Watching people participate in the study may also give a sense of how people may try to bilk the system. You may realize that a particular group of questions lend themselves to participants just breezing through and mentally cheating on their answers. These possibilities don't always occur to us in the study design phase when we're concerned about making each individual question perfect. But seeing someone else go through the study in its entirety, in real time, often gives us that fresh perspective.

In addition to thinking aloud, it helps to ask participants a few post-pilot questions at the end about their experience with the study itself (again, rather than whatever you are testing). Some examples may include:

- How clear/unclear were the instructions? Questions? Tasks?
- Was there any point in the study where you might have considered quitting without finishing? Where?
- Did the study feel too long or too short? Were the time expectations accurate?
- How could the study be improved overall?

Some of these questions may best be asked in the context of walking through the study with them a second time, focusing specifically on these details.

4.1.3 Full pilot with data checks

After, or in conjunction with conducting technical checks and usability checks with a handful of people, this stage of the pilot is a full run-through with a larger group of pilot participants. Data checks are similar to technical checks, but the focus is more on the quality and "sanity" of data rather than whether individual data were submitted and returned correctly. Think of it in terms of looking at data in the aggregate—looking at the bigger picture rather than individual pieces of data. Let's take the example of the pets study task:

"You remember the ferret food you like to buy starts with a 'Z'. Find out the weights of the two bags of this food available for purchase."

Let's say that the answer choices looked like the following:

2
4
8
10

The intended correct answer to the task was "4" at the time that the study was designed, meaning 4 pounds (the unit of measurement was purposely omitted for the sake of this example). But what if 70% of the participants answered "8"? This could be due to a number of different reasons:

- *Timing issue:* The live Web site was changed from when the study was designed to when it launched. For example, they started only offering 8 pound bags of food or added a second option of the 8-pound bag that users saw first.
- *Alternative answers/paths:* There may have been a different path to a different answer than the path you anticipated or expected users to take, e.g. there was a promotional link off the home page that brings users to another page with more or different options for ferret food.
- *Technical glitch:* The tool was coded accidentally to display the answer choice "8" twice and omitted "4" (the correct answer) altogether. Normally you'd have caught this when doing the technical checks, but perhaps it wasn't clear until looking across a large amount of data.

- *Misinterpretation:* Participants misinterpreted the question or looked at the answers quickly and assumed that the task was asking for price and not weight. In this example, units of measurement were missing from the answers so they chose "8", thinking that they were indicating the purchase price of $8.00 and not a weight of 8 pounds (also should be caught with usability checks).
- *Abandonment:* "8" was the first choice in the list, and choosing it was the participants' only way of bailing out of the task because there was some prototype or study issue that prevented them from completing the task. Alternatively, perhaps it was a legitimate design flaw and people couldn't find the answer using the Web site so they chose the first answer available. Cases like this reinforce the need for a "None of the Above" or "Give Up/Can't Find" answer so that you aren't left wondering whether this was a legitimate response or whether there was a problem with the study design or implementation. It also demonstrates why it's helpful to randomize answer choices where appropriate so if you never catch this problem, at least the effects would be spread out evenly across data rather than biasing it in one direction.

> **TIP**
> As a caveat and reminder, steer away from randomizing any set of answers that have a natural order to them, such as in the pets example where numbers are being used for weights.

It's important to take a good look at pilot data to catch any irregularities such as the one illustrated in the previous example. Here are some more tips and examples.

- Look for themes in answers and choices, e.g., a vast majority of participants failed a particular task or took an unexpected path to an answer.
- Look for improbabilities; when collecting task time, make sure that the majority of participants weren't taking unusually short or long periods of time to complete certain tasks.
- Cross-reference data when taking a high-level view of it; if the majority of the participants who got the task wrong rated the task as very easy, was it because they *thought* they got it right, but were mistaken (the worst kind of usability issue)? Was it because the anchors (e.g., "strongly disagree" and "strongly agree") on the rating scales were accidentally reversed? Was it because they misinterpreted what they were looking for?
- If you find contradictions between verbatim responses and how easy they rated a task to be, investigate this further.
- Also look for excessive drop-off rates and themes regarding where participants are dropping off in the study.

As you can see, there may be many explanations for an unexpected piece of data, which is where your investigation work comes in. It especially underlines why you should do other types of pilots in conjunction with this one, such as sitting with people as they attempt to go through it (usability checks) or quality assurance testing the study to make sure it's functioning properly (technical checks).

HOW MANY PILOT PARTICIPANTS DO YOU NEED?

The number of participants appropriate for this stage of piloting should be proportional to how many you anticipate for "real" study results. It also depends on the complexity and criticality of the study. There's no perfect formula, but if you were to take us hostage in a usability lab until getting an answer, we'd generally recommend piloting with about 10% of the number of participants expected to complete the real study.

If our 10% answer is not enough to release us from your captivity, here is our very nonscientific recipe for you.

- About 10% of the expected results return, unless that would mean less than 10 or more than 200 people
- Add in an additional pinch of participants for each factor: especially business-critical studies, studies with a complex subject matter, and/or complex study design

Here are a few examples.

- **Exhibit A:** We were expecting about 100 participants for a quick validation of a redesigned widget that was usability tested in a lab already. Here we looked for about 10% pilot group, or about 10 people. If it were a particular critical study and any more complicated, we might have upped that number to 20 or so.
- **Exhibit B:** We were hoping for about 500 or so responses in the real test, but this was a very complex test with many moving parts (multiple versions of the study, multiple prototypes, complex subject matter, great deal of pressure from business partners). In this case our 10% guideline would have given us 50 participants, but we wanted to be sure so we upped it to about 80.
- **Exhibit C:** There is an expected turnout of 10,000 responses (not likely, but possible, and we're making this one up). In this case, 10% is probably excessive. We'd likely learn what we need to learn with a couple hundred responses instead. It might take a good deal of time and effort to get a few hundred pilot participants, but if the study is important enough that we've arranged for 10,000 responses to the real test, then a pilot group of 200 is worth it, proportionally.

Keep in mind that if the study runs smoothly with the full pilot group and nothing needs to be changed, their data can be counted toward the final results!

We gave you a number of things to look out for when conducting a full pilot with data checks. But the moral of the story is that you're eyeballing data for anything that looks fishy. Once data are collected, it will take a few hours at most. And don't worry—if you are afraid of missing any potential problems in the pilot phase, we have some tips in Chapter 5 to help you clean up "real" study data when it starts to roll in.

4.1.4 Preview of results

The final reason to do a pilot is to preview the results. This is instrumental in making sure that you are collecting everything necessary to answer the research questions and goals.

The first step is to take pilot data and perform the exact analyses that you plan to with the real data set. Going through this exercise has allowed us to see if there are any gaping holes in data and whether the data really address what we've intended.

Let's take the example of a true intent study, where actual users are intercepted when visiting a Web site on their own and asked to report their intentions and/or experiences using that Web site. To make it easy, let's assume a hypothetical example in which we're conducting a true intent study of a bookstore Web site and, upon exiting, users get a survey.

The first question is, "What did you come to this Web site to do?" The answer choices are:

- find a book
- find music
- find stores and hours
- sign up for a membership card
- find events/book signings
- apply for a job

We ask them to rate how successful they were with the task and to include comments. We feel confident that this is a perfect study design! We did an extensive task analysis, and these categories cover all of the reasons that someone may need to visit the site.

Flash forward to study data. We start to graph all of the reasons people checked off for coming to the bookstore Web site against the ratings they gave it. Then we see that 62% of the participants came to the site to find a book. This makes sense, but we notice in the confidence intervals (more on this in Chapter 6) that there is a large variation in the ratings. Upon further examination, pockets of people rated finding a book very high, whereas others rated it very low. After reading the comments we realize that the category of "Find a book" wasn't granular enough. People seemed to have difficult experiences with finding a book by author or subject, whereas finding a book by title was a great experience. But darn, we don't have ease of use ratings for either of those specific subtasks. We also realize when looking at the results that it would have been helpful to break down data by participants who were avid readers and who use competitor Web sites regularly, but alas we didn't collect this background information. If only we realized this before launching the study!

You can see that sometimes going through the motions of the real analysis will enlighten you with ideas for a better study design. Running a pilot affords the ability to do this so that you're not stuck later with answers to the wrong questions.

Piloting also provides the ability to "code" answers ahead of time. For example, let's say that we provide an open-ended comments field so that participants could express their thoughts about their experiences. Pilot data give us a comprehensive sense of the types of answers that may arise from those comments fields. We can then take those types of comments and code them into categories, for example:

> "A = Search functionality does not have ability to restrict to genre"
> "B = Author search does not account for misspellings"
> "C = ISBN search field is one character short"
> Etc., etc.

The list may not account for every possibility, and that's okay. We can just add to the list later when encountering a new response type. Mainly we're doing some work up front to make the analysis quicker and easier later.

Finally, doing this preview of the analysis means that you'll have prepared the templates already so that the *actual* analysis is a matter of simply copying and pasting data into spreadsheets. This helps move the process along efficiently, especially when you have eager clients and business partners awaiting the results!

4.2 TIMING THE LAUNCH

Once you have carefully worked out the issues with the study through piloting, the study is ready to be launched. This is an exciting time, but don't let your excitement or client demands cloud your judgment; it's important to consider the appropriate time to launch, as well as the number of launching phases appropriate for the study.

We do not cover here the mechanics of the actual study launch, as that varies greatly depending on what tool and services (e.g., panels) you're using.

4.2.1 Finding the right time to launch

The key to timing the launch is understanding the target users. It may take some work to understand the impact that timing may have on participation, as well as the quality and results of the study. This could mean steering away from a time of day, a particular day, week, or even month or fiscal quarter. Here are some examples.

- **Time of day:** Let's say that the audience is working professionals, such as company employees who mostly work a 9-to-5 day. We've seen from our own studies that it's better to launch the study first thing in the morning while employees are getting acclimated or during the lunch hour. There will be more participants and perhaps better quality if they are elicited at less busy times in the day. Similarly, when eliciting participation from personal email addresses, you may want to launch in the evening, just after dinnertime.

- **Day of the week:** We've seen with user groups such as call center representatives that Mondays are a worse day to get their participation, as they are fielding constant calls about questions that customers had over the weekend.
- **Week:** The last week of the month is the busiest for some groups of people. For example, store managers may have to reconcile monthly inventories or sales personnel may have to meet sales quotas.
- **Month/time of year:** An example of this in the United States would be with tax accountants. You don't want to test tax software changes at the height of the tax season in March and early April!

In addition to their lack of availability, these examples show that for those who do participate, their level of stress or time urgency may be elevated. Therefore, the quality of the results can be impacted as well. We've seen people rushing through more and mentally cheating, and their perceptions even being skewed toward the negative.

On a related note, not only do participants' level of stress and busyness affect results, but external factors can also impact results. We have seen in some of our studies that something such as market conditions can affect perceptions of the design. In fact, we ran one study that evaluated a financial services design for 2 days. On the first day, the market was fine. On the second day, the market had just tanked, and participants' perceptions of the same exact design were significantly lower! You wouldn't want to test security software the day after a virus breaks loose or to test the Boston Red Sox Web site the day after they win or lose the World Series. (Unless you're looking to; see the related sidebar.) Monitor external factors related to the product's domain and anticipate how they may affect the results. It's always a good idea to build some padding into the timeline in case you may need to put the study on hold for unexpected events or extend the study time frame in order to smooth out some of the noise in data associated with those unexpected events.

TESTING DURING CRITICAL INCIDENTS

We warn you against testing during critical incidents, unless of course that is what you're trying to do. Sometimes those incidents draw unique user groups and unique tasks and can be an opportune time to identify usability issues. For example, e-commerce sites being tested during December (before the holidays) might provide a different flavor of insight than at other times during the year. So just be aware of what's happening during the test and make sure that it correlates back to the original goals of the study.

4.2.2 Singular and phased launches

One decision you'll have to make is whether the study should have one singular launch or phased launches. A singular launch is the easiest approach. Some benefits include:

- Everyone in the sample has an equal opportunity to participate at the same time
- It can be planned easily around a particular event or occurrence
- It reduces the overall time required to conduct the study

TIP
A phased launch is also sometimes referred to as a "slow start" or "rolling start."

However, in some circumstances it might make better sense to employ a phased launch.

The idea behind a phased launch is to break the launch into pieces so that participants are not invited all at once. This can be done in as many or as few groups as you'd like, depending on the goals and targeted users. The amount of time between phases is also up to you.

Here are some reasons that you would want to do this:

- You're not completely confident that the study tool and/or prototype will pass the "stress test" of having hundreds of people using it at once. Depending on the servers being used, who is supporting them, and the extent of functionality (and thus server calls), some Web sites have been known to crash or drag when being used by large numbers of people at the same time. Phasing the launch will help avoid this problem.
- You want to avoid filling up the quotas quickly with one particular type of participant. Let's say that there is a 50-person cap on female participation and a 50-person cap on male participation (referred to as "quotas"). If invitations are sent out to 300 people all at once, the "eager beavers" will come first and may fill up these 50-person quotas very quickly. These types of participants may have common characteristics, such as being incentive driven, having hidden agendas, or just having a certain personality type. Any of these factors may lead them to dominate and influence the results. Phased launching allows all demographic groups and user types to participate because the study is being released to groups at a time. So there may be some eager beavers in each group, but sending the invites to smaller groups of people in phases (in this example, say, 20 people at a time) will allow other people to participate as well within each phase.
- You want to account for any external factors influencing the results. Remember our story in the last section about how the down market affected participants' reaction to a product? If you do phased launches over a few days or weeks, data will naturally account for the multiple emotional climates reflected in the subjective ratings. Because data will be aggregated, perceptions from any one single phase will not dominate the results (depending on the spread of participation and how many phases have been launched).

■ You have a last opportunity to change the study design. If you spent the appropriate time on study piloting, the launch should run smoothly. However, in the real world, no matter how careful we are, we still may miss something important until after the fact. Phased launches provide the opportunity to catch any problems with real data and fix them before the next launch. You might have to discard that group's data, but at least you didn't launch all at once with an unrecoverable problem.

We recommend using phased launches if you have the time and budget built into the study plan. But if any of the points above aren't particularly applicable or concerning, then a singular launch should do the trick.

4.3 MONITORING RESULTS

Whether launching the study in a single or multiple phases, be prepared to monitor the results. It's a bad time to go on vacation! Monitoring is usually the easiest and one of the more interesting parts of the process. It's important to be proactive in the event that things are not working out as planned.

Most of the vendor tools allow you to monitor the study in real time, although some provide more information than others. The most useful tools are those that allow you to do things such as

■ view how many have completed the study or are currently participating
■ view dates/times people participated
■ view how many have abandoned the study and at what sections/ questions
■ view the extent to which quotas are being filled
■ view the demographic makeup of the participants
■ download or view the results to date while the study is still live

When viewing this information in real time, you can take steps to address any issues or concerns. If there's a problem with participation rates, for example, you may consider sending out additional invitations or reminders to nonrespondents or adding more phases to the launch. If the respondent types are appearing unbalanced, you might add more screening questions or lower the quotas. If data quality isn't great, you may want to place more speed traps in the study or target a different panel or group of people. Finally, just monitoring the results might supply a little nugget of information that you can pass on to clients or business partners. This will help manage expectations so that they can start planning for additional time and budget needed for changes to be made. But beware! Don't let them jump to conclusions and start making any changes to the design until all data are in and analyzed.

> **TIP**
> If you make any in-field changes during the launch phase that would cause incomparability with prior data, make sure either to "start over" with results at the time of the implemented change or to distinguish new data as separate from the old in the analysis.

WHAT'S AN ACCEPTABLE PARTICIPATION RATE?

Response rates vary widely and wildly. It depends on what's being tested and who it's being sent to. If the study is being sent to people who you've personally met or tested with before and who have a vested interest in you, the product, or in having their feedback heard, the rates will be higher than typical. Essentially the more targeted the participants are, the higher the participation rate will be. However, don't be surprised by a 5 to 10% participation rate. Although online studies are fun (we think) and very different from surveys, people mentally lump them in with surveys. As mentioned in Chapter 3, incentives may help but then you need to be more careful with participants who misrepresent themselves and mentally cheat throughout the study. Make sure to review Chapter 2 and plan to invite enough people to account for this.

4.4 SUMMARY

This chapter discussed how to pilot and launch the study effectively. Keep the following things in mind during this process.

- Check for technical issues such as data passing and submission, error conditions, branching, and anything else that might cause the study to break. This can be done by a few people going through the study multiple times and in multiple environments.
- Always do a small pilot for usability checks. Sit with a couple of people and have them think aloud as they attempt the study. This will give you a sense of flow, timing, and usability issues with the test itself.
- Run a larger scale pilot to check for data quality issues such as improbable values, oddities, and contradictions in the success rates, ratings, and comments.
- Set up spreadsheets and perform the intended analysis on pilot data, which may further provide insight into any problems with the study design.
- Make sure to avoid launching the study at times that may adversely affect the participation rate and quality of data. Consider whether to employ singular or phased launches.
- Monitor the results so that you are able to make swift, informed changes during the launch if necessary.

CHAPTER 5
Data Preparation

Data preparation is one of the most important steps in conducting an online usability study, yet it's often overlooked. It is easy to assume that all data are ready to be analyzed or there just isn't any time to clean up data prior to analysis. We have even been known to skip the data preparation phase because we are too excited to analyze data. Think of opening and starting up a brand new computer without reading any instructions. It might be more exciting, but it can also be a little risky.

After launching and receiving your data, we recommend setting aside at least a small amount of time for this additional step of preparing data, typically no more than a few hours. It will end up saving a lot of time and headaches down the road. Data preparation is about getting data ready for analysis by checking the quality of data, removing problematic participants and tasks, recoding variables, and even creating a few new variables.

Data preparation for an online usability study is a little different from typical online surveys because of the type of data collected. There are more opportunities to have problems with online usability data than with a traditional market research survey. Not only do you have to look at all self-reported data, but behavioral and clickstream data as well. This is usually a quick process. Think of it as very cheap insurance. This chapter reviews the basic steps in data preparation: downloading data, performing data quality checks, removing participants, removing tasks, recoding variables, and creating new variables.

5.1 DOWNLOADING/EXPORTING DATA

Data cleanup begins with downloading or exporting data into a format that you will use during analysis. All vendor solutions that we have used, including Keynote's WebEffective, UserZoom, RelevantView, and Loop11, allow exporting data into Excel or a format it can read. Some vendors also provide the capability to directly export data into statistical programs such as SPSS and SAS. We prefer

TIP

Create a backup copy of the original data set and store it in a place other than your hard drive. You never know when your hard drive might crash!

to prepare data in Excel and then transfer the cleaned up file into a statistical software application for in-depth analysis if needed. We strongly recommend that you keep at least one copy of original raw data with no modifications. You never know when you might need to go back to original data because you made a mistake in the cleanup file or analysis.

Downloading or exporting data is usually simple. Just make sure all data are included during export. With some vendors, clickstream data are stored separately from self-reported data, or the panel characteristics may be stored separately from study data. It's important to know exactly what you're downloading so that you can make sure you're not missing any data that you may need later.

The format of data is important. If given the choice, always opt for having one participant per row. Each column should be a different variable, such as Task 1 success, Task 1 ease of use rating, and Task 1 time. Avoid a format that includes the same participant along multiple rows. This will make the analysis very tricky and will invariably need to be transformed so there is only one participant per row. Also, if possible, choose to have all the variables in the same file. Once you start to work with multiple files, analysis will get confusing.

CAUTION USING PRECANNED GRAPHS

With some vendors it's possible to download the results directly into PowerPoint in the form of various charts and graphs. This includes some of the key graphs, such as overall task success, self-report variables, and task times. We recommend resisting this temptation because you haven't scrubbed data yet. The only exception could be when you're absolutely certain that data are clean as a whistle.

5.2 DATA QUALITY CHECKS

Once you open the data file, the first thing you should do is check the quality of data. In other words, you want to make sure data were coded correctly. We hope you took our recommendations and performed a data quality check as part of the piloting phase. Whether you did or not, we still recommend that you do some simple quality checks before conducting any analysis. For example,

- Perform a frequency analysis to make sure all variables are within a possible range of values. For example, if a Likert scale question on satisfaction is based on a 1 to 5 scale, and you notice values of "0", you know you have an issue with how data were coded.

- Check missing values. Some missing values may be coded as "0". It's important that all missing values be represented as blank or null values. Otherwise, you will be factoring missing data values in the analysis.
- Take a look at the task times. Make sure the times are expressed in seconds and look reasonable. If there are some task times with 0 seconds, you should be suspicious, particularly if the task was performed successfully and verbatim comments were entered.
- Check clickstream data, particularly with respect to page views. Make sure there is a reasonable range of page views, particularly in the case where participants were successful in a task but had far fewer page views than the minimum necessary to complete the task. Also, actual pages visited should make sense from a task perspective. If there are a large percentage of participants who seem to have visited a Web page that does not make sense, there could be an issue with how that page was captured.
- Check the variables that are based on conditional logic. For example, some questions may only be given if the participants indicate they had difficulty on a task. If you see verbatim comments entered for tasks that were highly rated, there may be a problem.
- As a final check, we recommend you take a glance at automatically generated data graphs. While you're not going to use them, they're a helpful way to do a quick quality check.

THE QUICK APPROACH TO DATA QUALITY CHECKS: SORTING

If you're hard-pressed for time and you want to perform a quick data quality check, use the sort function. Simply sort each variable and try to spot outliers in data. You are most likely to encounter coding problems at the top or bottom of the list. For example, page views with counts of 0 will bubble up to the top (or bottom), and rating scale data that are out of range will also pop out.

One big caveat with sorting is to make sure you are sorting on the entire data set and not just one variable. In other words, make sure each participant's data remain intact. In Microsoft Excel terms, this means highlighting your entire data set and choosing Data > Sort and then the appropriate variables to sort by. Don't just click on one column header!

5.3 REMOVING PARTICIPANTS

After performing a data quality check, we recommend looking at data to determine whether specific participants should be removed from the study. This is not about deciding that you don't like the way someone answered a particular question (this would be unethical). Rather, this is about potentially removing specific participants who didn't complete the study as intended, either because they didn't put forth a fair or complete effort or they misrepresented themselves. It's important that you take necessary steps to remove noise that may be masking what is truly happening in the study. Ultimately, any decisions you make need to be documented and explained as part of any write-up or presentation.

5.3.1 Incomplete data

One reason to remove a participant is incomplete data. For example, it's possible that a participant responded to very few of the questions and didn't perform any of the tasks. This participant either was not trying very hard or there was an issue with data collection. This would certainly be valid grounds for removing the participant from the data analysis. Luckily, most vendors will allow you to make specific questions and tasks required, eliminating this issue. The downside of making a question required is that dropout rates increase. Furthermore, many vendors only pass along data from completed studies, often referred to as the number of "completes." This is a problem we rarely run into, but as a general guideline we would recommend that if a participant failed to perform most or all tasks, we would consider them candidates for removal.

5.3.2 Participants who misrepresent themselves

Ideally, you will be able to screen out participants who misrepresent themselves at the beginning of a study. However, sometimes participants who misrepresent themselves can sneak into your study. Assuming they answered the screening questions appropriately and you're not going to hire a private detective to find out if they are who they say they are, what can you do? Well, one option is to compare their responses in your survey to another existing data set. If you're using an online panel, you should be able to compare their responses in your study with their profiles. For example, a participant might indicate that she is an older woman, but the user profile states that he is a younger man. Chances are that this participant figured out how to answer the screener questions to qualify for the study. Of course, there is also the possibility that a spouse or friend is using their profile. In this situation, you need to make a judgment call about whether to include the participant—after all, they simply could have just passed the study on to their spouse or friend.

5.3.3 Mental cheaters

Unfortunately, not all participants try their best. About 9% of the participants may be "mental cheaters" and, depending on the panel, this can range up to 16% (Miller, 2008). This means a participant is performing to satisfy the technical requirements of the study, such as completing all required questions. But they aren't giving any thought to their responses. They're simply flying through the study as fast as they can to get the incentive. This is perhaps the most common reason to remove a participant. There are several ways to identify mental cheaters.

Extremely poor or abnormal performance

Perhaps the most common reason to remove a participant is when their performance is so bad or bizarre that you are certain they are a mental cheater. For example, when participants:

- Failed all tasks, even the most simple
- Completed all tasks in an extremely short amount of time, and most, if not all, resulted in failures
- Had a very small number of page views for each task, even when the task required many page views

Speed traps

If you used a speed trap (described in Chapter 3.8.3), you will need to review data. If a participant failed the speed trap, consider removing that participant. This is particularly important if they missed more than one speed trap. If the participant only missed a single speed trap, depending on the context of that speed trap, you may decide to remove their data for that one section only.

Inconsistent responses

Another useful way to identify mental cheaters is to look at the consistency of responses. You may have included questions that are essentially the mirror opposite of each another. If the participant is paying attention, he/she will answer the questions consistently. If cheating, he/she will not. Similar to speed traps, you should use your own judgment about whether you want to remove the entire participant or only data for a particular section.

USING SUS RESPONSES AS A CONSISTENCY CHECK

One of the qualities of the system usability scale (SUS) is how questions flip between positively worded and negatively worded. Because of this, if participants are cheating, they might score all the answers a "5", which would result in a SUS score of 50 out of a maximum of 100 (see Chapter 6.2.3 on how to calculate a SUS score). This is highly unlikely behavior if the participant is actually reading every question. It essentially means they find the product very easy and very difficult to use. In this case, we recommend not including this participant's data in the analysis of SUS.

5.3.4 Tips on removing participants

One of the most important things to do before removing any participants is to leave a clean trail of what you do and why you are doing it. We recommend:

- Always keep a copy of the original data set. This is data exactly as you received it before any editing has occurred.
- Document the rules you used to remove participants. This is easy to overlook but very important (and worth repeating)!

- Instead of removing data, consider converting numeric values to a character or string format so that it will not be used in analysis. This can be done easily by adding a character next to the number such as "&1.56". By doing this you will still have data in case you need to refer to it, but it won't be included in any numeric analysis.

5.4 REMOVING AND MODIFYING DATA FOR INDIVIDUAL TASKS

It's much more common for a participant to disengage from just a few tasks than the entire study. Disengagement usually happens in longer online usability studies, perhaps more than 15 or 20 minutes long. Participants might get bored or be in a hurry to finish. Whatever the reason, we recommend that you take a close look at task-level data. Bottom line—don't throw out the baby with the bath water.

5.4.1 Outliers

Outliers are extreme points in data and are the result of atypical behavior. Outliers need to be examined before any conclusions about data can be made. The most common type of outlier in an online usability study is task time data. We typically remove task time data when a participant has an extremely short or long task completion time. When the task times are impossibly short (usually 3 seconds or less), the participant is almost always cheating (just trying to get through the study as quickly as he/she can to receive the incentive).

Task times that are impossibly long usually mean that they took a coffee break or even went home for the evening. We often observe task times in excess of 10,000 seconds, translating to roughly 3 hours. If you have access to page views, it is helpful to compare very long task times with page views. In many cases, the exceedingly long task time is not reflected in actual activity on the Web site. In cases such as these, we believe it is perfectly acceptable to remove data for that particular task.

Alternatively, if you do not have access to their page visits, you can use a couple of data-driven rules for removing exceedingly long task times. One option is to remove any task times that are 3+ standard deviations above the mean. This means that you are essentially removing the top 0.3% of the time observations. A second option is to sort time data and look for natural breaks. A natural break is where there is a large gap in the times. For example, you might have a lot of users who completed the task in less than 100 seconds, then a large gap (natural break), with a few users taking 500 or more seconds. In this case, we would consider removing data for those participants that took longer than 500 seconds to complete the task.

There are more sophisticated techniques for identifying outliers, the most common of which is called Grubb's test (Grubbs, 1969). While this is not available in Excel, it is offered in some more advanced statistical software packages.

5.4.2 Contradictory responses

It's not uncommon to discover contradictions in how a participant responds to a particular task. For example, a participant might rate a task as very difficult, but provide a glowing description of how easy the task was to complete. Alternatively, a participant might describe how many pages it took to complete the task, but the number of page views is far fewer than they have described. What should you do about this? In our experience, we have found a couple of general guidelines to be useful.

- If only a small number of participants exhibit contradictory responses on a single task, such as fewer than 5%, we tend to disregard this issue and not look into actual data.
- If a large number of participants (perhaps more than 25%) show a consistent pattern of contradictions between their ease of use rating and their verbatim response, it is critical you look at how the task was performed. It is possible that data were not coded correctly, participants were confused by the question(s), or there was something in the Web site or prototype that generated this inconsistent response. In any case, you need to play the role of detective and find out what happened. Trying to reproduce the problem is a good place to start. In any case, you will have to make a decision about whether to throw out some data or relaunch the study after the fixes have been made.

5.4.3 Removing a task for all participants

It is hoped that you piloted the study and discovered any potential issues with the tasks prior to launch. Occasionally though, problematic tasks can sneak in, particularly when there is a delay between piloting and launching. Problematic tasks are usually the result of some external factor impacting the nature of the task and have nothing to do with the participant's performance. For example, if we wanted to evaluate how participants find the current price of the book "Measuring the User Experience" on a live Web site and we provide a set of answers based on the current price at launch (such as "about 40 dollars" or "about 30 dollars"), and the actual price had actually dropped during the data collection phase, the correct answer is no longer valid. Also, a task might no longer make sense because the information is no longer available or no longer relevant. In these cases, it is important that you replicate the task to better understand why so many participants got the same wrong answer or exhibited the same pattern of results.

The decision to remove an entire task for all participants should not be made lightly. By removing a task, you eliminate task data that is not valid; however the experience of that particular task is still reflected in the overall assessments. Therefore, the overall assessments of their experience may have been quite different had they never performed the task. Perhaps similar to a surgeon deciding to amputate a limb, we recommend that you get a second opinion on which, if any, tasks to eliminate. Fortunately though, task data can always be added back into the analysis.

5.4.4 Modifying task success

Modifying task success involves recoding the answer of a specific question from incorrect to correct or vice versa. Think back to your days in school when, on a rare occasion, all the students complained that one of the incorrect questions on the exam was actually correct, the teacher might have given all students credit for that particular question. The same applies in online usability studies. There are situations in which you discover that a majority of participants all responded with the same incorrect answer and may have even rated the task as very easy to complete. It is possible that their response is actually valid. We do our best to reproduce the task and give them every benefit of the doubt.

5.5 RECODING DATA AND CREATING NEW VARIABLES

This section reviews common ways to create new variables and guidelines for recoding variables. Recoding and creating new variables will make your analysis more meaningful by focusing on data that matter to your audience. We like to think of the original set of variables as the building blocks.

5.5.1 Success data

The most common way to recode success variables is to convert text data to numbers, so "1" represents task success and "0" represents task failure (see Figure 5.1). Some applications return values of "success" and "fail" for each task. This is based on the participant's response compared to the responses you have marked as correct. Converting success data from string to numeric format is required to perform basic statistical functions such as frequencies, cross-tabs, or chi-square analysis. Also, you can calculate averages and confidence intervals as long as data are numeric.

Success data can also be used in combination with other performance metrics. In some cases, it is not enough to be successful. Rather, the user should be successful within a particular time constraint or even within a certain number

FIGURE 5.1
An example showing how task success is represented in data and calculation of overall task success.

		fx	=AVERAGE(B2:F2)			
	A	B	C	D	E	F	G
	Participant	**Task 1**	**Task 2**	**Task 3**	**Task 4**	**Task 5**	**Overall Success**
1							
2	P1	1	1	1	1	1	100%
3	P2	1	1	1	0	1	80%
4	P3	1	0	0	1	1	60%
5	P4	0	0	0	1	0	20%
6	P5	0	1	0	1	0	40%
7	P6	1	0	1	1	0	60%
8	P7	0	0	1	1	1	60%
9	P8	0	0	1	1	1	60%
10	P9	1	1	1	1	1	100%
11	P10	1	1	0	1	1	80%
12	Average	60%	50%	60%	90%	70%	66%

	A	B	C	D
	Participant	Task1_success	Task 1_time	Task1_new success
1	Participant	Task1_success	Task 1_time	Task1_new success
2	P1	1	30	1
3	P2	1	43	0
4	P3	1	42	0
5	P4	0	56	0
6	P5	1	21	1
7	P6	1	37	1
8	P7	1	44	0
9	P8	0	67	0
10	P9	1	30	1
11	P10	1	28	1
12	Average	80%	40	50%

D2 f_x =IF(AND(C2<40,B2=1),1,0)

FIGURE 5.2
An example showing how new task success can be calculated using both task success and completion time. A total of 50% of the participants completed the task successfully in less than 40 seconds.

of page views. Calculating success based on more than one variable is fairly easy. Figure 5.2 is an example of how to calculate a "new success" variable based on task success and completion times. In this example, a task is scored successful if participants got the right answer (column B) and completed the task in less than 40 seconds (column C).

5.5.2 Time variables

As far as recoding time variables, the only potential thing to look out for is how the time is expressed. Nearly all of the tasks that we see are fairly short and therefore are expressed in seconds. If you happen to be evaluating tasks that typically run longer than 5 minutes, we recommend converting seconds to minutes. This recommendation is only for the presentation so that the audience does not have to do any mental arithmetic.

TIP
Times are often stored in Excel in hours:minutes:seconds format, but when doing calculations using those times (e.g., calculating an elapsed time), it's easier to convert them to seconds. Check our Web site for examples of converting Excel times in hours:minutes: seconds format to seconds.

Another new time variable you might want to create is completion times meeting specific thresholds. For example, you may know that a large percentage of your users drop out of a specific transaction if it takes longer than 45 seconds to complete. If this is the case, you can assign each participant a "1" if they were under the 45-second threshold or a "0" if they were above the 45-second threshold (see Figure 5.3). You don't have to use the same threshold for each task. Because some tasks may be inherently more complicated than others, you can just as easily use different thresholds for different tasks. Determining specific time thresholds is a conversation between you and the business sponsors/clients. Ideally, the thresholds are based on past research and tie directly to return on investment.

FIGURE 5.3
An example showing task completions based on time thresholds.

	A	B	C	D	E	F	G
					Task1_45sec_	Task2_45sec_	Task3_45sec_
1	Participant	Task 1	Task 2	Task 3	Threshold	Threshold	Threshold
2	P1	30	60	20	1	0	1
3	P2	43	56	19	1	0	1
4	P3	42	55	30	1	0	1
5	P4	56	75	27	0	0	1
6	P5	21	45	16	1	0	1
7	P6	37	44	40	1	1	1
8	P7	44	56	27	1	0	1
9	P8	67	67	34	0	0	1
10	P9	30	70	29	1	0	1
11	P10	28	51	33	1	0	1
12	Average	40	58	28	80%	10%	100%

E2 =IF(B2<45,1,0)

FIGURE 5.4
An example showing the classification of task completion times.

C2 =IF(B2>59, "3", IF(B2>39, "2", IF(B2>0, "1")))

	A	B	C	D	E	F	G
1	Participant	Task 1	Task 1 category				
2	P1	30	1				
3	P2	43	2				
4	P3	42	2				
5	P4	56	2				
6	P5	21	1				
7	P6	37	1				
8	P7	44	2				
9	P8	67	3				
10	P9	30	1				
11	P10	28	1				
12	Average	40					

Restricting yourself to classifying a participant above or below a specific completion time is not always useful. In some cases, you may want to classify each participant into time intervals, such as "fast," "medium," or "slow." Figure 5.4 shows how to create a new variable based on different time intervals. In this example, if a participant is slower than 59 seconds he is categorized as a "3," greater than 40 seconds he is classified a "2," and less than 40 seconds he is a "1." It is important to keep in mind that you are converting data from ratio to ordinal. In practical terms, this means that you cannot take averages or run t tests between various groups. There are a different set of statistics that apply to ordinal data.

5.5.3 Self-reported variables

Self-reported variables such as overall satisfaction, ease of use ratings, and task confidence do not usually require recoding. The one exception may be when self-reported variable scales run from both positive to negative and negative to positive. For example, you may ask participants to rate the ease of use from

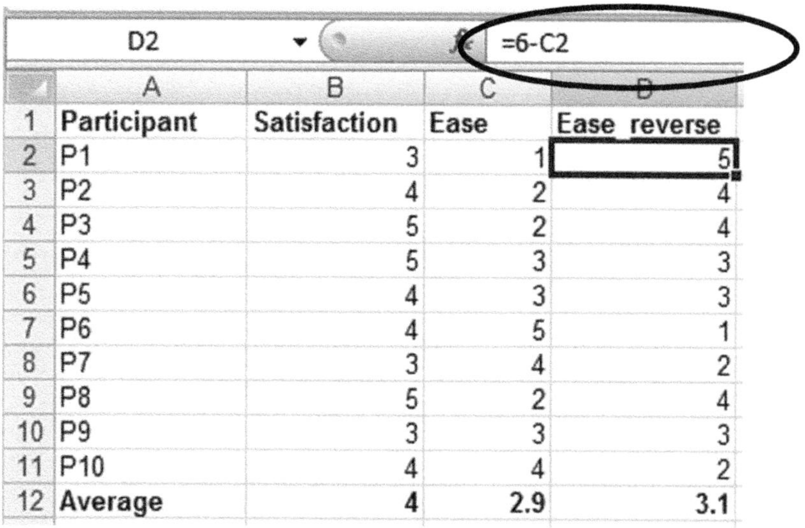

D2		▼	f_x =6-C2	
	A	B	C	D
1	Participant	Satisfaction	Ease	Ease reverse
2	P1	3	1	5
3	P2	4	2	4
4	P3	5	2	4
5	P4	5	3	3
6	P5	4	3	3
7	P6	4	5	1
8	P7	3	4	2
9	P8	5	2	4
10	P9	3	3	3
11	P10	4	4	2
12	Average	4	2.9	3.1

FIGURE 5.5
An example showing how to flip scales on an ease-of-use rating variable (based on a five-point scale) so that larger numbers represent greater ease ratings.

1 (very easy) to 5 (very difficult). Conversely, at another point in the study you may ask someone his/her likelihood of using the Web site in the future, from 1 (not at all likely) to 5 (very likely). The direction of the scales should not be used to trick someone or make them pay attention. Rather, the direction of the scales should be intuitive to the respondents.

When reporting these data, it's useful to have all variables run from negative evaluation to positive. This will help your audience when they glance at your charts and can equate larger values as better. Figure 5.5 shows how to recode an ease-of-use rating variable so that larger numbers are better (easier) and smaller numbers are worse (more difficult).

5.5.4 Clickstream data

Most vendor solutions provide a rich set of clickstream data. Clickstream data are a detailed log of how participants navigate through the Web site during a task. The log typically includes the pages visited, time spent on each page, how they arrived on the page, and where they went next. From an aggregate perspective, clickstream data provide tremendous insights into how easily the site is navigated, what pages are causing the greatest confusion, and what pages are critical in reaching a desired destination.

There's not a lot of preparation to do with clickstream data as you might have with other data. In our experience, it's usually easier to analyze clickstream data within the vendor tools themselves because of superior visualization techniques. Figure 5.6 is an example from Keynote's WebEffective tool of how participants navigated to the Punta Cana beach resort on the www.clubmed.com Web site. You might notice that 4 out of 13 participants went from the home page to the village finder, whereas 7 participants went straight from the home page to the Punta Cana resort overview page.

FIGURE 5.6
A visualization of partial clickstream data using Keynote's WebEffective tool. Copyright © 2009 Keynote Systems, Inc. All rights reserved.

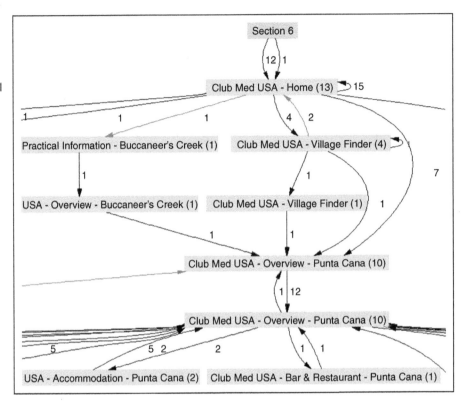

There are a few things to keep in mind as you start to play with clickstream data. First, if you end up removing any participants from original data or remove any tasks for specific participants, you need to do the same with the automatically generated figures. In other words, the cleanup you performed on overall data has to exactly match the clickstream analysis. This is usually done through a filter operation, where you can only include certain participants in the analysis. Second, it is important to look at the individual pages that are being analyzed. Check to make sure that each page visited is actually a unique page. For example, some Web sites that take advantage of flash or frames do not represent themselves accurately on clickstream data. It is possible that the tool you are using could be counting each frame as a separate page.

Some tools will allow you to clean up clickstream data. This is very important, as there easily can be hundreds of pages visited multiple times, by hundreds of participants. The first thing we recommend is cleaning up the URLs by labeling the pages so that they make sense to you. For example, you may be able to only label the URL and not all the associated java script functions or simply include the page titles. Next, combine multiple URLs that represent the same page. Sometimes the same page might have different URLs. If you are not sure, just visit the pages and compare. Finally, we recommend combining groups of pages to assist in the interpretation and analysis. Sometimes you just might want to see what general areas the participants went to from the home page, without having to consider all the other individual pages.

5.6 SUMMARY

The first step in preparation is downloading data. Most important, make sure that you save copies of the original and the complete data set before any cleanup begins in case you make a mistake. A validity check of data involves making sure all data were coded correctly. The best way to run a quick validity check is to perform a frequency analysis for all variables, making sure that the values for each variable are in the appropriate range.

Once you feel data have been represented accurately, it's time to get your ax. The first cuts are participants that did not complete major parts of the study (incompletes) or misrepresented themselves in the screener (fraudulents). The best way to identify fraudulent participants is to compare their responses on the screening questions with previously provided panel characteristics. The second set of cuts includes mental cheaters. These are participants who provide the minimum amount of effort to receive the incentive. Identifying cheaters is done by looking at extremely poor performance, missing speed traps, or inconsistent responses. Removing an entire participant from the study should not be taken lightly, and your decisions should be well justified and documented so that it can be communicated to your audience.

After you have removed all the bad apples from the study, it is time to turn your attention to the individual tasks. Outliers with completion times are the most common offenders. It is well worth your while to set up minimum and maximum thresholds for time data, as otherwise the extreme outliers will influence results heavily. In some cases you may want to consider removing task data when there is obvious confusion based on an inconsistent response pattern, particularly between verbatim responses and rating scales. Other times, task success needs to be modified to include alternative correct answers. This is particularly the case when evaluating live Web sites.

After data are cleaned up, it is time to create a set of commonly used metrics based on the existing set of variables. Commonly created success metrics include overall task success and task success based on some other factor such as task completion times. Task completion times can be transformed into new metrics based on meeting specific time thresholds and categorized into time intervals such as fast, medium, and slow. Self-report variables are often used to create top-2 and bottom-2 box scores to identify participants who have a solid positive or negative experience. Different self-report variables can also be combined easily to create overall experience variables. Clickstream data are usually manipulated within vendor tools due to their superior visualization tools. It is important that any participant or task that was removed also occurs in any clickstream analysis.

CHAPTER 6
Data Analysis and Presentation

If you're familiar with traditional lab usability testing, you know that the majority of what you learn from a test comes from direct observation of the participants in the study. In an online study, you don't have that direct observation. You might have 1000 different people doing your study simultaneously. Even if you had the *technical* ability to somehow watch "over the shoulder" of those participants, it's not humanly possible. That's where your analysis of data from the online study comes in. That data, and your analysis of it, have to take the place of direct observation. It has to provide a retrospective view "over the shoulder" of your participants.

This chapter is all about making sense of data from your online study. We describe techniques you can use to detect trends in data and differences among tasks, conditions, or groups of participants. Keep in mind that your analyses should be driven by the goals of the study. As discussed in Chapter 2, you might have several different goals for your study, but from a data analysis perspective they tend to fall into two general categories:

1. *Identifying usability issues with a design*. The primary objective here is to improve the design as part of an iterative process.
2. *Comparing different designs or versions*. This might involve comparisons among design alternatives as part of an iterative process, comparison among competitors' Web sites, or perhaps establishing baseline usability metrics for *future* comparisons.

Data from your online study provide the building blocks that you can use in addressing these goals. The way you use these building blocks may differ depending on what your goals are. For example, task success data are basic building blocks that you can use in several different ways. In an iterative process focused on identifying usability issues, tasks with the lowest success rates can point to issues in the design. The main analysis in this case is simply calculating a mean success rate for each task. You might then use the verbatim comments for each of those problem tasks to help zero in on the exact usability issues. However, task success data can play a slightly different role in making comparisons among different designs. Instead of focusing on individual tasks, you will tend to look across the tasks to see how one design fared in comparison to another. You're more likely to do statistical analyses to determine which designs are statistically better or worse than others. In many cases, the decision you're trying to make is which design to carry forward. Once you've made that decision, you might then use some of the other techniques (e.g., identifying problem tasks, studying the verbatim comments) to improve that design.

You can think of data from an online usability study—the analysis building blocks—as falling into three broad categories:

- **Task performance data** include all the information related to the tasks the participants performed, such as task success, task times, and task efficiency. These tell you about the *behavior* of the participants.
- **Self-reported data** include all the information from any rating scales, preference selections, rankings, comments, and any other answers that the participants provide. These tell you about the *reactions* of the participants. These data might be collected at the individual task level or at the session level.
- **Clickstream data** include any information collected "behind the scenes" about the participants' interaction with the Web site, such as the pages they visited, how long they spent on each page, what links they clicked on, and their use of specific site features, such as search. Like task performance data, these tell you about the *behavior* of the participants, but from a different perspective.

The following sections provide more details about these three broad categories, including discussions of how to analyze and summarize each of the types of data. Once we've covered these "analysis building blocks," we'll look at the analysis from a broader perspective, including how to use these data in addressing the goals of your study.

6.1 TASK PERFORMANCE DATA

Your online study might have one task or many tasks. The tasks could be simple and straightforward or complex and multifaceted. The participants might have been given the tasks or they might have made them up. Whatever the characteristics of the tasks, much of what you will learn comes from them. The most important kinds of task performance data are task success, task times, and measures of task efficiency.

6.1.1 Task success

With many tasks, whether the users were successful is a clear binary decision: either they accomplished the task or they didn't. But in some cases, there may be more than one correct answer or there may be shades of gray between success and failure.

Binary task success

To take a real example, consider our study of an online photo clip-art gallery. In this study, each of the tasks involved finding the full-size version of a thumbnail image they were shown. In the example shown in Figure 6.1, the participant's task is to find the image of the light bulb shown in the top window by navigating in the lower window. In this screenshot, the participant has navigated to the correct category using the outline on the left; that yielded thumbnails of the

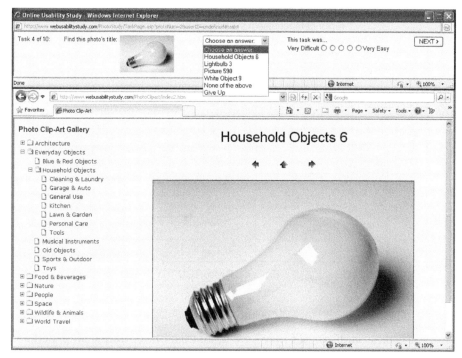

FIGURE 6.1
Screenshot showing that the participant has navigated to the correct photo and is ready to choose the answer.

images in that category. Clicking on the thumbnail of the light bulb yielded a full version of the photo along with its title.

There can be little doubt in the participant's mind about whether they got to the right answer. The photos match exactly and the exact wording of the title of the photo appears in the drop-down list of answers. Because this task has a very clear end state, binary task completion (success or failure) is appropriate. With relatively simple tasks like this, you also tend to get very low task failure rates, as shown in Figure 6.2.

In this study, there were three conditions, as determined by the behavior of the Table of Contents (TOC) in the left frame. As can be seen from Figure 6.2, even though the task failure levels were low for all three conditions (under 10%), the participants were significantly more likely to get the right answer when using the Static TOC or Auto-collapse TOC.

SHOULD YOU REPORT RATES AS "TASK SUCCESS" OR "TASK FAILURE"?

You'll notice that sometimes we talk about task success rates and sometimes about task failure rates. Obviously, they're complementary. A task success rate of 96% would have a task failure rate of 4%. We usually focus on task success, but if the success rates are very high, sometimes it's useful to focus on task failure, making it easier to see any differences that may be significant.

FIGURE 6.2
Task failure data from the photo clip-art study for tasks where target photos were in the upper half of the outline.

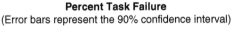
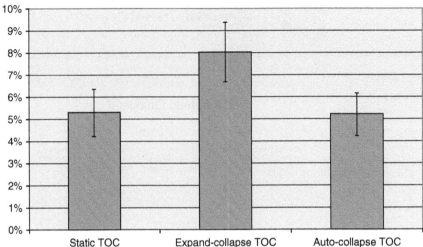

Percent Task Failure
(Error bars represent the 90% confidence interval)

Static TOC   Expand-collapse TOC   Auto-collapse TOC

Tasks with multiple correct answers

In some online studies, tasks may have more than one correct answer, perhaps by design (see Section 3.4). For example, you might want to use the answers given by the participants to provide some information about how they arrived at those answers. An easy way to do this, particularly if you have control over the prototype or site being tested, is to arrange for different answers depending on how the participant got to the answer. For example, assume that a Web site supports both a traditional navigation mechanism and a search mechanism for getting to the content. You could have different content pages, or answers, depending on which way the user got there. Figure 6.3 shows what task success data might look like for such a study.

In this example, you can see that participants were far more successful with certain tasks (2, 4, and 6) than with others (1, 3, and 5). But you can also see that search played a much more significant role in the success with some of the tasks (3 through 6) than with others (1 and 2).

Breakdown of task completion status

Sometimes it's instructive to look at the task completion states in more detail. Specifically, you might want to look at the different ways that participants failed to complete the tasks. Two common ways that participants fail are by giving an incorrect answer or giving up. Giving an incorrect answer could indicate that the participant was just guessing, but it could also indicate that they really thought that was the answer, i.e., the site somehow led him or her to conclude that was the answer. Giving up, particularly when it's associated with a relatively long task time, might indicate that the participant was getting frustrated with the site and had reached the point where it didn't appear to be fruitful to continue with the task.

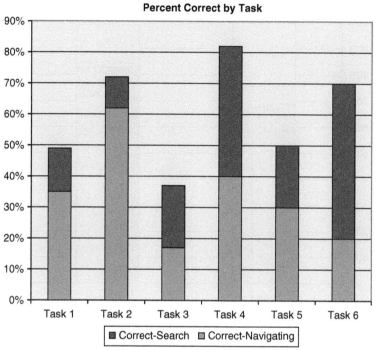

Percent Correct by Task

Correct-Search   Correct-Navigating

FIGURE 6.3
Task success data for a
hypothetical study with
two different ways of
getting to the correct
answers.

FIGURE 6.3
Task success data for a
hypothetical study with
two different ways of
getting to the correct
answers.

Figure 6.4 shows an example from our online study comparing the NASA and Wikipedia sites about the Apollo Space Program.

Note that not only were participants more successful using the Wikipedia site, they also were less likely to give up and less likely to get the wrong answer. High percentages of incorrect answers or "give-up's" should be studied further to determine the cause.

WHAT'S A NORMAL "GIVE-UP" RATE?

Many factors influence the likelihood of a participant giving up on a task, including how difficult the task is, how obtuse the Web site is, and how motivated the participant is. But we were curious about the range of give-up rates that we've seen in our online studies. Figure 6.5 shows the frequency distribution of give-up rates from online usability studies that looked at a total of 29 conditions (Web sites) and used a total of 329 tasks. Each of these conditions had at least 25 participants and some had 1000+. The mean give-up rate was 10% and the median was 6%. The 25th percentile was 2% and the 75th percentile was 12%. The lowest average give-up rate for any one condition was 1% and the highest was 43%.

This would suggest that a give-up rate for a task below about 10% can be considered "normal," whereas a give-up rate above about 15% might be considered high, particularly if you believe the task should be relatively simple.

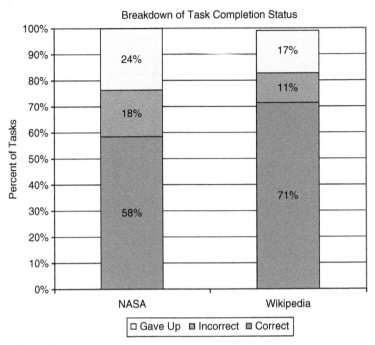

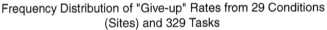

FIGURE 6.4
Task completion status information for an online study of the NASA and Wikipedia sites about the Apollo Space Program.

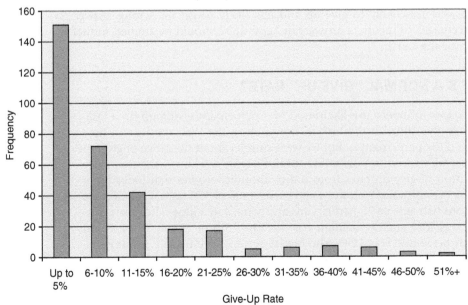

FIGURE 6.5
Frequency distribution of give-up rates for 29 conditions and 329 tasks.

Calculating task success rates

Assuming your study has more than one participant and more than one task, there are two ways of calculating task success rates:

- Percent of *tasks* each *participant* completed successfully
- Percent of *participants* who completed each *task* successfully

In the first case you're collapsing across tasks and in the second you're collapsing across participants. Let's look at an example. Consider the data shown in Table 6.1.

This is based on a sample of actual data for one of the conditions from our study of an online photo gallery. (There were actually 400+ participants per condition rather than just the 20 shown here.) Each participant attempted 10 tasks, which are shown as the columns, and we're looking at task success data for 20 participants, shown as the rows. The entries in the table are either 0's (indicating task failure) or 1's (indicating task success). The averages on the right, which are averaging across the columns (tasks), represent the percent of *tasks* that each participant accomplished successfully. The averages at the bottom, which are averaging across the rows (participants), represent the percent of *participants* who accomplished each task successfully. Both are useful sets of averages, depending on

Table 6.1	A portion of task success data for one condition from the online photo gallery study. A "0" means task failure and a "1" means task success.

Participant	Task 1	Task 2	Task 3	Task 4	Task 5	Task 6	Task 7	Task 8	Task 9	Task 10	Average
P1	1	1	0	1	0	1	1	1	1	1	80%
P2	0	1	1	1	0	1	1	1	0	1	70%
P3	0	0	0	1	1	1	1	1	1	1	70%
P4	1	1	1	1	1	0	1	1	1	1	90%
P5	1	0	0	1	1	0	1	1	1	1	70%
P6	1	1	1	0	0	1	1	0	1	1	70%
P7	1	1	1	1	1	1	1	1	1	1	100%
P8	1	1	1	0	0	1	1	1	1	0	70%
P9	0	0	1	1	0	1	1	0	1	1	60%
P10	1	0	1	1	0	1	1	0	1	1	70%
P11	1	1	1	1	1	1	0	1	1	1	90%
P12	1	1	1	0	1	1	1	1	1	0	80%
P13	1	1	0	1	1	1	1	1	1	1	90%
P14	0	0	1	1	0	0	1	1	1	1	60%
P15	1	0	1	1	1	1	1	0	1	0	70%
P16	0	0	1	1	1	0	1	1	1	1	70%
P17	1	1	1	0	0	1	1	1	1	1	80%
P18	1	1	1	1	1	1	1	1	1	1	100%
P19	1	1	1	1	1	1	1	1	1	0	90%
P20	1	1	0	1	1	1	1	1	1	1	90%
Average	**75%**	**65%**	**75%**	**80%**	**60%**	**80%**	**95%**	**80%**	**95%**	**80%**	**78.5%**

TIP

Data shown in Table 6.1, and the sample calculations done with it, are available to download from our Web site.

your goals. The averages of those two sets of averages will always be the same (78.5% in this example), assuming there are no missing data.

Focusing on the averages for the *tasks* is useful if you're trying to identify the tasks that participants had the most trouble with (e.g., Tasks 2 and 5 in this example). Focusing on the averages for the *participants* is useful if you're trying to identify participants (or demographic groups of participants) who were having the most difficulty (e.g., participants 9 and 14 in this example). Finally, focusing on the *overall* average is useful if you're trying to compare data for different conditions, designs, or sites.

Confidence intervals

Showing confidence intervals for task success (or failure) data is probably one of the most important things you can do to help the viewer of your results get a sense of what's important in data and what differences to pay attention to. Confidence intervals for task success data are calculated in two different ways depending on whether you're looking at the percent of *tasks* that the participants accomplished successfully or the percent of *participants* who accomplished each task successfully.

WHAT'S A CONFIDENCE INTERVAL AND WHY SHOULD YOU CARE?

Suppose you conducted an online study with 20 participants and found that their overall task success rate was 70%. How confident can you be that if you did the same study again, with 20 new participants, you would get the same answer? That's what a confidence interval can help you determine. It gives you an indication of how accurately the mean from your sample represents the true population mean. In other words, if you were to run your study with hundreds of thousands of participants (essentially the "population") and calculate the mean task success rate, how close would the mean task success rate from your sample of just 20 participants come to it?

You can calculate a confidence interval for continuous data using the CONFIDENCE function in Excel. It takes three parameters:

- **Alpha**, for the confidence level desired, which is usually 0.05 (for a 95% confidence interval) or 0.10 (for a 90% confidence interval).
- **Standard deviation** of the sample (which can be calculated using the STDEV function).
- **Size** of the sample (which can be calculated using the COUNT function).

Suppose that for your study with 20 participants, the 95% confidence interval for your overall task success rate (70%), calculated using this formula, is 8%.

That means that you can be 95% sure that the *true mean* for the task success rate is 70 ± 8%, or somewhere between 62 and 78%. Another way to put it is that if you were to do your same study 100 times, you would expect the mean task success rate to fall between 62 and 78% about 95 of those times, but about 5 times it would fall outside of that range. So a confidence interval really does tell you how confident you can be in the accuracy of the mean being reported.

Calculating a confidence interval for the percent of *tasks* that the participants accomplished successfully is relatively straightforward. Assuming there's a reasonable number of tasks (e.g., four or more), you can treat the task success rates for each participant as continuous data. That means you can use the CONFIDENCE function in Excel. For the sample data shown in Table 6.1, the 90% confidence interval for the mean task completion rate per participant is 78.5% (the overall mean) ± 4.5%, or 74 to 83%. Likewise, the 95% confidence interval for the mean task completion rate per participant is 78.5 ± 5.4%, or about 73 to 84%. (The 95% confidence interval will always be wider than the 90% confidence interval.) These confidence intervals can be particularly useful if you want to compare across conditions or Web sites. For example, this is how the confidence intervals shown earlier in Figure 6.2 were calculated for each of the three conditions.

WHAT ARE CONTINUOUS DATA?

Continuous data are data that can be broken down into smaller units and still be meaningful. Time, weight, mass, and length are all examples of continuous data in the real world. In usability studies, task times, task success percentages (across multiple tasks), and ratings on multipoint rating scales are all considered continuous. Discrete, or categorical, data are data that can only be counted, such as the number of males or females in a study or the number of positive or negative comments.

WHAT ALPHA LEVEL SHOULD YOU USE?

What alpha level (or confidence level) should you use in calculating a confidence interval? The three commonly used alpha levels are 1% (for a 99% confidence interval), 5% (for a 95% confidence interval), and 10% (for a 90% confidence interval). The level you choose depends on how willing you are to be wrong. At a 1% alpha level, the true mean could fall outside of the confidence interval 1% of the time, whereas at a 10% alpha level, the true mean could fall outside of the confidence interval 10% of the time. We most commonly use a 10% alpha level in our online studies.

In many situations, you want to calculate confidence intervals for the success rate *for each task*. This is particularly useful when you're making comparisons between tasks (e.g., was the success rate for Task 2 significantly lower than that for Task 9?).

Calculating these confidence intervals for each task requires a somewhat different approach. Continuing with sample data from Table 6.1, let's assume you wanted to create a graph showing the task completion rate for each task, along with a 90% confidence interval for each. Let's look at Task #1 as an example. The completion rate for it was 75%, which means that 75% (15) of the 20 participants completed that task successfully. It's technically possible to use the CONFIDENCE function in Excel to calculate a 90% confidence interval for that task completion rate. If you do that, you get a 90% confidence interval of 16.3%. But there's a problem. When looking at an individual task like this, your data are binary: either each person succeeded (1) or didn't (0). And when you have binary data, you shouldn't use the CONFIDENCE function because it assumes your data are continuous. With binary data, the confidence interval should be calculated using what's called the binomial distribution. And you should make some corrections to take into account the smaller sample sizes we often have in usability studies.

Thankfully, how to do all of this has already been figured out for us. Sauro and Lewis (2005) have shown that with binary data like this, the best method of calculating a confidence interval is using something called the Adjusted Wald Method. (Impress your friends at your next party by asking them if *they* know what the Adjusted Wald Method is.) The easiest way to do that calculation is to use either the calculator that Jeff Sauro has provided on his Web site (http://www .measuringusability.com/wald.htm) or the spreadsheet on the Measuring UX Web site (http://www .measuringux.com/AdjustedWald.htm).

> **TIP**
>
> To show confidence intervals on a graph in Excel, right click on one of the bars (or data points) in the graph and choose "Format Data Series"and then click on the "Y Error Bars" tab. The cells in your spreadsheet representing the confidence interval should then be chosen as both "+" and "-" "Custom" error amounts. This will create error bars representing the confidence intervals.

The smaller the sample size, the more important it is to use the Adjusted Wald Method to calculate the confidence interval for the completion rate of a single task. Once you get to a sample size of 80–100 participants or so, there's not much practical difference between using the Adjusted Wald Method and using the CONFIDENCE function in Excel.

Figure 6.6 shows the completion rates per task. The 90% confidence intervals for each task were calculated using the Adjusted Wald Method and plotted as error bars on the graph. It's apparent from studying this graph that Tasks 2 and 5 had significantly lower completion rates than Tasks 7 and 9.

HOW DO YOU INTERPRET ERROR BARS ON A GRAPH?

What conclusions can you come to by comparing the error bars (confidence intervals) for different means, as shown in Figure 6.6? Here are a few simple rules you can follow:

- If the error bars for two means *do not overlap*, you can safely assume that the means are *significantly different* statistically (at the alpha level chosen for the confidence intervals). So in Figure 6.6, for example, the error bars for Tasks 5 and 7 do not overlap, indicating that the means are significantly different (at the $p = 0.10$ level).

- If the error bars for two means *widely overlap*, you can safely assume that the means are *not significantly different*. Tasks 3 and 4 in Figure 6.6 are a good example.
- If the error bars for two means *slightly overlap*, you need to do some additional testing to decide if they are significantly different. The easiest way to decide is by using a *t* test (see Section 6.1.3). Tasks 5 and 6 in Figure 6.6 might be a good example.

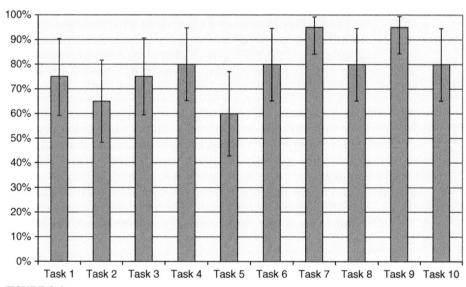

FIGURE 6.6
Mean task completion rates for data from Table 6.1, plus the 90% confidence interval for each, calculated using the Adjusted Wald Method.

6.1.2 Task times

As described in Chapter 2, sometimes how quickly users can get their tasks done is just as important as their task success. In fact, sometimes the two measures go hand in hand. Consider the case of a portable automated external defibrillator, which is used to administer shock to a victim of sudden cardiac arrest. To be most effective, the first shock should be delivered within 3–5 minutes of the cardiac arrest. The appropriate measure of task success is actually a combination of delivering the shock correctly (e.g., with the electrodes placed properly) *and* within a certain period of time. Although most of us don't deal with design for these kinds of life-and-death situations, we do often deal with cases where time is important to the user. Users often have several Web sites to choose from (e.g., to make travel arrangements), and they will tend to prefer sites that allowed them to get their tasks done successfully *and* quickly.

So how do you analyze task time data? While it may sound easy to just look at the average time that the participants spent on each of the tasks, in practice it's not quite that simple.

All task times or only successful times?

One of the complicating factors is whether you should look at the times for *all* tasks or only tasks that participants *got right*. There are logical arguments on both sides.

- **All tasks:** Reporting the times for all tasks is more representative of what the participants actually experienced. They actually spent that time even when they weren't successful, so why should you throw that data out? Reporting all times also makes time data more independent of success data.
- **Only correct tasks:** Reporting times for only tasks where they got the right answer is more reliable. It reflects how long it actually took the participants to do those tasks. When the participants failed at the tasks, you don't know what they did or what state they got to, so you don't know what that time really means.

You can easily find advocates of both approaches in the usability community. While we see value in both approaches, we more often come down on the side of reporting times for *all* tasks, regardless of whether they were successful. In an online usability study, the participants almost always decide for themselves when to give up on a task or guess at an answer. So time data from an online study don't have an artificial component that time data from a traditional lab usability study sometimes have, where the moderator decides to "call" a task for some reason (the participant is getting frustrated, not making progress, etc.).

Another reason for including time data for all tasks involves the case where only a small percentage of the participants actually succeeded at a task, but they happened to do so relatively quickly. Most of the people who failed actually spent much longer on the task. In that case, looking at time data for successful tasks only would give a biased view of the times actually spent on the task.

Let's look at a real example of time data for all tasks vs only for correct tasks. Figure 6.7 shows time data from our study of an online photo clip-art gallery. There were 10 tasks, each of which involved finding a different photo in the gallery.

These means are based on data from 1334 participants, which explains why the confidence intervals are so small. All participants attempted all 10 tasks, which were presented in a random order to each participant. Note that these data have already been "cleaned" to remove outliers (e.g., participants who got interrupted in the middle of a task), which is particularly important for time data. More about that in the next section.

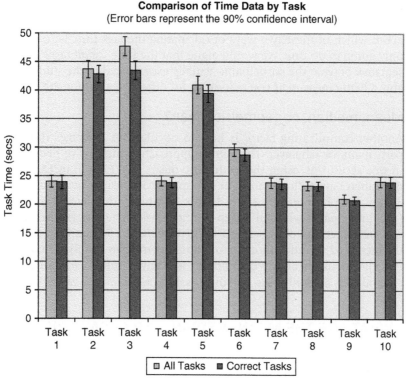

Comparison of Time Data by Task
(Error bars represent the 90% confidence interval)

FIGURE 6.7
Task times from an online photo gallery study calculated based on all tasks or only tasks that the participants got correct.

The first thing that strikes you from Figure 6.7 is that times calculated the two ways are extremely similar to each other. What's not apparent from the graph, because of the scale, is that in every case the time calculated using only the correct tasks is shorter than the time calculated using all tasks—sometimes only a half second shorter. The other thing that becomes apparent after studying the graph is that for all tasks except one (Task 3) the two times are not significantly different from each other (the error bars overlap). That means there's more variability simply due to the "noise" in the data than there is due to the way the time is calculated.

But for one task—Task 3—there is a significant difference, with the time from *all* participants (including the ones who got it wrong) significantly longer than the time from just the participants who got it correct—about 4 seconds longer. This task also had one of the lowest success rates of all 10 tasks. All of the tasks involved finding a photo in the gallery based on a thumbnail they were shown. Task 3 involved finding a photo of a boat in a harbor with the sun setting behind it. Part of the challenge of each task was deciding what aspect of the image was used to determine the category it belonged to. So participants might have wondered whether this photo was a "sunset" photo, a "sun and clouds" photo (both of which were categories in the gallery), or perhaps a "nautical" or "boats" photo (categories not in the gallery, but that may not have been obvious).

The participants who got Task 3 wrong (which includes those who gave up on it) spent significantly longer on the task than those who got it correct. We think that's a useful piece of information and not one we would have learned if we hadn't done an analysis of the times both ways. However, the question remains about which of these two ways of calculating the task time is "better" if you're only going to do one. We would argue that the time for *all* tasks is more representative of what the participants actually experienced in the study and is probably a better measure if you're looking for differences among the tasks.

Mean, median, or geometric mean?

Another complicating factor is how to calculate an "average" time for a task, participant, or whatever. The simple approach, which we've been using so far in this section, is using the arithmetic mean (=AVERAGE in Excel). But time data often have a "long tail." For example, let's consider *raw* time data for Task 3 from the photo gallery study, before "cleaning" the data to remove outliers (e.g., participants who fell asleep during a task). The longest time for this task was 4,204 seconds, or over 1 hour! When you have a long tail like this, it impacts the mean (62.9) much more than it does the median (36.5) or geometric mean (38.5). The mean of any distribution is always "pulled" toward the long tail. (Technically, a distribution like this is said to be *positively skewed*.)

WHAT ARE THE MEAN, MEDIAN, AND GEOMETRIC MEAN?

The *mean* of a set of numbers is what most people think of as the average. You calculate it by adding up all the numbers and dividing by how many there are. Or you use the AVERAGE function in Excel. The *median* of a set of numbers is the middle number if you put them in order from lowest to highest. If you have an even number of them (in which case there's not a middle number), it's halfway between the two numbers on either side of the midpoint. Or use the MEDIAN function in Excel. The *geometric mean* of a set of numbers is the mean of the natural logarithm of the numbers, converted back to a base 10 number. Before you start having nightmares about high-school math, just remember that it's a way of reducing the impact of very large or very small numbers in calculating a mean. Or use the GEOMEAN function in Excel.

For the photo gallery study, we decided that 300 seconds (5 minutes) was the maximum amount of time that a participant would reasonably spend actively working on any one task. (These were actually quite simple tasks.) So part of the "scrubbing" of data was to eliminate any times over 300 seconds. (See Chapter 5.) Note that this was done *universally*, without regard to which task it was or which condition of the study. Also note that the removed time was simply treated as a missing value; other data points for that task (e.g., ratings, success) were retained. There were 19 of these times out of the total set of 1334 times for Task 3. The new mean was 47.7 seconds, the new median was 36.0 seconds, and the new geometric mean was 36.9 seconds. Removal of times longer than 300 seconds had almost no impact on the median and geometric mean, but a significant impact on the mean (going from 62.9 to 47.7 seconds). This 24% change in the mean was based on removing only 1% of the data points. The important lesson from this is that you should either "clean" your time data based on a rule that's consistently applied or you should use the median or geometric mean rather than the mean. We generally prefer to clean data and then use the mean, mainly because it's simpler to do other manipulations then, such as calculating confidence intervals for the mean, and it's a bit easier to explain to your audience.

WHAT IF YOU GET A #NUM! ERROR WHEN CALCULATING A GEOMETRIC MEAN?

One of the amazingly helpful error messages you can get in Excel is a "#NUM!" error when doing a calculation. (We always thought that "#NUM!" looks like what you see in comic strips when someone hits their thumb with a hammer.) Unfortunately, that can happen very easily when using the GEOMEAN function. (Not the hammer thing, but maybe a similar reaction.) One of the somewhat hidden features of the GEOMEAN function is that it's limited to 30 numbers. Thankfully, there's a work-around. Assume you have a column of numbers in Excel, in column "A", that you want to calculate the geometric mean for, and it's more than 30 numbers. Create a new column next to it, in "B", and put the following formula in the first cell (B1):

    =LN(A1)

That tells Excel to take the natural log of the number in cell A1. Copy that formula down for as many rows as you have data in column A. Let's assume there are 100 of them. Then, somewhere else on the spreadsheet, enter the following to get the geometric mean:

    =EXP(AVERAGE(B1:B100))

(You would change B100 to indicate how many data points you actually have.) This is taking the average of the natural logs of the original numbers and then converting it back to base 10. (EXP is the inverse of LN.) (Those who tuned out because of nightmares about high-school math can safely tune back in now.)

Confidence intervals

In the same way that average task success rates can be calculated either per participant or per task, so can average task times. Consider the sample task times shown in Figure 6.8.

The assumption is that data in Figure 6.8 have already been cleaned according to whatever rule was adopted for the study (See Chapter 5). You can then calculate the mean times per participant (the means on the right) and the mean times per task (the means across the bottom). You can also use the CONFIDENCE function in Excel to calculate a confidence interval for the overall mean time (36 seconds) and for each task. The overall confidence intervals are shown on the right,

Microsoft Excel - SampleTimes-ConfInterval.xls

File Edit View Insert Format Tools Data Window Help Adobe PDF

N2   =CONFIDENCE(0.1,STDEV(L2:L21),COUNT(L2:L21))

	A	B	C	D	E	F	G	H	I	J	K	L	M	N	O	P
1	Participant	Task 1	Task 2	Task 3	Task 4	Task 5	Task 6	Task 7	Task 8	Task 9	Task 10	Mean		90% Confidence Interval:		
2	P232	14	35	83	18	16	93	26	43	30	27	39		3.5		
3	P233	31	104	40	22	22	33	27	32	20	20	35				
4	P234	26	45	114	35	47	26	24	24	18	43	40		95% Confidence Interval:		
5	P235	15	83	47	14	15	44	27	20	15	21	30		4.2		
6	P237	12	46	68	19	33	17	30	30	15	19	29				
7	P238	24	72	32	17	45	37	22	97	19	20	39				
8	P239	41	46	73	12	21	19	28	23	18	24	31				
9	P240	179	74	68	22	92	49	49	45	35	26	64				
10	P241	37	24	9	39	82	99	42	31	40	25	43				
11	P242	20	91	48	28	23	51	41	17	19	18	36				
12	P243	49	60	43	35	61	36	24	26	51	68	45				
13	P244	18	40	14	21	28	62	36	16	20	15	27				
14	P245	22	24	44	32	58	41	20	29	22	26	32				
15	P247	20	116	34	15	16	28	26	15	26	25	32				
16	P248	17	22	14	18	26	26	30	18	13	32	22				
17	P249	25	23	69	24	19	21	39	59	27	28	34				
18	P250	20	16	68	24	16	34	21	79	23	24	32				
19	P252	27	99	53	34	82	23	22	20	16	42	42				
20	P253	17	23	11	14	48	30	20	16	15	16	21				
21	P254	47	55	47	23	132	29	30	26	25	35	45				
22	Mean	33	55	49	23	44	40	29	33	23	28	36				
23																
24	90% C.I.:	13.2	11.4	9.8	2.9	11.7	8.2	3.0	8.1	3.5	4.5					
25	95% C.I.:	15.8	13.6	11.7	3.5	14.0	9.8	3.5	9.6	4.2	5.4					

FIGURE 6.8

Sample times (in seconds) for 20 participants and 10 tasks, along with the means by participant and task, as well as the confidence intervals.

and the confidence intervals for each task are shown across the bottom. Because time is a continuous variable, you can use the CONFIDENCE function in Excel for both sets of calculations.

6.1.3 Efficiency

So far we've looked at task success and task time separately. But in many cases what you care about most is the two of them together. That's what efficiency measures are all about: a way of combining task success and task times into a single measure that represents task success per unit of time. A participant who gets five tasks correct in 5 minutes is being more efficient than one who gets five tasks correct in 10 minutes.

Number of tasks correct per minute

One simple measure of efficiency, which we find most managers, developers, and other nonusability geeks can relate to easily, is the number of correct tasks per minute. You can calculate this for each participant:

Number of correct tasks/total time

Total time is usually expressed in minutes but can be whatever units you want. Since this can be calculated for each participant, you can then build a confidence interval for its mean.

Table 6.2   A portion of data from the online photo gallery study showing the condition each of these 20 participants was assigned to, how many tasks they got right, the total time they spent, and their efficiency (# correct per minute).

User ID	Condition	# Correct (Out of 10)	Total time (min)	# Correct per min
P182	Auto-collapse TOC	9	3.72	2.4
P183	Auto-collapse TOC	10	3.48	2.9
P184	Expand-collapse TOC	10	6.70	1.5
P185	Auto-collapse TOC	10	5.71	1.8
P186	Static TOC	5	10.10	0.5
P187	Auto-collapse TOC	9	4.89	1.8
P188	Expand-collapse TOC	9	5.68	1.6
P189	Expand-collapse TOC	10	4.85	2.1
P190	Expand-collapse TOC	10	3.17	3.2
P191	Static TOC	10	5.38	1.9
P192	Auto-collapse TOC	10	4.51	2.2
P193	Static TOC	10	3.99	2.5
P194	Auto-collapse TOC	10	5.50	1.8
P195	Auto-collapse TOC	10	4.83	2.1
P196	Expand-collapse TOC	10	6.03	1.7
P197	Expand-collapse TOC	10	3.45	2.9
P198	Static TOC	9	10.62	0.8
P199	Static TOC	10	6.93	1.4
P200	Expand-collapse TOC	10	4.05	2.5
P201	Expand-collapse TOC	4	3.69	1.1

Let's look at an example. Consider the data shown in Table 6.2, which are a small portion of data from our study of the online photo clip-art galleries.

In this study, each of the participants attempted the same set of 10 tasks, although in random orders. For this efficiency measure to be meaningful, it's important that each participant be presented with the same set of tasks. It's also easier to understand the measure if the tasks are reasonably comparable to each other (e.g., in this study they all involved finding a specific photo in the gallery). So for each participant you simply divide the number of tasks they got correct by their total time in minutes. The resulting efficiency measure is shown in the last column of Table 6.2. Note that even with just this sample of 20 participants (out of the 1334 in the study), this efficiency measure ranged from a low of 0.5 tasks correct per minute to a high of 3.2. Of course, higher levels are better. Note that a participant who got no tasks correct would always get an efficiency score of 0 regardless of their time.

Figure 6.9 shows what the complete set of task efficiency data looks like split by condition. In this study, task success data showed a tendency for the Expand-Collapse TOC condition to be slightly *less accurate*, whereas time data showed that the same condition took users marginally *longer*. The combined effect of the two was that the Expand-Collapse TOC condition was significantly less efficient than the other two conditions ($p = 0.03$ and 0.02 by t test).

FIGURE 6.9
Efficiency data (correct tasks per minute) from our online photo gallery study.

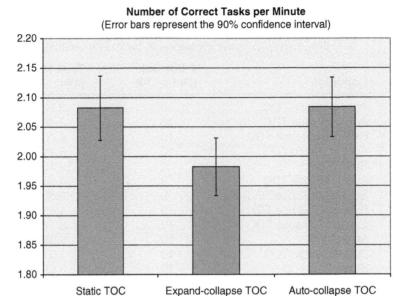

Number of Correct Tasks per Minute
(Error bars represent the 90% confidence interval)

Static TOC   Expand-collapse TOC   Auto-collapse TOC

HOW DO YOU DO A *T* TEST?

A *t* test allows you to see if two means are significantly different from each other. Consider the sample data in Figure 6.10, which shows the times for two different tasks for 10 participants. You could do a *t* test to see if those two means (31.3 and 37.3 seconds) are significantly different from each other.

The TTEST function has four parameters:

- The range of the first set of numbers (B2:B11 in this example)
- The range of the second set of numbers (C2:C11 in this example)
- The number of tails for the test, which in almost every case should be 2
- The type of test, which should be 1 if it's a "within-subjects" design (as in this example) or "2" if it's a "between-subjects" design

What's the "within-subjects" and "between-subjects" stuff about? It's the same as it was back in Chapter 2: "within-subjects" simply means the numbers are paired—the two members of each pair came from the same person. In this example, there were 10 participants, each of whom did both Task 1 and Task 2. In a "between-subjects" design, the two sets of numbers would have come from two groups of people.

The answer that you get from a *t* test, 0.01 in this example, tells you the probability of the difference between those means being due to chance alone.

Lower numbers (closer to zero) are more significant. By convention, any probability less than 0.05 is widely considered to be significant. Some people consider a probability between 0.05 and 0.10 to be significant and some don't. We usually report a probability in that range as "marginally significant." Any probability greater than 0.10 is widely considered to be nonsignificant. The way to report the result of the t test in this example would be to say something like, "The two means are significantly different from each other ($p = 0.01$, by t test)."

Percent task success per minute

A very similar method of calculating efficiency is to divide the task success *rate* by the *mean* task time. The Common Industry Format (ISO 9241–11) for usability test reports specifies that task completion rate per unit of time (typically minutes) is one of the core measures of efficiency. If each participant in a usability test attempts the same number of tasks, then this is equivalent to the number of correct tasks per minute that we just discussed. The advantage of this percentage method is that it also works when the participants are presented with different numbers of tasks. Simply divide each participant's task success *rate* (percent) by their *mean* task time in minutes. (Other units of time can be used if needed.) The result is usually expressed as a percentage, although technically it's a percentage per minute. Note that it's possible (and in some studies common) for this percentage to go above 100% for participants who are very accurate and quick.

Microsoft Excel - t-test-example.xls

File Edit View Insert Format Tools Data Window Help

D2 ▾ = =TTEST(B2:B11,C2:C11,2,1)

	A	B	C	D	E
1	Times (sec)	Task 1	Task 2	t-test	
2	P1	28	36	0.01	
3	P2	30	31		
4	P3	28	39		
5	P4	31	45		
6	P5	30	33		
7	P6	42	38		
8	P7	24	28		
9	P8	29	33		
10	P9	38	42		
11	P10	33	48		
12	Means:	31.3	37.3		
13					

FIGURE 6.10
Example of doing a t test in Excel.

6.2 SELF-REPORTED DATA

In many online studies you care less about the actual *performance* of the participants (task success, times, etc.) and more about their *perceptions*. These perceptions are what users are most likely to remember, and consequently are most likely to influence their future behavior. That's what we're calling self-reported data, because you're asking the participants to tell you about their reactions and attitudes. The most common ways to do this are using various kinds of rating scales or checklists, open-ended questions, and overall assessment tools (e.g., standard questionnaires).

6.2.1 Rating scales

Rating scales can be used at various points in an online study: at the beginning, before or after each task, and at the end. These can take on many forms, with some addressing specific *features* of the Web site or task (e.g., navigation, search, site map) and others addressing specific *reactions* to the Web site (e.g., visual appeal, page load times, likelihood to return to the site). For any of these ratings, some type of Likert scale or other scales with anchors at the two ends are most commonly used. Most of these scales generally have at least 5 points and sometimes up to 9 or 10.

Analyzing these kinds of ratings is quite simple. One of the reasons that we usually present them with labels at the two ends of the scale and not in between is that it allows you to treat the ratings as if they were interval data. The advantage of interval data is that you can calculate means and confidence intervals. For example, consider the task ratings shown in Table 6.3.

For this example, let's assume the rating scale was this:

> This task was…
> Very Difficult 0   1   2   3   4 Very Easy

Those numbers shouldn't be shown to the participants (e.g., they could just be a series of radio buttons), but that's the way we have coded the values internally. It will usually make life easier for you if you code rating scales starting at 0 rather than 1. (It just makes it simpler if you ever want to look at the ratings as percentages of the maximum possible rating—more on that later in this chapter.)

For the sample data shown in Table 6.3, we've calculated mean ratings per participant (on the right) and per task (across the bottom) using the AVERAGE function in Excel. We've also used the CONFIDENCE function to calculate a 90% confidence interval for the mean rating for each task (also across the bottom). We can then create a graph of these mean task ratings as shown in Figure 6.11.

| Table 6.3 | Sample task ratings, with means and 90% confidence intervals, for five tasks and 10 participants. |

Participant	Task 1 rating	Task 2 rating	Task 3 rating	Task 4 rating	Task 5 rating	Means
P1	4	2	1	0	3	2.0
P2	3	3	3	1	4	2.8
P3	3	1	2	1	4	2.2
P4	3	1	2	2	3	2.2
P5	4	2	3	1	4	2.8
P6	2	1	2	2	3	2.0
P7	3	3	2	0	4	2.4
P8	3	3	3	2	4	3.0
P9	2	2	2	1	3	2.0
P10	3	3	3	2	4	3.0
Means	**3.0**	**2.1**	**2.3**	**1.2**	**3.6**	**2.4**
90% CI	0.35	0.46	0.35	0.41	0.27	

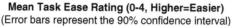

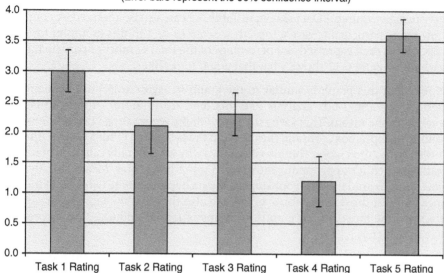

FIGURE 6.11
Mean task ratings for
data shown in Table 6.3.

There are a few things to notice about the format of this graph:

- We've labeled it as a "Mean Task Ease Rating." People create all kinds of crazy rating scales, so you never know what they mean or what direction they're going. Because higher numbers on our scale mean that the task was perceived as easier, we're reminding the viewer of that by calling it a "Task Ease Rating."
- We've also included the reminder "(0–4, Higher=Easier)." Again, we're just reminding the viewer what the scale was and what direction it ran.
- We've included error bars to represent the 90% confidence interval for each of the means, and we reminded the viewer of what the error bars mean (since there's not a standard for what error bars are used to represent).

In terms of the actual contents of the graph, you can see right away that Task 5 was perceived as significantly easier than any of the others, Task 1 was next easiest, then Tasks 2 and 3, and finally Task 4 was perceived as being significantly more difficult than any of the others. (Reminder: If two error bars don't overlap, you can assume those two means are significantly different.)

Top-2-box scores

Another popular technique for summarizing the results of rating scales, especially satisfaction ratings, is the use of "top-2-box" scores (sometimes abbreviated as "T2B"). The theory behind this technique is that you're trying to identify respondents who really gave a positive rating as opposed to a neutral or negative rating.

For example, on a rating scale of 1 to 7, the top-2-box scores would be 6 and 7. (The technique can also be used as "bottom-2-box" to focus on respondents who gave negative ratings.) Data shown in Table 6.3 can also be analyzed by counting how many participants gave a top-2-box score (3 or 4 in this example) for each task. This is then expressed as a percentage of the total number of participants for each task. Figure 6.12 shows what that graph looks like.

Notice that this graph is similar to the graph in Figure 6.11 but not identical. Results of a top-2-box analysis like this tend to be more "extreme" than an analysis of the means. That's why the task with the worst rating (Task 4) shows up with a 0% top-2-box score and the task with the best rating (Task 5) shows up with a 100% top-2-box score. This also illustrates why we generally calculate means of ratings, when it's appropriate, rather than top-2-box scores. Means usually give you more "granularity" in your summary data because you're using *all* of the ratings, not just those in the top 2 boxes. We also find that the larger your sample sizes are, the more similar graphs of means of ratings and top-2-box scores are to each other.

Top-2-box scores are particularly useful when you're dealing with ratings that are ordinal (e.g., rank order data). With ordinal data, you don't know, for example, if the "perceived distance" from the item in first place to the item in second place is the same as the "perceived distance" from the item in second place to the item in third place. So in that case you can't (or shouldn't) calculate a mean of the rankings. But it is perfectly appropriate to use top-2-box percentages.

FIGURE 6.12
Graph of top-2-box scores for data from Table 6.3.

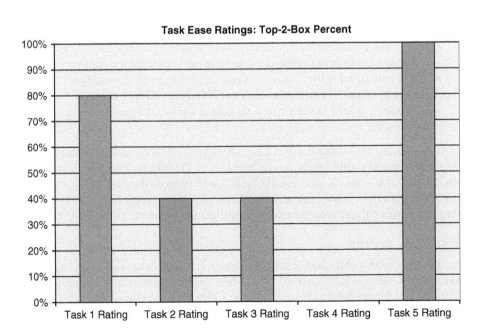

Let's consider a specific example of post-session rating scales from our online study that looked at the Web sites of the two major candidates in the 2008 U.S. presidential election, Barack Obama and John McCain. Each participant was assigned randomly to do the same set of tasks on one of these sites. Two rating scales asking for assessments of the site as a whole were included at the end of the study:

- "Overall, how easy or difficult was it to find the information you were looking for? (Very Difficult to Very Easy)"
- "Overall, how visually appealing do you think this Web site is? (Not at All Appealing to Very Appealing)"

Each of these was a seven-point rating scale. A portion of the data is shown in Table 6.4.

The means of these ratings for each site can then be calculated using the AVERAGE function in Excel, and confidence intervals can be calculated using the CONFIDENCE function. The results (for the full set of data) are shown in Figure 6.13.

Comparison of the confidence intervals shows that the Obama site received significantly higher ratings for Ease of Finding Information than the McCain site. Confidence intervals for the Visual Appeal ratings slightly overlap, but a t test shows that the Obama site received significantly higher ratings on that scale as well ($p = 0.04$).

> **TIP**
> When making a graph like that shown in Figure 6.13, make sure the bars that the viewer is most likely to want to compare are next to each other. In this example, the viewer is most likely to want to compare the means for the two *sites* on each of the ratings, not the means for the two *ratings* on each of the sites.

Table 6.4	Overall ratings from a portion of data from the study comparing Obama and McCain Web sites.		
Participant	**Site**	**Ease of finding info**	**Visual appeal**
P01	Obama	3	3
P02	McCain	2	1
P03	McCain	5	5
P04	Obama	6	6
P05	Obama	6	5
P06	Obama	1	1
P07	McCain	5	5
P08	McCain	7	7
P09	McCain	2	6
P10	McCain	3	2
P11	Obama	7	7
P12	McCain	2	4

FIGURE 6.13
Graph of overall ratings from the online study of Obama and McCain Web sites.

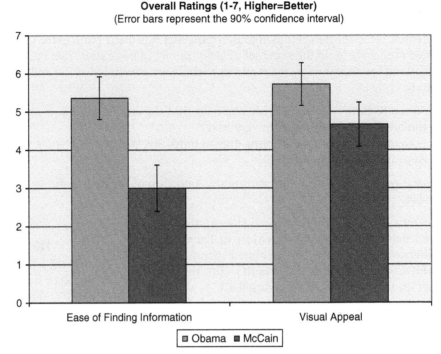

Overall Ratings (1-7, Higher=Better)
(Error bars represent the 90% confidence interval)

Ease of Finding Information   Visual Appeal

▣ Obama ▪ McCain

PIVOT TABLES ARE YOUR FRIEND

We used to think that only spreadsheet geeks used pivot tables in Excel. Why would we ever want to pivot our tables anyway? But then we learned that pivot tables can be your new best friend. Table 6.4 is a great example of when a pivot table can be really handy. Let's consider how to calculate the means of the "Ease of Finding Information" rating for the Obama and McCain Web sites. One way to do that would be to sort the spreadsheet on the "Site" column and then manually identify the two sets of ranges for the two means that need to be calculated using the AVERAGE function. But that can be a pain if you have more than just two conditions or data are still being collected.

That's where pivot tables come in. The basic steps in creating a pivot table are to select data you want to include, run the "PivotTable and PivotChart Report" wizard in Excel, and then drop the appropriate fields into the blank pivot table. In our example, you would drop the "Site" field on the part of the blank pivot table that says "Drop Row Fields Here" and the "Ease of Finding Info" field on the part that says "Drop Data Items Here." This will initially show you the *counts* of how many "Ease of Finding Info" ratings there are for each of the sites (18 for McCain and 25 for Obama in our example). But right clicking on one of those counts will let you change the "Field Settings" to "Average" instead of "Count." Data will update to show the means: 5.4 for Obama and 3.0 for McCain in our example. That's it. If you update data on the original spreadsheet (e.g., by adding more data points), simply come back to the pivot table, right click anywhere in it, and choose "Refresh Data" to update the pivot table.

It's also possible to use the same pivot table to show standard deviations and counts for the "Ease of Finding Info" ratings for both sites. And that's what you need to use the CONFIDENCE function to calculate the confidence intervals. A detailed example and demonstration of how to do this can be found on our Web site.

As described in Chapter 3, a variation on the simple rating per task is to ask the participants to rate how easy or difficult they *expect* each task to be before they actually do it and then ask them to rate it again on the same scale after they do the task to indicate how easy or difficult it *actually* was (Albert and Dixon, 2003). Consider the data shown in Table 6.5.

This shows the mean task ease ratings from before and after each of five tasks. The "Before" rating is an assessment of how difficult the participants expect the task to be based on their previous experience with tasks of that type. You expect some tasks to be more difficult than others. For example, it should be easy to get a stock quote on IBM, but it would probably be difficult to rebalance your entire portfolio to match a new projected retirement date. The "After" rating is an assessment of how easy or difficult the task actually was. One way of plotting these results is shown in Figure 6.14.

In this scatterplot, the mean Before ratings for each task are shown on the *x* axis and the mean After ratings are shown on the *y* axis. You can then look at the four quadrants of the graph:

- *Big Opportunity:* These are the tasks (T3 in this example) where participants expected it to be difficult and it was difficult. No big surprises, but potentially opportunities for pleasantly surprising users if these could be improved.

Table 6.5   Mean "Before" and "After" task ease ratings for five tasks.

Task	Mean before rating	Mean after rating
T1	3.2	3.0
T2	1.4	2.6
T3	1.5	1.4
T4	2.5	1.2
T5	3.6	3.7

FIGURE 6.14
A graph of data shown
in Table 6.5.

- *Fix It Fast:* These are the tasks (T4 in this example) where participants expected it to be easy but it was actually difficult. These are the ones you really need to focus on improving.
- *Don't Touch It:* These are the tasks (T1 and T5 in this example) where participants expected it to be easy and it was easy. No surprises, but make sure you don't mess these up in making any changes.
- *Promote It:* These are the tasks (T2 in this example) where the participants expected it to be difficult, but it actually was easy. These are the big wins. You should consider promoting how easy it is to do these tasks.

We've found that this is a very helpful way of presenting the results because it makes it easy to see which areas need to be addressed first.

6.2.2 Open-ended questions, comments, and other verbatims

Performance data (task success and time) and ratings can help you identify areas that participants had the most trouble with, but the comments they provide can help you understand *why* they had difficulty. These kinds of open-ended questions or comment fields are usually included at two levels in an online study: for each task and at the end of the study.

Task-based comments

A common technique is to provide participants with the option of entering comments for every task. In addition, it's common to have conditional logic in the design of the study such that the participants are *required* to provide a comment or explanation if they gave the task a particularly poor rating (e.g., a "0" or "1" on a scale of task ease from 0 to 4) or if they give up on the task.

Let's look at a specific example. In our online study comparing the PETCO and PetSmart Web sites, there were four tasks that participants were asked to perform on one of the sites:

1. Find a particular type of ferret food.
2. Find a store in a specific area that offers grooming.
3. Find out how much it costs for ground shipping of a gift card.
4. Find out how many types of pine cat litter are available.

The task ease ratings for each of these tasks on the two sites are shown in Figure 6.15.

The pine cat litter task had the lowest (worst) rating for Site A and was rated as significantly more difficult than the same task on Site B. Any participant who gave one of the two lowest scores on the task ease rating was asked what they found difficult about the task. Out of the 18 participants who used Site A, 3 of them gave one of the two lowest ratings to this task and provided the following responses about what was difficult:

- "I couldn't find any search option for scent. There was only a 'scented' and 'unscented' category."
- "Unable to find pine litter by itself. Search engine would not allow … put me back to cat litter."

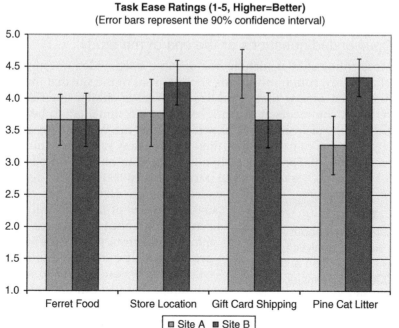

Task Ease Ratings (1-5, Higher=Better)
(Error bars represent the 90% confidence interval)

Ferret Food   Store Location   Gift Card Shipping   Pine Cat Litter

Site A   Site B

FIGURE 6.15
Task ease ratings from the pet-supply Web sites study.

- "Didn't notice the ability to select litter options by clicking on the category break-down above the search results at first. After a minute, I found it though."

Note that all three of those responses mention the Search function. A quick check of the Web site shows that entering a search for "pine cat litter" on the site takes you to a landing page about cat litter rather than a more traditional listing of rank-ordered results. So just from these three comments we've been able to identify a usability problem with the site's search mechanism.

Unless you have an unusually large number of participants in your study or they had an unusually difficult time with some of the tasks, the number of task-level comments you get generally won't be overwhelming and you can simply inspect them to detect any themes, such as the "search" theme from the comments given earlier. If you do get a large number of task-level comments, refer to the next section for tips on analyzing large numbers of verbatim comments.

Comments at the level of the individual task can be particularly helpful because they're usually very targeted, like the examples given earlier. One of the challenges with interpreting some verbatim comments is understanding the actual problem that a participant had. Comments from the end of a study sometimes are too general to be particularly helpful (e.g., "Information was confusing"— What information? Where? How was it confusing?). In a traditional usability test, the moderator can probe further to get at the details, but not in an online study. You have to try to capture what you can using the mechanisms of the study, which is why task-level comments, particularly triggered by a lower task ease rating, can be very helpful.

Open-ended questions at the end of the study

Most online studies include one or more open-ended questions at the end of the study, commonly asking about aspects of the site that the user liked or didn't like, aspects that could be improved, or similar questions. Similar to verbatim comments at the task level, these comments can be an incredibly rich source of insight into how to improve the Web site. In a study with a large number of participants, there can be many verbatim comments to try to make sense of. For example, in our study of an online photo clip-art gallery, a total of 945 participants (69%) provided responses to an open-ended question asking about challenging or frustrating aspects of the site. Entire books have been written about techniques for extracting information from textual sources like this, a process usually called text mining or text analytics. What we outline are some very simple techniques that you can use to help analyze a relatively large number of verbatim comments from a usability study.

TIP

For more information about text mining and text analytics, see the books by Feldman and Sanger (2006) and Spangler and Kreulen (2007).

Let's take the 945 comments from our study of an online photo gallery as a case study in this process. Although there were three conditions in this study, the only difference among them was the behavior of the table of contents in the left navigation frame. Because the actual contents and organization of the photo clip-art gallery were the same in all conditions, we will look at the comments about challenging or frustrating aspects of the site for the three conditions combined.

The first thing we usually do is use Excel or Word to sort the comments in alphabetical order. One thing you learn quickly in analyzing verbatim comments like this is that the participants take the questions very literally. One advantage of sorting the comments alphabetically is that now all of the comments that simply say something like "No," "None," "Nope," or "Nothing" are near each other. (This is in response to the question "Were there any aspects of the Web site that you found particularly challenging or frustrating?") While you should note how many of these comments there were, for the purposes of extracting meaning from the comments, they can be removed. That reduces our number of comments from 945 to 650.

The next step is to use a program, Web site, or other utility that lets you analyze the frequency of words in these comments. We have links to several of them on our Web site. For this example, we'll use the Advanced Text Analyser on UsingEnglish.com (http://www.usingenglish.com/members/text-analysis/). (It requires membership, but that's free.) After pasting the comments into a text box on the site, you can generate a list of the most frequent words in the text, excluding common English words ("a", "the," "and," etc.). Table 6.6 shows the top 20 words in terms of frequency.

The first thing that's apparent from this list is that something about the categories used on the site (e.g., Architecture, Everyday Objects, Nature, etc.) must have been confusing to the participants. Some of the other frequent words, such as "pictures," "photo," and "photos" are understandable given the subject matter of the site. Some of the words, such as "architecture," "building," "china," "wildlife," "sunset," and "animals" all refer to specific categories used on the site, apparently that the participants had trouble with. One of the particularly interesting words in the list is "search." In many situations, when you identify a frequent word, you need to go back to the original comments containing that word to make sure that you understand the context. In the case of "search," checking the original comments yields a number of suggestions related to a "Search" feature:

- a search feature would help
- doesn't have a search option
- lack of search facility
- needs image search functionality
- should be a search option
- Sometimes it was difficult to figure out the category of the photo. Perhaps a tag search or something like that would help.

Table 6.6	Twenty most frequent words in frustrating comments about the site from the photo gallery study.

Word	Count
categories	117
category	89
pictures	86
architecture	75
multiple	43
easy	36
photo	33
into	29
search	27
items	26
photos	26
finding	25
folders	25
didn't	24
building	23
china	22
different	22
wildlife	21
sunset	19
animals	18

FINDING ALL COMMENTS THAT CONTAIN A SPECIFIC WORD

One of the useful functions in Excel for dealing with verbatims is the SEARCH function. Assume that the comments you want to analyze, such as the frustrating comments in our photo gallery study, are in a column of cells in a spreadsheet. You can then use the SEARCH function in the column next to it to identify all the comments that contain a specific string *somewhere in the cell*. The two parameters for the SEARCH function are the string you're trying to find (e.g., "category") and the cell that you want to check for that string. So you would put that function in the cell next to the first comment and then copy it down for as many cells as there are comments. If the cell *does not* contain the string, you'll get a #VALUE! error. That's okay. Any cells that *do* contain the string will give you a number, which represents the position in the text of the cell where the string starts (e.g., a "1" means that it starts at the beginning). You can then sort the two columns using the column containing the SEARCH functions as the sort key. All the comments that yielded "#VALUE!" will fall at the bottom while the ones containing the target string will be at the top.

Using this process certainly won't capture all of the key points in the verbatims, but it will help you find many of them. Of course, you'll probably want to go beyond just the top 20 words like we did in this example. We usually study at least the top 50 words (with the common English words removed) to see what insights we can get from them, referring back to their context in the original comments as needed. This process will allow you to start grouping the comments into logically related categories.

USING WORD CLOUDS TO VISUALIZE FREQUENT WORDS

An interesting way to visualize frequent words in any collection of text is using what are called "word clouds." While the Advanced Text Analyser on the UsingEnglish.com site can create word clouds, they're not nearly as visually interesting as the word clouds created by Wordle.net. Figure 6.16 shows an example of a word cloud created using Wordle.net for frequent words in the frustrating comments from the photo gallery study.

In a word cloud, the size of a word represents its frequency in the text. But the interesting thing about Wordle.net is the extremely wide variety of fonts, colors, and layouts that it supports. In fact, you can create word clouds that are quite striking. Like the Advanced Text Analyser, Wordle.net provides an option for removing common English words (and those from many other languages), but the two sites must use different lists of common words. The word cloud shown here includes a number of words (e.g., "great," "wall," "world," "travel") that must have been treated as common words by the Advanced Text Analyser. The lesson from this is to try at least a couple of different tools for analyzing word frequency to see if they yield different results.

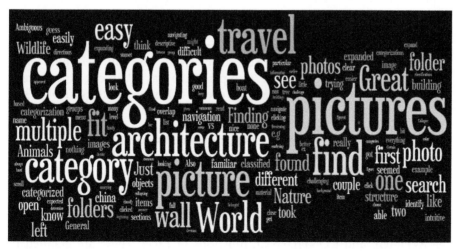

FIGURE 6.16
Word cloud created using Wordle.net of frequent words used in the frustrating comments from the photo gallery study.

6.2.3 Overall assessment tools

As discussed in Chapter 3, several standard assessment tools are available in the usability literature (e.g., SUS, QUIS, CSUQ, USE). The System Usability Scale (SUS) has become particularly popular because it is reliable with small numbers of participants (Tullis and Stetson, 2004) and is relatively short (10 rating scales). Because of its popularity, some benchmark data providing SUS scores from a wide range of studies are available for comparison purposes. (See our Web site.) The exact wording of the SUS rating scales, as we have adapted them for Web sites, is as follows.

1. I think that I would like to use this Web site frequently.
2. I found this Web site unnecessarily complex.
3. I thought this Web site was easy to use.
4. I think I would need assistance to be able to use this Web site.
5. I found the various functions in this Web site were well integrated.
6. I thought there was too much inconsistency in this Web site.
7. I would imagine that most people would learn to use this Web site very quickly.
8. I found this Web site very cumbersome/awkward to use.
9. I felt very confident using this Web site.
10. I would need to learn a lot about this Web site before I could use it effectively.

Each of these statements is accompanied by a five-point scale of "Strongly Disagree" to "Strongly Agree." Note that half of the statements are positive and half are negative, which is part of what seems to make SUS effective.

CALCULATING SUS SCORES

Calculating the SUS score from ratings on the 10 scales is straightforward, although a bit tedious to do by hand. That's why we've provided an Excel spreadsheet to do the calculation on our Web site. SUS scores are truly percentages of the maximum possible SUS score. They range from 0 (the worst possible score) to 100 (the best possible score). In looking at the SUS scores from 129 different conditions in 50 different studies in the usability literature, we found that the average SUS score was 66. The 25th percentile was 57, the median was 69, and the 75th percentile was 77. In our experience, most "average" Web sites generally get overall SUS scores in the 60's or 70's.

Let's look at an example of SUS scores from a real study. In our Apollo study, we compared the Wikipedia and NASA sites about the Apollo Space Program. Participants did the same tasks on one of the two sites. At the end, they were given the SUS questionnaire. Table 6.7 shows a portion of the individual SUS scores.

The means and confidence intervals for these scores can be calculated using the AVERAGE and CONFIDENCE functions in Excel. These are graphed in Figure 6.17 (for the full data set).

Table 6.7 Some individual SUS scores from our study of Apollo
Program Web sites.

NASA	Wikipedia	NASA	Wikipedia
7.5	50.0	17.5	32.5
72.5	55.0	22.5	47.5
37.5	75.0	15.0	77.5
27.5	60.0	47.5	82.5
85.0	85.0	7.5	65.0
17.5	45.0	72.5	82.5
15.0	92.5	60.0	87.5
25.0	50.0	45.0	82.5
30.0	55.0	10.0	55.0
52.5	27.5	57.5	90.0

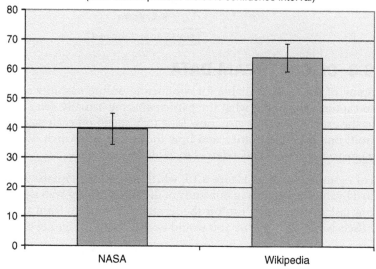

Mean SUS Scores by Site
(Error bars represent the 90% confidence interval)

FIGURE 6.17
Graph of the means
of SUS scores from
our Apollo Program
Web sites study.

Obviously there's a dramatic difference in the SUS scores, with the NASA
score (39.7) significantly lower than the Wikipedia score (64.0). In a case
like this, where there's a pretty big difference between the means
and we have a reasonably large sample size, we find it's
sometimes useful to graph the frequency distribution of the scores. That's shown in Figure 6.18.

Studying Figure 6.18 makes it even clearer
what a dramatic difference there is between
the two sets of SUS scores, with scores for the
NASA site peaking at the lower end and those
for the Wikipedia site peaking in the middle and
upper end.

TIP

Check our Web site for details on
using the FREQUENCY function in
Excel for calculating a frequency
distribution, such as shown in
Figure 6.18.

FIGURE 6.18
Frequency distribution of SUS scores from our Apollo Program Web sites study.

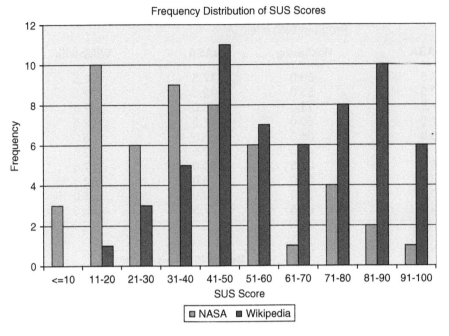

6.3 CLICKSTREAM DATA

Some of the tools available for conducting online usability studies allow you to capture data about what the participants are actually *doing* on the site, such as the exact pages they visit, how long they spend on each page, the transitions from one page to another, and how they use a site search mechanism. In the aggregate, this is usually referred to as clickstream data.

For example, consider Figure 6.19, which is part of a visualization of pages visited by the participants in our study of the TerraPass.org Web site. There was only one task in this study: "Explore the TerraPass Web site to learn about how carbon offsets work and whether you would be interested in signing up."

Here you can see the paths that participants followed to get to a page and the associated percentages of participants, as well as the paths that they took away from this page and those percentages.

USING CLICKSTREAM DATA TO DEFINE TASK SUCCESS

Some of the online study tools allow you to define whether participants were successful with a task by whether they reached one or more predefined pages as they were doing that task. This works well if the task is such that it can only be accomplished by reaching one or more specific pages *and* if you can safely assume that once a participant reached one of those pages he or she would realize the answer is there. We've seen many cases where a participant reached a page that contained the answer but didn't see the answer or didn't realize that it was the answer.

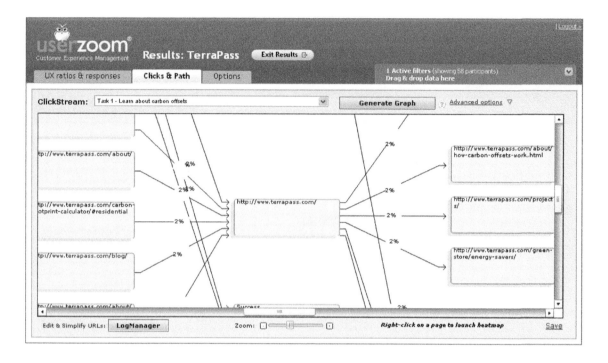

FIGURE 6.19
A portion of clickstream data from our study of Terrapass.org.

Another way of visualizing the click behavior on the site is using a heatmap representing where the participants in the study clicked on any given page. For example, Figure 6.20 shows a click heatmap for the TerraPass home page. The "hot" areas of this visualization represent where the participants in the study clicked the most often on the home page: in the left navigation area on "Gift Ideas" or "Carbon Offsets" or in the "For Businesses" area under the large "ad" about energy-saving gifts (whose content changes).

To take another example, let's look closely at clickstream data from our study of a pet-supply Web site (Site B from the study). One of the metrics that can be calculated from clickstream data is the number of pages the participants visited for each task. Because some tasks will inherently require more pages to accomplish than others, one thing you usually want to factor out is that inherent difference in the tasks. That's done by determining the minimum number of pages that could be visited to accomplish the task successfully. (For sites that have a Search function, this count is usually made by navigating rather than searching.) For each task, you then subtract the minimum number of pages from the actual number visited. Figure 6.21 shows that difference for each of the tasks in the study.

You can see that Task 1 (finding a particular type of ferret food) took significantly more "extra" pages than any of the others. While that could certainly indicate

FIGURE 6.20
An example of a "click heatmap" from UserZoom of the USA.gov home page.

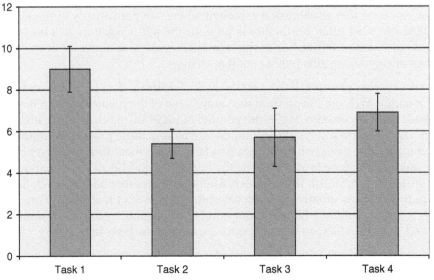

FIGURE 6.21
Number of pages visited beyond the minimum number needed to accomplish each task for Site B from the pet-supply Web site study.

Number of Pages Beyond Minimum
(Error bars represent the 90% confidence interval)

challenges that participants had with Task 1, it could also be due to the fact that the tasks were presented in the same order to each participant so that Task 1 was always first and participants were still getting oriented to the site. This reaffirms the value of presenting tasks in a random order to each participant when possible. The other thing apparent from Figure 6.21 is that Task 2 (finding a store) took significantly fewer extra pages than Task 4 (finding pine cat litter). Because practice effects certainly can't explain that difference, it would be wise to study the differences between the two tasks to see why Task 2 was done more effectively than Task 4.

Another interesting analysis from this study involves the use of site search. On average, participants tried to search a total of about three times during the study. Only 2 participants out of 24 (8%) *never* tried the site search mechanism. Five years ago we rarely saw participants turn to a site search mechanism to find the answer to something. Now it's rare that participants don't try a site search at least once. This is what we call the "Google effect." Figure 6.22 shows the mean number of searches per task.

It's not an error in the graph that there are no searches shown for Task 2 (finding a store). None of the participants used the site search mechanism for that task. Instead, they all used the Store Locator. The higher usage of search for Task 1 could again be due to the fact that it was always the first task and the participants were "testing" the search to see how well it worked. It's also interesting to look at the use of search as a function of whether the participant got the task right (regardless of which task it was). Figure 6.23 shows the percentage of participant tasks that used search, split by incorrect and correct tasks.

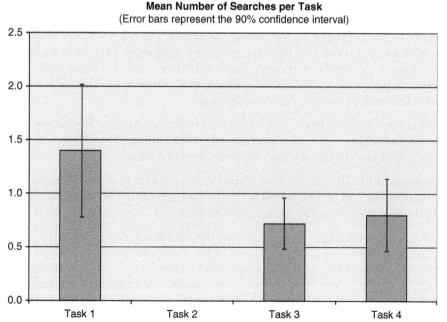

Mean Number of Searches per Task
(Error bars represent the 90% confidence interval)

FIGURE 6.22
Mean number of searches for each task for Site B from the pet-supply Web site study.

FIGURE 6.23
Percent of participant tasks where search was used as a function of whether they got the right answer.

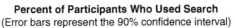

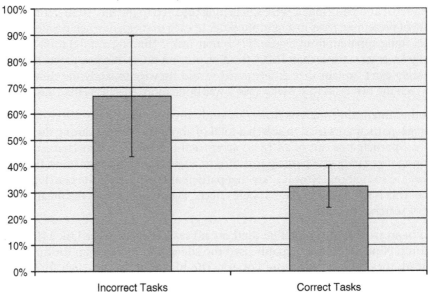

Percent of Participants Who Used Search
(Error bars represent the 90% confidence interval)

You can see that the participants used search significantly more often on incorrect tasks than on correct tasks. Note that these confidence intervals were determined using the Adjusted Wald Method, as the data are binary (either the participant used search or not). (See Section 6.1.1) The confidence interval for incorrect tasks is much larger because there were fewer incorrect tasks than correct tasks. Does this mean that the use of search actually caused the participants to be more likely to get the wrong answer? Maybe, but that's not the only possible explanation. It could also be that participants were more likely to use search on the harder tasks and that they were also more likely to fail at those tasks. In any event, it would be worth studying the search function to see if there are aspects of it that may be causing problems for users.

What you can learn from clickstream data is limited mainly by your own ingenuity and willingness to dive into the data. For example, Table 6.8 shows a small portion of raw clickstream data from the TerraPass study.

Analysis of the clickstream data reveals that a total of 18 different pages in the TerraPass site had at least two visits by the participants in the study. These pages, in descending order of visits, are listed in Table 6.9.

Of the 58 participants who completed the TerraPass study, 45 of them (77%) succeeded while 13 (23%) failed. One of the many additional analyses you could do of clickstream data is to see if certain pages on the site were more often associated with success vs failure. The participants' task was to learn enough about carbon offsets to decide whether they would be interested in signing up. Given the overall level of success (77%) vs failure (23%), you can then look at selected pages on the site

	Table 6.8	Portion of clickstream data for the first three participants in the TerraPass study. The URLs visited are shown along with the participants' indication of whether they succeeded at their task.

N	CodeUser	Alias	LogTime
1	C17S1_101	http://www.terrapass.com	Nov 19 2008 6:41PM
2	C17S1_101	http://www.terrapass.com/	Nov 19 2008 6:41PM
3	C17S1_101	http://www.terrapass.com/green-store/ carbon-offsets/	Nov 19 2008 6:42PM
4	C17S1_101	http://www.terrapass.com/projects/	Nov 19 2008 6:43PM
5	C17S1_101	http://www.terrapass.com/faq/	Nov 19 2008 6:43PM
6	C17S1_101	Success	Nov 19 2008 6:44PM
1	C17S1_103	http://www.terrapass.com	Nov 19 2008 6:44PM
2	C17S1_103	http://www.terrapass.com/	Nov 19 2008 6:44PM
3	C17S1_103	http://www.terrapass.com/green-store/gifts-for-her/	Nov 19 2008 6:44PM
4	C17S1_103	http://www.terrapass.com/Merchant2/merchant. mvc?Screen=I	Nov 19 2008 6:45PM
5	C17S1_103	http://www.terrapass.com/green-store/carbon-offsets/	Nov 19 2008 6:45PM
6	C17S1_103	http://www.terrapass.com/green-store/ led-christmas-lights/	Nov 19 2008 6:45PM
7	C17S1_103	http://www.terrapass.com/about/	Nov 19 2008 6:46PM
8	C17S1_103	Success	Nov 19 2008 6:47PM
1	C17S1_104	http://www.terrapass.com	Nov 19 2008 6:52PM
2	C17S1_104	http://www.terrapass.com/	Nov 19 2008 6:52PM
3	C17S1_104	http://www.terrapass.com/ earch/?cx=0016832740263211079	Nov 19 2008 6:53PM

to see how their percentages of success and failure compare to that. For example, a total of 18 participants visited the TerraPass "Projects" page. With a total of 18 participant visits, the "expected" outcome would be that 14 of those participants (77%) would eventually succeed while 4 would fail (23%). But a detailed analysis of clickstream data reveals that only 10 eventually succeeded (56%) while 8 eventually failed (44%). A χ^2 test (the CHITEST function in Excel) can be used to determine if that observed frequency is significantly different from the expected frequency. In fact, results indicate that the failure rate is significantly worse than expected ($p = 0.02$), pointing to a potential problem with that page, at least in terms of informing users about what carbon offsets are. However, of the 19 participants who visited the "How Carbon Offsets Work" page, 89% were successful while only 11% failed, indicating that participants generally found that page useful in accomplishing their task.

6.4 CORRELATIONS AND COMBINATIONS

Sometimes the most interesting things you learn from an online usability study come from combining or comparing the different types of data (e.g., task success, task times, ratings, SUS scores). For example, discovering that a task has a particularly low success rate but a high task ease rating might reveal that the

Table 6.9	List of pages in the TerraPass site with at least two visits by participants in the online study.	

Page	Visit count
http://www.terrapass.com/	136
http://www.terrapass.com/green-store/carbon-offsets/	47
http://www.terrapass.com/projects/	24
http://www.terrapass.com/about/how-carbon-offsets-work.html	23
http://www.terrapass.com/about/	15
http://www.terrapass.com/carbon-footprint-calculator/	15
http://www.terrapass.com/carbon-footprint-calculator/#air	9
http://www.terrapass.com/green-store/	8
http://www.terrapass.com/carbon-footprint-calculator/ #residential	7
http://www.terrapass.com/carbon-footprint-calculator/action	7
http://www.terrapass.com/buy-carbon-offsets/	5
http://www.terrapass.com/projects/listing.html	5
http://www.terrapass.com/projects/our-principles.html	4
http://www.terrapass.com/about/ourstory.html	3
http://www.terrapass.com/faq/carbon-offsets/	3
http://www.terrapass.com/projects/categories.html	3
http://www.terrapass.com/carbon-footprint-calculator/#road	2
http://www.terrapass.com/faq/	2

participants didn't realize they were getting the wrong answer to the task. And in some situations, you just want to get an overall sense of how a site did in the test, which can be done by combining some of the data in appropriate ways.

6.4.1 Correlations

Correlations involve looking at how one variable, such as task success, tends to change in relationship to another variable, such as task ease rating. Let's consider three variables from the study of the photo clip-art gallery: task success, task time, and task ease rating. We're going to look at them by task, as shown in Table 6.10.

A handy feature of Excel is the "Analysis ToolPak," which can be added via the "Tools > Add-ins" menu if you don't see the "Tools > Data Analysis" menu option. One useful function it provides is a correlation function. Selecting the data shown in Table 6.10 and choosing the "Correlation" function from the Data Analysis dialog box result in the correlation matrix shown in Table 6.11.

Table 6.11 shows values of the correlation coefficient ("r") between the pairs of variables. A correlation coefficient can range from −1.0 (perfect negative correlation) through 0 (no correlation) to +1.0 (perfect positive correlation). The diagonal values in Table 6.11 are 1.0, as any variable correlates perfectly with itself. The other values are the interesting ones. Task Success doesn't correlate particularly well with either the Task Ease Rating (0.36) or the Task Time (−0.43). But the Task Ease Rating and Task Time correlate almost perfectly (−0.99). Figure 6.24 shows the scatterplots corresponding to these correlations.

Table 6.10	Task success rates, task ease ratings, and task times, by task, from the photo gallery study.		
	Task success	**Task ease rating**	**Task time (sec)**
Task 1	81%	4.5	24
Task 2	88%	3.4	42
Task 3	84%	3.5	46
Task 4	88%	4.5	24
Task 5	86%	3.7	40
Task 6	88%	4.2	29
Task 7	94%	4.5	23
Task 8	89%	4.5	23
Task 9	90%	4.6	21
Task 10	92%	4.4	24

Table 6.11	Correlation matrix for data shown in Table 6.10.		
	Task success	**Task ease rating**	**Task time (sec)**
Task success	1.00		
Task ease rating	0.36	1.00	
Task time (sec)	−0.43	−0.99	1.00

We've added the trend line to the scatterplot of Task Time vs Task Ease Rating to reflect the near-perfect negative correlation between those variables: the longer a task took, the worse the task ease rating. That's not surprising, as these were very simple tasks (mean task times were all under 1 minute) and the amount of time that a task took should be pretty apparent to the participants. They must have used that as a key factor in deciding their task ease rating. What's more interesting is to study the other two scatterplots. In the case of Task Ease Rating vs Task Accuracy, most of the tasks cluster along a diagonal line from lower left to upper right, with the exception of one "outlier" task in the upper left, which is Task 1.

For the most part, tasks with higher task ease ratings also had higher task accuracies, but not for Task 1. It had a high task ease rating but a low accuracy. Similarly, in the case of the Task Time vs Task Accuracy, most of the tasks cluster along a line (or perhaps a curve) from the upper left to the lower right, again with one exception: Task 1, which is in the lower-left corner. Tasks that were more accurate generally were also faster, but Task 1 was *less* accurate and faster. Something is odd about Task 1.

TIP

You can add a trend line to a scatterplot in Excel by right clicking on any data point and choosing "Add Trendline" from the pop-up menu.

Task 1 involved finding the title of the full version of the photo of a bird shown in a thumbnail, as illustrated in Figure 6.25. The title of the target photo was "Bluebird on Branch."

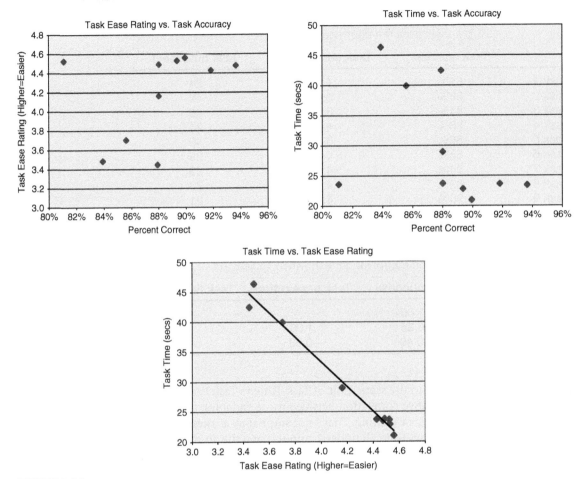

FIGURE 6.24
Scatterplots of Task Ease Rating vs Task Accuracy, Task Time vs Task Accuracy, and Task Time vs Task Ease Rating from the photo gallery study.

The answer options provided to the participants were as follows:

- Bird 48
- Bird on Branch
- Bluebird on Branch
- Pic-622
- None of the above
- Give up

While 81% of the participants chose the correct answer, "Bluebird on Branch," 17% chose "Bird on Branch." The next-highest percentage for an incorrect answer option for *any* task (not counting "Give ups") was only 5%. Why did some of the participants quickly come to the (incorrect) conclusion that "Bird on Branch" was the right answer? There are two likely reasons:

1. They were simply guessing and in reading down the list of answer options, "Bird on Branch" was the first one that sounded like it might be right.
2. They didn't read the title of the photo closely and picked "Bird on Branch" because it looked pretty much like what they saw.

FIGURE 6.25
Target photo for Task 1 in the photo gallery study.

In this case, studying the correlations among data from the study revealed an outlier task, Task 1. Further investigation of that task revealed what was perhaps a flaw in the study design: the inclusion of a distractor answer, "Bird on Branch," which was simply too similar to the correct answer (and might especially be problematic if a participant had to navigate away from the Web site to an answer page first rather than see the two simultaneously). While you want your distractor answers to seem plausible, your purpose isn't to "trick" the participants with them.

In other studies, we've seen these kinds of "outlier" tasks reveal some of the most important insights from the study. For example, in one study we had selected the distractor answers in such a way that a participant who failed to do a key step in a sequence of steps would arrive at that distractor answer (which was completely different from the correct answer). What we saw, similar to the example just given, was very low accuracy for that task coupled with shorter task times and higher task ease ratings. In fact, many of the participants were failing to include that critical step and thus arriving at the wrong answer, but they were blissfully unaware of their mistake. This type of error is often much more insidious because the user may not detect it until much later (if at all), perhaps when the consequences are more serious.

6.4.2 Combinations (or deriving an overall usability score)

Sometimes you just want to get to the bottom line with an online usability test: How well did it do? It's almost like people asking that question want a *grade* reflecting how well the site did. While we don't generally come up with a grade, there are some ways of deriving an overall usability score that come close.

One of the easiest ways of calculating an overall usability score is to convert key measures from the test (e.g., task success, task time, task ratings) to percentages and then average them together. This can be done either at the task level or for the overall study. For example, consider the data shown in Table 6.12, which is a small portion of data from our online photo study.

This shows the three key task measures from that study: task ease rating (1–5), percent correct, and task time in seconds. Averaging these together in an appropriate way would give you an overall sense of the results at the task level.

Table 6.12 Small portion of participant data from the online photo study showing condition, mean task ease rating, percent correct, and mean task time in seconds.

Participant	Condition	Mean task ease rating	Percent correct	Mean task time (sec)
P382	Static TOC	4.0	100%	20
P383	Static TOC	4.4	100%	24
P384	Auto-collapse TOC	4.4	100%	19
P385	Expand/collapse TOC	4.0	100%	47
P386	Static TOC	3.8	90%	26
P387	Auto-collapse TOC	4.2	100%	29
P388	Auto-collapse TOC	4.1	90%	33
P389	Expand/collapse TOC	3.2	100%	19
P390	Static TOC	4.9	100%	23
P391	Expand/collapse TOC	4.1	80%	50
P392	Static TOC	4.3	90%	22
P393	Static TOC	4.4	100%	17
P394	Auto-collapse TOC	4.0	100%	41
P395	Static TOC	3.2	100%	25
P396	Auto-collapse TOC	4.6	100%	44

To average these together, we will first convert each of them to a percentage of the *best possible score*. The task accuracy, or percent correct, already is such a percentage, so it doesn't need to be transformed. The task ease ratings were done on a scale of 1–5, where 5 was a perfect score. These can be converted to a percentage by subtracting 1 from the score (to change the scale to 0–4) and dividing by the new maximum possible score, 4. In that way, a score of 1 on the original scale becomes 0% and a score of 5 on the original scale becomes 100%. The task times are slightly trickier because they don't have predefined end points to the scale, and because the scale is reversed relative to the other two: higher time values are worse. The technique we've used to transform time data is to divide the minimum (shortest) time value by each time to be transformed. For example, although it's not shown in Table 6.12, the shortest mean task time was 10 seconds. This transformation method converts that shortest time to 100% and all the other times to some percentage less than that. In that study, the longest mean task time was 81 seconds, which becomes 12%. The result of these transformations for data in Table 6.12 is shown in Table 6.13.

Finally, we've simply averaged the three percentages together (percent correct, time %, and task rating %) to arrive at a combined task percentage, which is shown in the last column of Table 6.13.

In the photos study, the main thing we were interested in was how the three conditions, reflecting different approaches to the navigation table of contents, compared to each other. Figure 6.26 shows a graph of this combined task measure as a function of condition. (This is another example where a pivot table can be used in Excel to easily calculate these means for each of the conditions. See Section 6.2.1.)

Table 6.13 Data from Table 6.12 with percentage transformations added.

Participant	Condition	Mean task ease rating	Percent correct	Mean task time (sec)	Time percent	Task rating percent	Combined task percent
P382	Static TOC	4.0	100%	20	84%	75%	86%
P383	Static TOC	4.4	100%	24	70%	85%	85%
P384	Auto-collapse TOC	4.4	100%	19	85%	85%	90%
P385	Expand/collapse TOC	4.0	100%	47	35%	75%	70%
P386	Static TOC	3.8	90%	26	65%	70%	75%
P387	Auto-collapse TOC	4.2	100%	29	58%	80%	79%
P388	Auto-collapse TOC	4.1	90%	33	50%	78%	73%
P389	Expand/collapse TOC	3.2	100%	19	89%	55%	81%
P390	Static TOC	4.9	100%	23	72%	98%	90%
P391	Expand/collapse TOC	4.1	80%	50	33%	78%	64%
P392	Static TOC	4.3	90%	22	77%	83%	83%
P393	Static TOC	4.4	100%	17	100%	85%	95%
P394	Auto-collapse TOC	4.0	100%	41	40%	75%	72%
P395	Static TOC	3.2	100%	25	66%	55%	74%
P396	Auto-collapse TOC	4.6	100%	44	38%	90%	76%

Because we were able to calculate this combined task percentage for each participant, we were also able to come up with confidence intervals for means using the CONFIDENCE function in Excel. You can see that this overall task measure came out significantly better for the Static TOC and Auto-collapse TOC conditions than it did for the Expand/Collapse TOC condition.

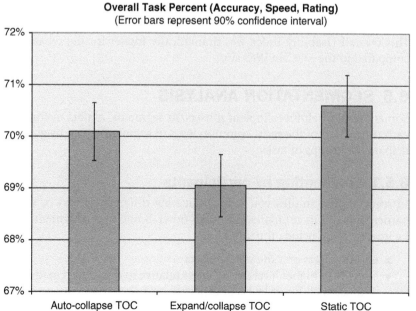

Overall Task Percent (Accuracy, Speed, Rating)
(Error bars represent 90% confidence interval)

FIGURE 6.26 Combined task percentages for the three conditions from the online photo gallery study.

FIGURE 6.27
Overall Usability Index
(percentage combination
of accuracy, speed, and
SUS score) from the
Obama and McCain Web
sites study.

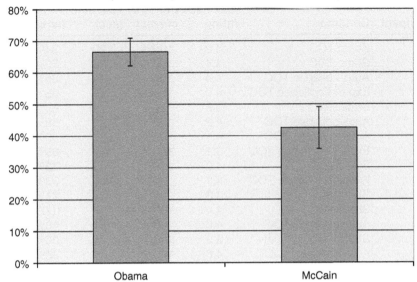

Overall Usability Index
(Percentage combination of accuracy, speed, & SUS score)
(Error bars represent the 90% confidence interval)

This percentage transformation technique can also be used to combine task- and session-based data from a study. For example, in the study of the Obama and McCain Web sites, this technique was used to combine task accuracy, task times, and SUS scores into an "Overall Usability Index." Task times were transformed using the method described earlier. Because both task accuracy and SUS scores are already percentages, there was no need to transform them. Results are shown in Figure 6.27.

This Overall Usability Index was dramatically higher for the Obama Web site compared to the McCain Web site.

6.5 SEGMENTATION ANALYSIS

Sometimes it's helpful to look at subsets, or segments, of data in comparison to each other. Two of the most common ways of segmenting are by groups of participants or groups of tasks.

6.5.1 Segmenting by participants

In some online studies you care about how different groups or segments of participants did in comparison to each other. Some of the segments you might be interested in include the following:

- Existing users of a site vs new users
- Users with higher levels of expertise relative to the subject matter of the site vs those with lower levels of expertise
- Users with more Web experience vs those with less Web experience

- Younger users vs older users
- Users from one country or part of the world vs another

Analyzing and comparing your data by looking at appropriate segments can give you important insights into the design of the site and what works well or doesn't. For example, it's not uncommon to find that users with more expertise in the subject matter of a site generally perform better in a usability test than those with less expertise. But by studying data from participants with less expertise you may be able to identify ways in which the site could be improved for them, and perhaps even for the participants with more expertise.

It's also common to uncover problems with international use of a site by comparing results for users from one country to others. For example, in an online test of a U.S.-based car reservation system, we saw that users from outside the United States had lower task completion rates and worse subjective ratings than those from within the United States. Analysis of the comments and the site revealed that the reservation page had a postal code field for home address that was formatted to accept only numeric codes (as in the United States), but not alphanumerics (as in the United Kingdom and many other countries).

As another example, let's look at data from our study of the TerraPass Web site. One of the questions asked at the beginning of the study was how familiar the participants were with carbon offsets (which is the basic subject matter of the site). Of the 76 participants who started the study, 42 (55%) said they were "Very" or "Somewhat" familiar with them, whereas 34 (45%) said they were "Not at all" familiar with them. This can provide a meaningful way of segmenting the rest of the data from the study. When doing segmentation analysis, you should make sure that you have a reasonable number of participants in each segment.

You can then look at task performance data as a function of this segmentation. For example, Figure 6.28 shows the task failure rate and task times split by these two segments.

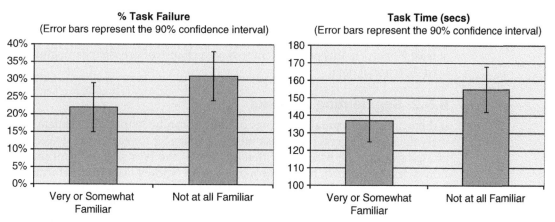

FIGURE 6.28
Task failure rate and task time as a function of familiarity with carbon offsets from the TerraPass study.

There's a tendency for participants less familiar with carbon offsets to have a higher task failure rate and longer task times. The differences did not reach statistical significance because of the relatively small sample sizes; more participants would be needed to determine if the differences are truly significant. But that shouldn't stop you from investigating whether there were certain aspects of the site that people who had less familiarity with carbon offsets found particularly confusing. That can be done by studying their comments about specific suggestions for improving the site. There was a very common theme in their suggestions, as the following samples illustrate.

- Most people just want to know WHAT a carbon offset is and it took me too long just to understand it. It needs to be up front because many people coming to the site might be just like me and have no clue what it is and why I should purchase it.
- Explain more up front and in plain terms what a Terrapass is and what carbon offsets are.
- Don't assume people have domain knowledge.
- I really didn't understand the concept.

The majority of comments from people with less domain knowledge expressed some form of the opinion that the site simply didn't do a very good job of explaining the basics: what a carbon offset is, why they should care, and what the TerraPass site is all about. Basically, this site suffers from the "preaching to the choir" syndrome: you need to already have some domain knowledge about carbon offsets in order to use the site effectively. However, that defeats a large purpose of the site, which one would assume is to get more people to buy carbon offsets.

Any data that we've discussed in this chapter can be segmented in this way: task success, task time, task ratings, overall ratings, SUS scores, verbatim comments, and clickstream data. Also, any data that you capture about the participants can be used as a basis for segmentation (e.g., age, gender, domain knowledge, Web experience). Generally, you want to limit your segments to perhaps two to four, but that's really more a function of how many participants you have in total and how many per segment. A reasonable rule of thumb is that you want at least 50 participants per segment to have a chance of getting meaningful or at least directional data.

6.5.2 Segmenting by tasks

If there are some natural groupings of tasks, it can be helpful to calculate summary data (task success, time, task ratings, efficiency) for each type of task. Task groupings might be based on different areas of the Web site, different interaction styles (e.g., search, navigation), or different types of tasks (e.g., information lookup, transactional). Ideally, there will be at least three tasks representing each group. When you plan to do this kind of analysis up front, try to have about the same number of tasks in each group. This analysis can be particularly helpful in identifying problem areas of a site.

6.6 IDENTIFYING USABILITY ISSUES AND COMPARING DESIGNS

As stated at the beginning of this chapter, the goals of an online study usually fall into two major categories: identifying usability issues with a design or comparing alternative designs. In many cases, you want to do both: determine which design "won," but also figure out how that design could be improved even more. Now that we've covered the analysis "building blocks," let's look at how they might be used in addressing these two types of goals.

6.6.1 Identifying usability issues

Perhaps surprisingly, if you ask 10 experienced usability professionals to tell you what a usability issue is, you'd probably get 10 different definitions. But the underlying theme you'd see in most of the definitions is that it's some aspect or feature of the product being tested that was confusing for at least some of the participants or that somehow contributed to their failure to accomplish a task in a reasonably efficient manner.

All data we've discussed in this chapter can be used as input to that process of identifying usability issues. Identifying usability issues is probably the most challenging part of analyzing results from any usability study, whether online or in a lab. Getting good at it takes lots of experience. The following sections describe some of the techniques we've found particularly helpful in identifying usability issues.

Focusing on problem tasks

Task-based data from an online study can point you directly to the tasks that the participants had the most trouble with. It's always helpful to look at the tasks that had the lowest success rates, longest times, or worst task ease ratings to try to determine why that happened. If your online usability study supports the collection of clickstream data, studying the exact paths of the participants who failed these tasks can be very enlightening. Where did they go wrong? Did they start down the wrong path from the home page or someplace further down? Did they try the site search function only to find that it didn't give them any useful results?

If you don't have clickstream data, your next best source of insight is probably any task comments provided by the participants. Closely study the comments from any of the participants who failed the task, took an unusually long time, or gave a low task ease rating. They should provide you with some good clues. Follow these clues yourself on the site to see if you can reproduce their thought process. As with clickstream data, try to identify where they went wrong and what aspects of the site led them astray. Was there some terminology that they didn't understand or something that they failed to see?

Analysis of errors

You often learn much more from the errors that participants make in a usability study than you do from the things they get right. As with usability issues, there's no universally accepted definition of exactly what an error is in a usability study. In fact, the definitions can get circular, with usability issues being things that lead to errors and errors being things that are associated with usability issues. But there are certain types of errors in a usability study that can be detected easily and that can help in identification of an underlying usability issue.

As mentioned in Chapter 3, one technique that we like to use in many online studies is to carefully choose the "distractor" answers for a task in such a way that their selection will tell us something about how the participant came to that erroneous conclusion. For example, assume that the test involved the use of an interactive tool for helping you decide which digital camera to buy. Digital cameras have many different characteristics, such as their zoom range, sensor size in megapixels, light sensitivity, weight, and cost. The participant's task is to find the least expensive camera that meets a particular set of these criteria. After manipulating some of the criteria, the participant is presented with a list of the cameras, which can be sorted in various ways. The participant might assume that the last criterion manipulated is the one that will be the sort order for the cameras. But what if the default sort order is always some characteristic that may not even be visible, such as how many are in stock. In that case, it might be appropriate to include as a distractor the camera that comes up by default at the top of the list, even though that's not the least expensive one that meets the criteria. If some participants choose that camera incorrectly, it's a reasonable assumption that it was because they didn't recognize that the default sort order wasn't what they expected.

Analysis of comments

Probably the best source of insight into usability issues comes from the verbatim comments of the participants, either from the individual tasks or from the end of the study. Participants who experienced problems with the site usually take the opportunity to tell you about the problems they had and what they think of the site. You might be surprised by how much detail some participants provide. The biggest challenges are detecting the common themes in the comments (see Section 6.2.2) and then determining what underlying usability issues (causes) they point to. Sometimes the causes are obvious, such as the example earlier from the TerraPass study where participants unfamiliar with carbon offsets clearly stated that their basic problem was simply understanding what the site was all about. But you'll also encounter many cases where the problems and underlying causes aren't so obvious. One of the most common complaints we've seen in an online usability test of a Web site is something like "poor organization of information." When you see relatively general comments like that, one approach is to see if there are other comments or clues that can lead to a better understanding of the problem. Is it mainly a problem with some of the terminology used on the site or is it how the concepts or pages are grouped together? Sometimes the best you can do is simply identify that the organization of the information just didn't work for some of the participants. You can't always find the answers to all the problems from one study. That's what iteration or simultaneously comparing alternatives is all about. Or that might be a case where you want to follow up an online study with a lab study to learn more about the cause.

6.6.2 Comparing alternative designs

As many of the examples in this chapter have illustrated, you tend to get the most information out of an online usability study if you can compare your results to *something*. The comparisons might be done within the study itself (e.g., the Obama and McCain Web sites) or they might be done to previous tests. Whenever we can, we try to set up online usability studies so that we can do comparisons within the study itself. This encourages our design partners on a project to come up with design alternatives that they want to try out. We think this is healthy, especially early in the design or redesign of a Web site, because it prevents you from getting "locked in" to a particular design too early. We like the distinction that Bill Buxton makes in his book (Buxton, 2007): Getting the design right vs getting the right design. All too often in design projects we settle on a basic design approach which we then iterate *ad nauseum* ("getting the design right") but then we miss some other significantly different design approach which would have been far better ("getting the right design").

We've done some online studies where we simultaneously tested as many as 16 different design alternatives for the same Web site! This approach helps "get the right design." But as we start to narrow down the design candidates, we then start making comparisons of more subtle differences. The photos study comparing the different navigation approaches for an online photo clip-art gallery is perhaps an example of this. But we've done studies where the differences were far more subtle than that. For example, in one study, we were comparing the exact timing of a fly-out menu: whether it should appear on click, automatically with no delay, a 250-msec delay, or 500-msec delay. And we actually got significant differences in task performance data: we found that the participants had a significantly higher task success rate when the menu appeared on click.

The other type of comparison we commonly make is to an earlier, or baseline, version of a Web site. If the new version isn't demonstrably better than the previous version, then why bother with the new version? (We think the people responsible for various Web sites often fail to ask this very basic question when deciding to "upgrade" their site to a totally new version.) We often start the process of redesigning a Web site (or portion of one) with an online usability study of the current site. That helps us identify problem areas that we need to focus on and it establishes a baseline of usability data to compare against.

Sometimes it's difficult to interpret the results of an online test of a single site without something to compare the results against. The following sections highlight some of the points to keep in mind when comparing alternative designs.

Make sure comparisons are valid

We once did an online study of two Web sites about inventors and inventions as an exercise for a class we were teaching. The tasks all involved finding information about the same inventors or inventions on one of the sites. It was a "between-subjects" design in that each participant used only one of the sites. One of the tasks involved finding information about an inventor who wasn't covered on Site A but was on Site B. We had intentionally included an answer option for *all* tasks that said "This information is not on this site." What we found was that the participants who used Site A (which did not include the information) had a dramatically lower task success rate, longer task time, and worse task ease rating for this task than those who used Site B. Site A also received significantly worse *overall* ratings that Site B. It could have been that Site A really was worse than Site B overall, but it's also possible that the one task that couldn't be done on Site A significantly influenced the participants' overall assessment of the site.

This is an example of a case where the comparison between the sites isn't really a fair comparison. Even if you exclude data for that one task from the analyses for both sites, the overall ratings were still influenced by it. Make sure that the tasks the participants do on each of the sites being compared truly are comparable.

You can also compare alternative designs that were tested at different times, as long as the tasks and other conditions are comparable. But sometimes external factors beyond your control change between two tests. An example from the financial world is that a Web site tested when the market is going up is likely to get more positive subjective ratings than one tested when the market is going down. That's why we like to test alternatives at approximately the same time whenever possible.

Use confidence intervals and *t* tests

As many of the examples in this chapter have shown, you should calculate and show confidence intervals for means whenever possible. These help you focus on the differences between designs that are truly significant. At a high level (e.g., overall task success rates for each of the alternatives tested), they can help you decide which alternative you should carry forward to the next design iteration or even whether you should take a design into production. At a more detailed level (e.g., success rates or subjective ratings for individual tasks), confidence intervals can help you identify certain tasks where one design worked significantly better than another. Even if that particular design wasn't the "winner" overall, understanding why it worked better for that particular task can inform possible improvements to the design that was the "winner."

In cases where confidence intervals for two designs are slightly overlapping, you'll usually want to do a *t* test to see if the difference is real. The bottom line is that you want to pay the most attention to the differences that are real. Those are the differences that you want to try to understand using any of the sources available to you—clickstream data, verbatim comments, and so on.

INTERPRETING STATISTICAL SIGNIFICANCE (OR LACK OF IT)

One of the most misunderstood aspects of statistics is the concept of statistical significance, and in particular the statement that there is a "significant difference" between two means. A statistically significant difference between two means simply indicates there is a strong likelihood that there *is* a difference between them—in other words, that the difference between them is not zero. It doesn't say anything about the *size* of the difference. The difference between mean task success rates of 89 and 91% can be just as significant as the difference between mean task success rates of 71 and 89%—it all depends on sample sizes and variability. But the first difference may have very little *practical* significance while the second one does.

Another of the subtleties of statistics is how to interpret the situation where two means are *not* significantly different from each other. For example, if the task success rates for two designs are not significantly different from each other, can you conclude that they are the same—that the true difference between them is zero? Sorry, but it doesn't work that way. You might have heard the expression in statistics that you can never accept the null hypothesis—only reject it or fail to reject it. The null hypothesis, in this example, is that there is no difference between the task success rates for the two designs. If you find that there is a significant difference between them, you're rejecting that null hypothesis. However, if you don't find a significant difference, you simply failed to reject that null hypothesis. It doesn't mean that they're the same.

6.7 PRESENTING THE RESULTS

We've tried to give many examples of how to present the results of an online study throughout this chapter. What we'll do now is just summarize some of the themes that you might have already detected and perhaps introduce a few new ones. We decided to do that in the form of a "Top Ten" list of tips for presenting the results. And, by the way, we're assuming you're making an actual presentation of the results rather than writing a long report that might just sit on someone's shelf gathering dust.

6.7.1 Set the stage appropriately

Your audience needs to understand the context of the online study, which means that you also must know something about your audience and what they already know. The less they know, the more stage setting you need to provide—about the site or prototype being tested, the goals of the study, the target users, and so on. But even when we're presenting to a pretty knowledgeable audience, such as the immediate project team, we find that it's helpful to include at least the basics of how the online study was conducted:

- What was tested (including one or more screenshots of the prototypes).
- How it was tested (including a screenshot of the online study itself).

- What questions were asked and what tasks were used.
- How the participants were recruited (e.g., a targeted email to a specific distribution list).
- What data were collected (e.g., task success, task times, clickstream data).

We commonly cover these points in a couple of slides, plus a couple of slides of screenshots. Make additional details about the method of study available in an appendix if you really want to.

6.7.2 Make the participants real

One of the disadvantages of an online usability study in comparison to a "live" usability study is that you can't see the participants. One of your goals in presenting the results of an online study is to make the participants "come alive" for your audience. One way to do that is to provide information about who the participants were: not just how many there were, but detailed characteristics derived from your demographic questions (e.g., age groups, gender, levels of relevant domain knowledge, frequency of use of the Web). You'll particularly want to focus on any details about segments of participants that you're going to use in your analyses. We usually have several slides summarizing the characteristics of the participants. You might even consider developing and using personas to represent the major categories of participants in the study. Another technique to make the participants "come alive" is to use their verbatim comments liberally throughout the presentation to reinforce your points. Of course, always be careful not to reveal any personally identifying information about your participants.

6.7.3 Organize your data logically

How you organize your data can make a big difference in how well your audience understands it. There's no universal way of organizing results from an online study that works well in all situations so be prepared to adapt. But a common technique we've used is to present data in a way that parallels the experience that the participants had, which usually means starting with task data (e.g., accuracy, time, ratings), moving on to session-level data (e.g., overall rating scales, SUS scores), and finally any data that you derived, such as an overall usability index. Don't overwhelm your audience with too many details. Just because you can slice and dice data in a hundred different ways doesn't mean you should.

6.7.4 Tell a story

Figure out what the important points you want to make are and make sure they don't get buried among everything else. If you're comparing three alternative designs and the important point is that the participants were significantly more effective in performing their tasks with one of them in comparison to the other two, make sure that point is crystal clear. Sometimes it may be more effective to drive that point home with several graphs showing different ways in which that design was more effective (e.g., better task success, shorter times), but if one graph makes that point particularly well (e.g., showing task efficiency), then just use the one. Verbatim comments from participants are also a great way to help tell a story and support your key points.

6.7.5 Use pictures

In many cases a picture really is worth a thousand words. One type of picture that you will undoubtedly use in your presentation is data graphs. Make sure they contribute to telling the story of what you learned from the study. The other type of picture that we find very helpful is an annotated screenshot of the site describing what happened at some critical point in a task. If you have clickstream data you might even be able to visually represent a "click heatmap" showing where the participants clicked on a critical page in performing a specific task.

6.7.6 Simplify data graphs

Data graphs should inform, not confuse. We find that it often takes quite a bit of experimentation with different ways of presenting data before we arrive at the best way of conveying the information. If presenting some data at the task level is too confusing, then summarize it across the tasks first and then dive in to specific tasks that illustrate key points. Just because you can create three-dimensional bar charts that dance and sing doesn't mean you should. Normal bar graphs and line graphs actually work pretty well, although that doesn't necessarily mean you should accept all the defaults in Excel.

> **TIP**
> Look at the books by Stephen Few (2004, 2006, 2009) for some good tips on presenting information graphically.

6.7.7 Show confidence intervals

You might have already noticed that just about every graph of means we've presented in this chapter has included confidence intervals for those means. Yes, they can be a bit of a pain to calculate, but they're really invaluable, both to you and to your audience. They help you focus on the differences that are real, and consequently they help your audience focus on them too. We've found that most of the people we present our findings to seem to "get" confidence intervals pretty quickly. They may not understand them from a statistical perspective or how they're calculated, but they understand that they mean the real value could actually be anywhere in that range. And seeing that the confidence intervals for two alternative designs don't overlap on some key measurement is an easy way to tell your story—much more effectively than a bunch of t tests or p values. By the way, you should pick a confidence interval (e.g., 90%) and stick with it.

6.7.8 Make details available without boring your audience

There's nothing worse than boring your audience with endless charts and graphs that nobody really cares about. If you didn't really learn anything useful from task time data, for example, just say that. Then make the details available in an appendix for anyone who wants to dive into it further. And because we don't want to bore the audience of this book, that's probably enough about this point!

6.7.9 Make the punch line(s) clear

Even if you've told your story clearly, the punch lines need to be even clearer. You need to summarize for your audience. Sometimes you get conflicting results from an online study (e.g., one set of data indicates that one alternative came out the best and another set indicates that a different alternative came out best). These things happen—quite commonly in fact. People are complex and their behavior is even more so. You need to help your audience understand what came out of the study and in some cases that means making an informed decision about what something from the study really means. Sometimes you'll be wrong, but you'll get better with experience, which is why you should encourage doing lots of studies with lots of alternatives—because you'll learn from all of them.

6.7.10 Clarify the next steps

An online study is almost never the end of the road. Provide a road map to show where the project should go next, or at least some directional suggestions. Don't assume that the next step should be another online study on a revised design. It's easy to get infatuated with one particular usability method and then keep using it. Maybe you should follow up the online study with a lab study to look at particular issues in more depth. A lab study lets you probe in ways that you just can't do in an online study. Maybe a particular demographic group had the most trouble in the online study. You might want to do some interviews, observations, or other types of contextual inquiry with those users to understand why they had those problems and how to address them. There are lots of ways to learn from users, and we should use whatever makes the most sense.

6.8 SUMMARY

The following are some of the key takeaways from this chapter.

- Task-based data, such as task success, task times, and ratings, can help you identify tasks that participants found particularly challenging, thus pointing to parts of the Web site that might be problematic.
- Session data, such as various overall ratings and verbatim comments, can help you get an overall picture of the experience that the participants had with the site, especially any areas that they found particularly challenging or that worked particularly well.
- Confidence intervals can be calculated for most of the measures we've discussed. They're a valuable tool to help focus on the differences that are real.
- Looking at correlations among data from your study (e.g., task success and task ease rating) can yield important insights. For example, a task with low success rates but high task ease ratings is possibly one where the participants didn't realize they were getting it wrong.

- Sometimes it's useful to combine several measures into a new combined measure, such as an overall usability score. This is particularly useful when comparing alternative designs, different versions, or competitors.
- Clickstream data can give you information about what parts of the site participants actually visited or used in performing their tasks. Comparing that to their task performance data can help you identify pages that helped participants achieve their goals vs those that did not.
- In identifying usability issues, your best clues are likely to come from an analysis of the tasks that participants did the worst on, the errors they made, and their verbatim comments.
- Analyzing and comparing data for different segments of participants can help you determine if some users are being served better by the site than others.
- When presenting results of an online study, try to tell a story, make your participants real, don't bore your audience with too many details, and point to next steps.

CHAPTER 7
Building Your Online Study Using Commercial Tools

As online usability studies have increased in popularity, a variety of commercial tools and systems have emerged to support these types of studies. This chapter is an introduction to four of them. You might be wondering if you *must* use a commercial tool to build an online study. The answer is "no." If you're interested in discount approaches to building an online study, go to Chapter 8. It's for the do-it-yourselfer who's willing to sacrifice some functionality to build a study cheaply (or even for free).

The following sections describe four commercial tools for building online studies: Loop11, RelevantView, UserZoom, and WebEffective. These are the tools we're familiar with that support the kinds of large-scale online usability studies we've been discussing in this book. Our criteria for selecting the tools were that they had to support:

- Testing of live Web sites or functional prototypes
- Presentation of tasks to the participants
- Automated collection of data, including at least some task metrics (e.g., task success, time, ratings)
- Collection of clickstream data
- Self-service use of the tool

We've used all of these tools ourselves, either for studies described in this book or other studies. For each tool, we provide an overview of what it's like to create an online study with it, what the study looks like from the participant's perspective, and what kind of data collection it supports. We also provide general information about the pricing of these tools. Pricing structures vary widely from one tool to another and, of course, are changing. In general, the more features a tool provides, the more it costs. We've used the following index to indicate the approximate cost of each tool:

- $ = up to about $600 (U.S.) per study
- $$ = up to about $6000 (U.S.) per study
- $$$ = up to about $12,000 (U.S.) or more per study

At the end of this chapter is a table comparing the features of these tools. We've also provided a detailed checklist of questions you can use in evaluating any commercial tool for building online studies.

The information in this chapter is current as of the writing of this book, but these tools are constantly being improved and new tools are being developed. Check our Web site for links to these tools and others.

RELATED TOOLS

A number of other commercial tools and services are available that are closely related to tools for building online usability studies. Some of these include the following.

- **C-Inspector.com**: A tool for testing the information architecture for a site. You upload a site map (the organization of the site) and define a set of tasks as well as their correct answers. You then recruit participants to do the study. Data collected include whether the participants were successful at the tasks, their average times, and their click paths.
- **Chalkmark** (http://www.optimalworkshop.com/chalkmark.htm): Allows you to present images of Web pages and corresponding tasks. Users click on the image to indicate where they would find the answer to the task. The system automatically records where the user clicked on the image and how long it took them.
- **FiveSecondTest.com**: Allows you to create very simple tests using images. Two types of tests are supported: users are asked to either list things they remember after viewing an image for five seconds or click on areas of an image shown for 5 seconds and then describe what those are.
- **MindCanvas** (www.TheMindCanvas.com): An online service that uses game-like methods to collect input from users. A number of different tools are available, including open and closed card-sorting exercises, methods for gathering emotional reactions to screens or images, and "where would you click" studies.
- **OpenHallway.com**: Based on the premise of "hallway usability testing," OpenHallway lets you create a test scenario for a site and then send a link to whoever you want. Their screen and voice are recorded while interacting with your site.
- **UserTesting.com**: Allows you to define a target demographic for your site and the tasks you want them to perform. Some of their testers (people who have registered on their site) who meet the target demographic then do the tasks on your site while their screen activity and voice are recorded.

- **Usability Exchange** (www.UsabilityExchange.com): An online service that matches Web site providers with a pool of disabled users who will conduct an online test of their site. You define tasks that the users should perform on the site and characteristics of the users, including their disabilities (e.g., degree of vision impairment). Users from their pool are then matched and given the study to perform online.
- **Usabilla.com**: Allows you to get feedback on any wire frame, mockup or Web page. Participants point and click on images to share their opinions using markers and notes.
- **Userlytics.com**: Allows you to specify a site to be tested, define the desired tester demographics, and specify tasks and questions to ask the testers. They then provide testers from their database whose screen activity, face, and voice are recorded while using your site.

New services in this field are coming out all the time. Check our Web site for the latest information.

7.1 LOOP11

http://www.Loop11.com
Cost: $

With Loop11 you can create online usability studies with multiple tasks using a live site or prototype. Various types of questions and rating scales can be interspersed with the tasks. When creating a task, you define one or more URLs for the page(s) that the participant should reach upon successful completion of the task. Loop11 will then automatically calculate and display task success rates. As shown in Figure 7.1, tasks are presented in a small toolbar area at the top of the window. The user navigates a prototype or live site in the main part of the window to accomplish the task. Once the user finds the answer, he or she clicks on the "Task Complete" button in the toolbar. Loop11 records all of the pages visited, including the one that the user was on when they clicked on the toolbar button. Loop11 supports a wide variety of question types (e.g., radio buttons, input boxes, check boxes). Task accuracy, time, and responses to any questions or ratings are recorded automatically.

7.1.1 Creating a study

You start by creating a new user test from the projects page. This page lists your projects currently under construction and already launched. Step 1 of creating a new user test, as shown in Figure 7.2, is to define some of the basic characteristics of the test, including its title, language, and introductory text.

Step 2 involves defining the tasks and questions of the user test. Figure 7.3 illustrates the creation of a new task, which includes the description of the task, its starting URL, and any URLs that should be considered as successful completion.

FIGURE 7.1
Sample online study of USA.gov created with Loop11. The task is shown to the participant at the top of the window.

You can also freely intersperse questions with the tasks. Questions can be presented in a variety of formats (radio buttons, check boxes, open-ended, etc.), options can be randomized, and an "other" field can be added.

In Step 3, you are given various final options related to the study, including the maximum number of participants, "Thank You" text, whether to allow multiple responses per computer, and whether to restrict participant IP addresses. In Step 4 you determine how participants will be invited to participate in the test, and in Step 5 you launch the test.

7.1.2 From the participant's perspective

When participants go to a Loop11 study, they would first be shown the introduction to the study that you defined, followed by a standard explanation provided by Loop11 of the mechanics of the study. Tasks are then presented to the participant as illustrated earlier in Figure 7.1. Questions are presented as illustrated in Figure 7.4.

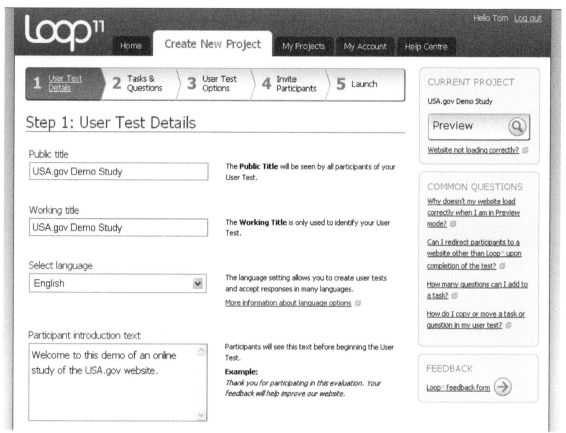

FIGURE 7.2
Step 1 of creating a new user test in Loop11.

7.1.3 Data analysis

Loop11 provides a "dashboard" that gives a high-level view of data from your study (Figure 7.5). This dashboard shows the average task completion rate across all participants and all tasks. It also shows summary data for each task, including task completion rate, average number of page views, and average time. Data can also be exported to CSV, XML, or PDF.

The "Tasks" tab in the Loop11 report contains detailed data on each task. For each task, it shows the task completion rate (and failure and abandon rate), the page views to complete the task, average time, and the most common pages where users succeeded, failed, abandoned, and first clicked. It also lists the most common navigation path from the starting page to task success. Note that task success is based on having reached one of the predefined "success" URLs for the task.

You can drill down to look at the click paths for individual participants and tasks by clicking on the "Participant Path Analysis" button. For example,

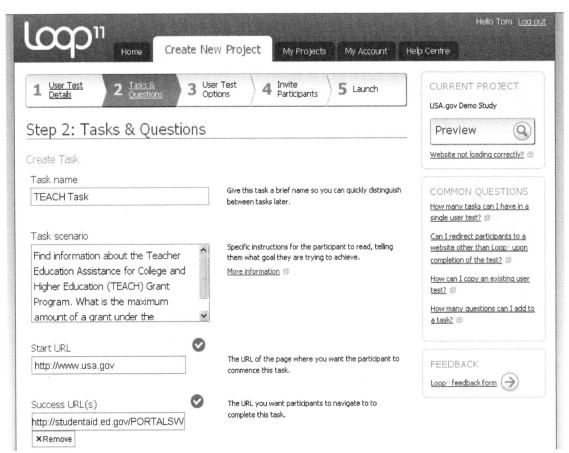

FIGURE 7.3
Creating a new task in Loop11.

Figure 7.6 shows the sequence of pages visited by Participant #2 in attempting the "Apollo Study Question" task. A thumbnail of the currently highlighted page (navigation step #6) is also shown.

The "Questions" tab shows results for the questions asked in the study (e.g., rating scales, multiple-choice questions) in the form of bar graphs. Finally, the "Participants" tab shows detailed data for each participant in the study, including the total time spent on the study, average time per task, average page views, and their page views and time per task.

7.1.4 Summary of strengths and limitations

Loop11 is a straightforward tool for creating and fielding online usability studies. You can create an unlimited number of tasks and questions per study; questions can be presented in a variety of formats. It supports the collection of most of the kinds of data discussed in this book, including task success, task times, rating scales and comments, and clickstream data. Unlike some of

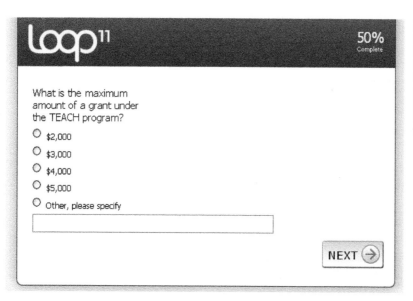

FIGURE 7.4
A question presented by Loop11. Note that the question replaces the Web site being evaluated. The Web site (or potentially a different one) will be brought back for the next task.

FIGURE 7.5
A dashboard showing overall results of a study in Loop11.

FIGURE 7.6
Clickstream ("Path Analysis") for one participant and one task in Loop11.

the other commercial services, it does not require the user to download any special software or custom controls. However, the simplicity of the Loop11 interface comes at the expense of some of the advanced features found in other commercial services, such as sophisticated scripting or "skip logic" and "display logic."

7.2 RELEVANTVIEW

http://www.RelevantView.com
Cost: $$–$$$

RelevantView is a fully featured online system for creating and administering a wide variety of online usability studies. Our sample study of pet-supply Web sites was created using RelevantView. As shown in Figure 7.7, tasks can be presented in a small window at the top of the screen. The user navigates a prototype or live site in the main window to accomplish the task. Once the user finds the answer, he or she clicks on an "Answer" button in the toolbar, which expands the window for selecting an answer. Note that tasks can also be presented in a small window on the left side of the screen, as illustrated in Figure 7.8. In this case, the options for answering the question are presented along with the task. As wide-screen monitors become more common, this may be an appropriate option for testing some sites.

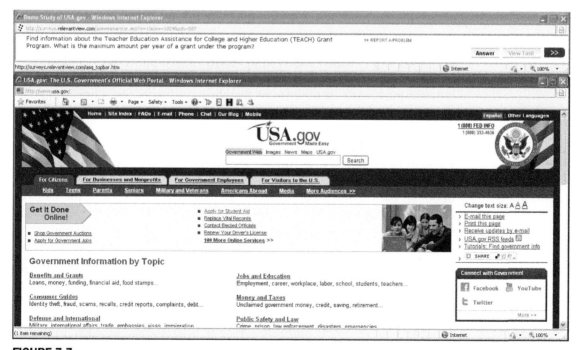

FIGURE 7.7
Example of an online study created with RelevantView.

FIGURE 7.8
An example of a task being presented in a left panel in RelevantView.

Similar to an online survey tool, RelevantView supports a wide variety of question types (e.g., radio buttons, drop-down lists, input boxes, check boxes). Responses to any questions or ratings are recorded automatically. Task accuracy is determined based on the answers that the participants give. Clickstream data can be recorded to identify the pages that a participant visits.

7.2.1 Creating a study

You start by creating a new "survey" on the Surveys page, shown in Figure 7.9. (Note that RelevantView refers to online studies as "surveys," which is the terminology used in this section.) This page lists all of your surveys, the status of each (e.g., being edited, in field, closed), and allows you to edit, preview, launch, close, duplicate, or delete surveys. Note that you can also download a survey to MS Word.

The first step of creating a new survey is to define some of the general properties of the survey, such as its name and a description. The Properties tab of the Survey Setup page (Figure 7.10) allows you to define global characteristics of the survey, such as whether all questions will be required, whether all task questions will be tracked with their clickstream-tracking technology, and whether a progress indicator will be shown. Other tabs allow you to customize various messages shown by RelevantView to the participants.

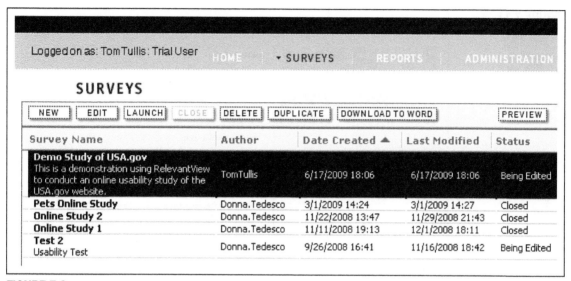

FIGURE 7.9
The Surveys page in RelevantView.

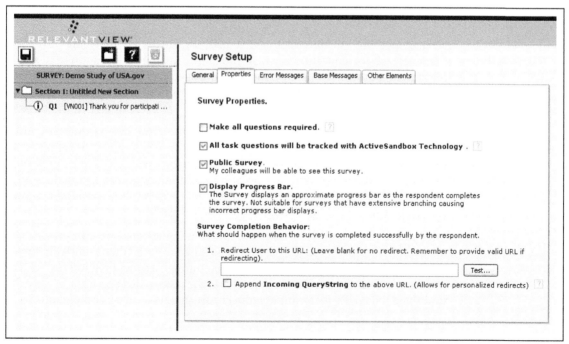

FIGURE 7.10
The Properties tab of the Survey Setup page in RelevantView.

FIGURE 7.11
The General tab of the
Question Setup page in
RelevantView.

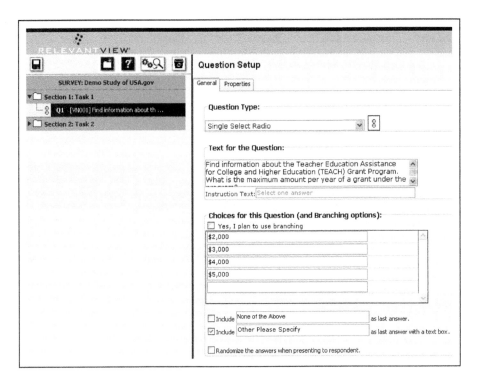

Next comes the creation of the first task, as illustrated in Figure 7.11. The
"General" tab for a question is where you define the type of question (e.g., single
select radio buttons, drop-down menu, multiselect), question text, and response
options. You can also randomize the response options and include a "none of
the above" or "other" options.

The "Properties" tab for a question is where you define the starting URL to be
shown along with the question, whether a response is required, whether clickstream data are to be recorded, and where the survey window is to be presented
in relation to the main window (top or left). In the case of displaying the survey
window at the top, you also define the text that will be shown on the two buttons in that window (e.g., "Answer" and "View Task").

After you've entered all your tasks and any other questions, you can preview the
survey from the Surveys page. Once you're satisfied, you can then launch the survey
using a Launch Survey wizard. This steps you through a series of questions, such as
whether you want to randomize the order of the tasks, when you want to close the
study, and what URL you want to redirect participants to upon completion.

7.2.2 From the participant's perspective

When participants go to the study, they are first presented with a general introduction, whose text can be modified using the "Base Messages" tab of the "Survey
Setup" page. That's followed by an introduction to the first task explaining how
the two windows work, including the two buttons that allow the participant to

toggle between two views: an initial view where the task window is small (as shown earlier in Figure 7.7) and an expanded view of the task window (which hides the Web site window) when the participant is ready to answer the question. The participant then steps through all of the tasks and questions in this manner.

7.2.3 Data analysis

The "Reports" page of RelevantView (Figure 7.12) provides access to a wide variety of reporting and export options for your surveys. The various options for the selected survey are accessed through the buttons across the top of the list (e.g., "Topline," "Verbatims," "Crosstab," "Clickstreams").

The "Topline" report allows you to drill down to basic response data for all the questions in your survey, as illustrated in Figure 7.13.

Selecting any one of the questions in the Topline report will display a graph and table of the responses for that question, as illustrated in Figure 7.14. Note that time data are not included in these Topline reports for tasks or other questions. Task time data would need to be derived from clickstream data.

RelevantView also allows you to generate a wide variety of "crosstab" reports, where you can select which response variable will be shown on the x axis and which will be shown on the y axis. For example, Figure 7.15 shows a sample crosstab report in which the participants' response to the gender question is shown on the x axis (Male or Female) and their rating of the difficulty of one of the tasks is shown on the y axis.

If clickstream data were recorded for the survey, then a clickstream report will be available, as illustrated in Figure 7.16. This shows the path (sequence of pages) that participants took through the site in performing the task. You have the option of looking at data for all participants, only those who completed the task, or only those who did not complete it. At each step, you can see what percentage of the participants went down each path from that step.

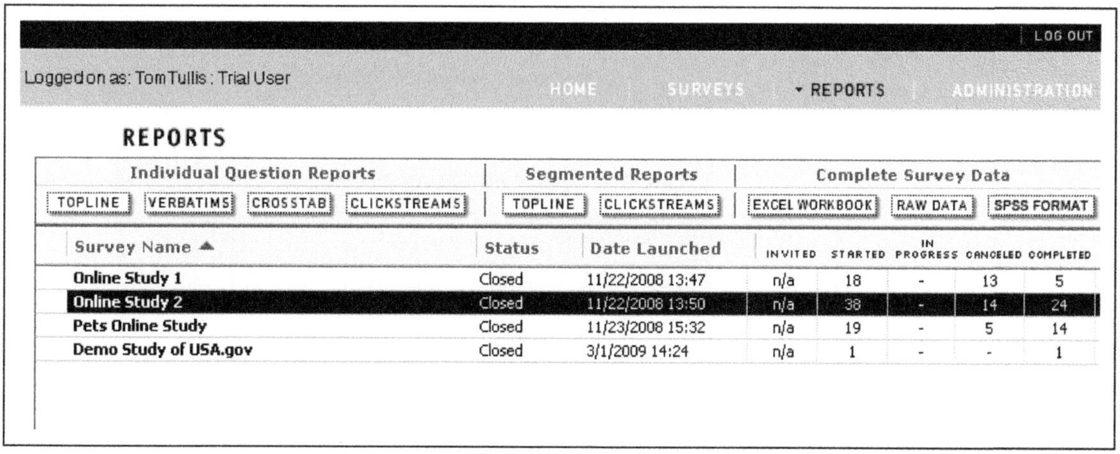

FIGURE 7.12
The "Reports" page of RelevantView.

FIGURE 7.13
A "Topline" report in
RelevantView.

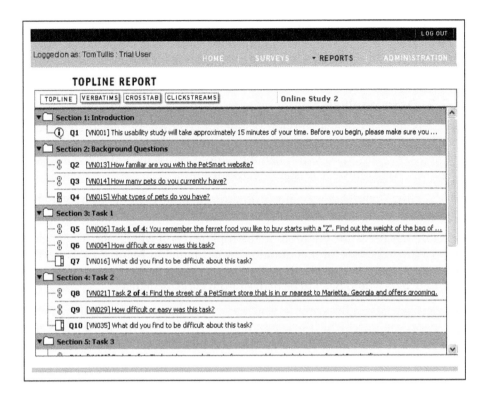

FIGURE 7.14
Detailed graph of data
for one question in
RelevantView. A tabular
version is also presented,
below the graph.

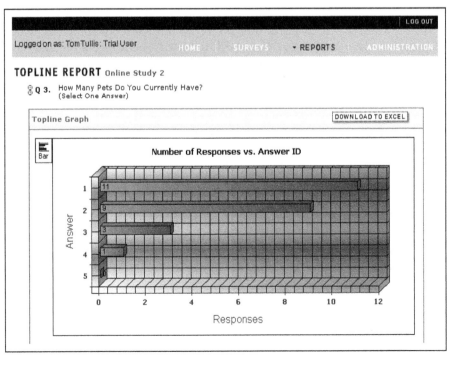

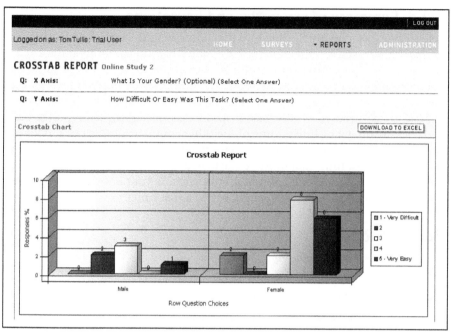

FIGURE 7.15
Sample "Crosstab" report in RelevantView.

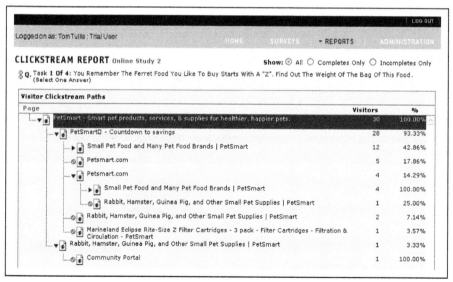

FIGURE 7.16
Clickstream data for one task in RelevantView.

Finally, RelevantView allows you to export your data in several different formats, including Excel, CSV, and SPSS. Each of these provides various options, including such things as raw clickstream data, raw responses, and browser data (e.g., browser used, screen resolution, browser window size).

7.2.4 Summary of strengths and limitations

RelevantView is a highly flexible tool that allows you to create a wide variety of online usability studies. It can be used to conduct baseline usability studies of live Web sites and competitive sites. Multiple tasks of various types can be presented to participants, as can a variety of questions and rating scales. RelevantView supports the collection of most of the kinds of data covered in this book, including task success (based on the answer to the task question), self-reported data, and clickstream data. Unlike some of the other commercial services, it does not require the user to download any special software or custom controls. One limitation is that task time data must be calculated from exported clickstream data. Also, the wide range of features available for creating your online study and analyzing data could be a little overwhelming to a first-timer.

7.3 USERZOOM

http://www.userzoom.com/
Cost: $$

UserZoom is a fully featured system for creating and administering a wide variety of online usability studies. Our sample study of the TerraPass Web site was created using UserZoom. As shown in Figure 7.17, tasks are presented in a small window at the bottom of the screen. The user navigates a prototype or live site in the main window to find the answer to the task. Task success can be determined

FIGURE 7.17
Sample online study in UserZoom. Note the task window across the bottom.

by getting the correct answer to a question or by having reached a predefined success URL. Task time is recorded automatically, as are clickstream data. A variety of questions and rating scales can also be used.

7.3.1 Creating a study

You start by creating a new project from the UserZoom Manager, as shown in Figure 7.18. Online projects are currently live; offline projects are not (and can be edited).

Clicking on the "Create New Project" tab takes you to the page shown in Figure 7.19 where you can define some of the basic characteristics of the study, including its name and language. You can also create the new study from scratch or from an existing study.

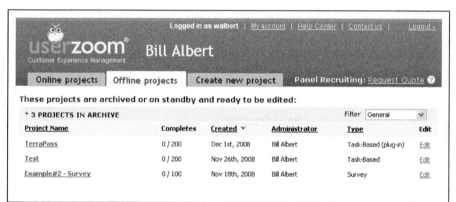

FIGURE 7.18
The Offline projects page in UserZoom. The Create New Project tab can be used to start a new project.

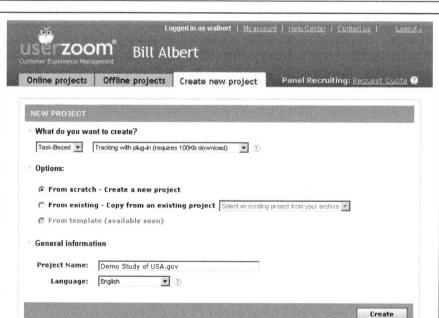

FIGURE 7.19
The first step of creating a new project in UserZoom.

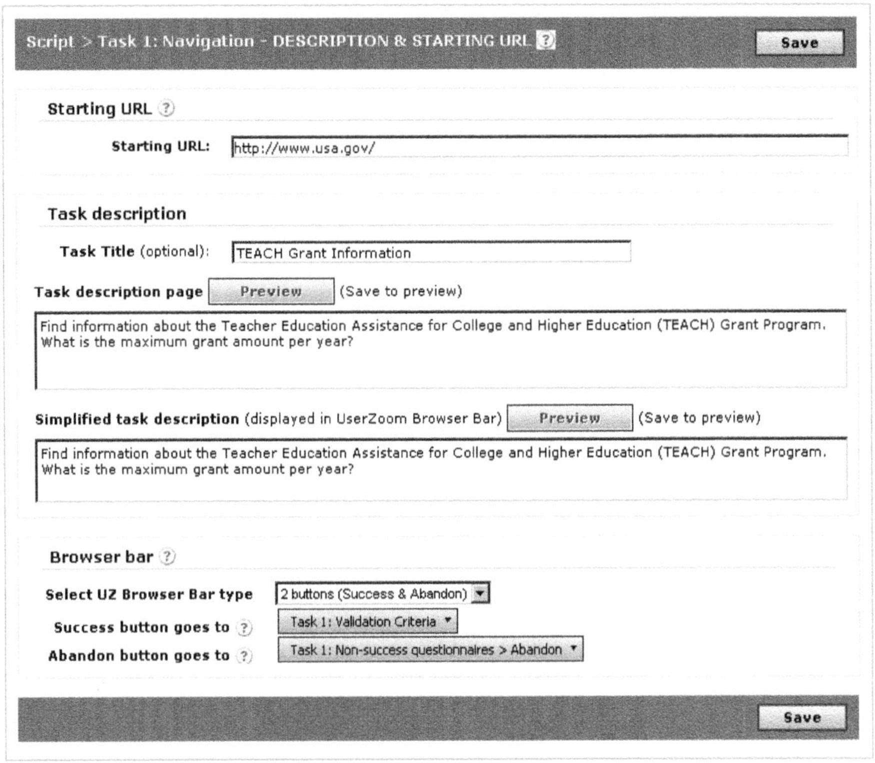

FIGURE 7.20
Creating a task in
UserZoom.

Next you begin creating your tasks, as shown in Figure 7.20.

When creating a new task, you first define the starting URL, question text, and what type of button bar will be shown. Next you determine how task success validation will be done. The main options are to validate by asking a question (e.g., the maximum amount of a TEACH grant) or by a success URL. When validating by a question, you have a variety of question types to choose from, including radio buttons, check boxes, and drop-down lists. When defining a multiple-choice question, you enter the question text and response options, define whether it is required or not, whether to randomize the response options, and which response or responses are correct (Figure 7.21). You also have options for allowing for an "other" option and for a comments field.

If you decide to validate task success by the participant having reached a given URL, you use the "Validate by URL" tab. This allows you to indicate one or more success URLs and the behavior desired for each (e.g., whether to let the participants continue browsing when they reach the URL or to intercept them at that point and display a success message). Additional questions can be added, such as various kinds of rating scales.

UserZoom also provides some "Quality Control" features for automatically performing some of the "data cleanup" functions discussed in Chapter 5.

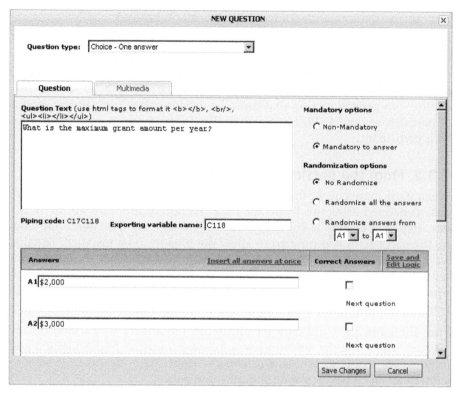

FIGURE 7.21
Defining the response options for a question in UserZoom.

As illustrated in Figure 7.22, it allows you to turn on a "Speeders Control" and/or a "Cheaters Control." The "Speeders Control" lets you exclude any participants who spent less than a defined number of seconds on a defined number of tasks. Likewise, the "Cheaters Control" lets you exclude any participants who did less than a defined number of clicks on a defined number of tasks.

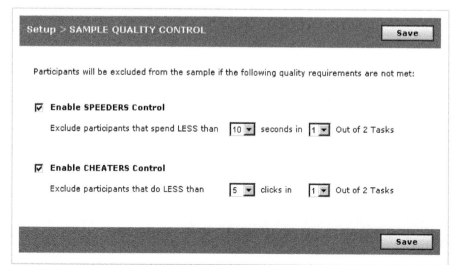

FIGURE 7.22
"Speeders" and "Cheaters" controls in UserZoom.

You can also randomize the order of some or all of the tasks.

When you're satisfied with your study design, you launch it using the "Start" link on the project summary page. You have several different options for the type of URL that would be sent to potential participants in the study. One option allows a panel supplier to append the participant's ID to the URL, another is a general version that could be used for all participants or groups of participants, and a third option has UserZoom generate unique URLs for each participant.

7.3.2 From the participant's perspective

When participants begin the study, they are presented with your introductory text, as defined using the "Welcome Page" section of the study editor. In the next step, if the study is collecting clickstream data via the UserZoom plug-in, the participant is prompted to allow the plug-in to be installed. The first task or question is then presented on a screen by itself. Once the participant is ready, the task is repeated in a small window at the bottom of the screen while the Web site is shown in the main window, as shown previously in Figure 7.17.

After the participant indicates having found the answer by clicking on the "Success" button in the task window, a full-screen version of the question and response choices is shown, as illustrated in Figure 7.23. In this case, we also allowed for an "other" response and for comments.

This process continues through the rest of the tasks and any other questions.

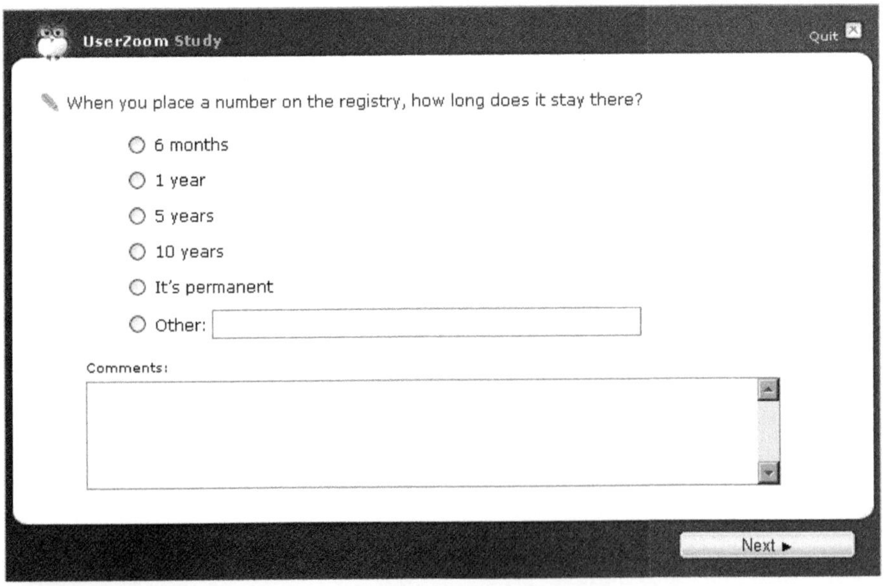

FIGURE 7.23
Task and response options in UserZoom.

When you place a number on the registry, how long does it stay there?

○ 6 months
○ 1 year
○ 5 years
○ 10 years
○ It's permanent
○ Other:

Comments:

7.3.3 Data analysis

The project summary page of UserZoom presents a summary of how many participants have started and completed the study in a table, as shown in Figure 7.24.

Detailed results can be viewed at any time by clicking on the "Analyze" link, which brings up the Results window, as shown in Figure 7.25. A left navigation panel allows you to look at the results for any part of the study. In this example, we're looking at the overall results for Task 1. The first pie chart shows the success rate for this task, and the second pie chart breaks down nonsuccess into its components (abandon and error). The tables on the right give more detailed data, including the task times, unique page views, and number of clicks.

Selecting an individual question from the left navigation panel shows detailed data for it, including both bar graph and tabular representations of the answers given to the question.

Selecting the "Clicks and Paths" tab in the Results window allows you to study click-stream data for each task, as shown in Figure 7.26. Right clicking on a given page allows you to view a heatmap of the clicks on that page, like the one shown earlier in Chapter 6 (Figure 6.20).

Finally, the "Options" tab in the Results window provides several options for exporting the results of the study. You can export raw data in several ways to an Excel spreadsheet or you can export a complete report to Word, including tables and graphs for all data.

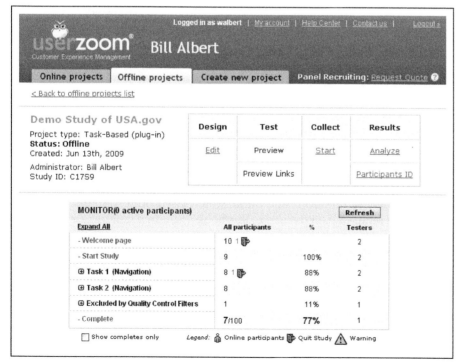

FIGURE 7.24
Project summary page in UserZoom showing status of participants.

FIGURE 7.25
Results window in
UserZoom showing
summary data for
Task 1.

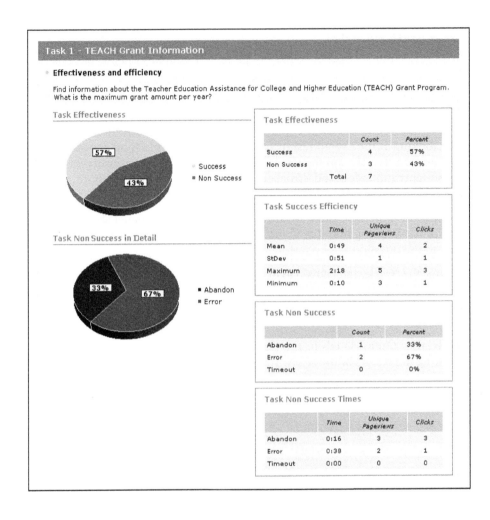

7.3.4 Summary of strengths and limitations

UserZoom allows you to create a wide variety of online usability studies. It can be used to conduct baseline usability studies of live Web sites, competitive sites, and prototypes. Multiple tasks of various types can be presented to participants, as can a variety of questions and rating scales. UserZoom supports the collection of most kinds of data covered in this book, including task success, task time, self-reported data, and clickstream data. Note that capturing clickstream data requires the participant to download a browser plug-in, which could be a problem for some users. However, UserZoom offers the option of inserting one line of JavaScript code to the site, which will track data without the need for download. Task success can be determined by the participant either answering a question correctly or reaching a predefined success URL. UserZoom also provides features that can help with data cleanup, including the ability to automatically screen out "Speeders and Cheaters."

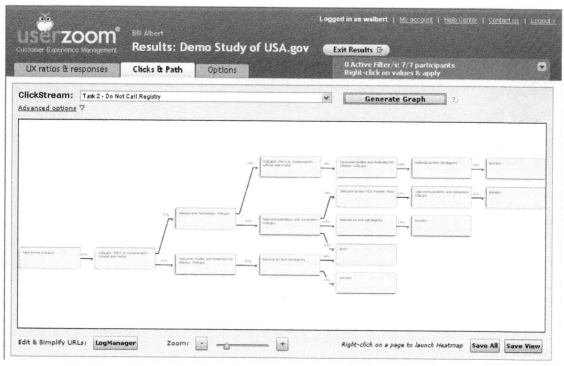

FIGURE 7.26
Clickstream display in UserZoom.

7.4 WEBEFFECTIVE

http://www.keynote.com/products/customer_experience/web_ux_research_
    tools/webeffective.html
Cost: $$$

WebEffective is a fully featured online system for creating and administering a wide variety of online usability studies. Our "true intent" study of MeasuringUX .com was created with WebEffective. As shown in Figure 7.27, tasks are presented in a small toolbar at the top of the screen (in this example). The user navigates a prototype or live site in the main window to accomplish the task. Once the user finds the answer, he or she clicks on an "Answer" button in the toolbar, which pops up a window for selecting an answer. Similar to an online survey tool, WebEffective supports a wide variety of question types (e.g., radio buttons, drop-down lists, input boxes, check boxes). Task accuracy, time, and responses to any questions or ratings are recorded automatically. Clickstream data can also be recorded to identify the pages that a participant visits.

7.4.1 Creating a study

You start by creating a new project using the WebEffective Portal (Figure 7.28). This page also allows you to view, edit, or delete any of your existing projects.

FIGURE 7.27

Example of an online study created with WebEffective. Copyright © 2009 Keynote Systems, Inc. All rights reserved.

When creating a new study, you start by defining some of its general characteristics (Figure 7.29), such as the number of participants needed, how windows are to be positioned, and the approach to pagination. This also lets you determine the placement of the taskbar: at the top of the screen, on the left, or as a small overlay on top of the main browser window.

Next you enter the text that will be used to introduce a participant to the study and then you start creating your tasks, as shown in Figure 7.30. For each task, you enter the text that will be used for introducing the task, the URL that the participant should be started on, and the type of response (e.g., radio buttons, drop-down list, check boxes). As illustrated in the example, if you choose "Single response (radio buttons)," you then define each of the options, including which one is the correct response (indicated by a check mark beside it). You can also define a number of other options, including whether an "other" option is provided, whether the options will be randomized, and whether a response is required.

You can intersperse a variety of question types (Figure 7.31) among the tasks as desired. Scripting is also supported, with conditional logic to display or skip questions depending on responses to earlier questions or on participant actions on the Web site being tested (e.g., clicking a button, reaching a given page). Randomization of task order is also possible.

You can preview the study at any time to see what it will look like to a participant. When you're ready to launch it, you change its status to Active. Once the

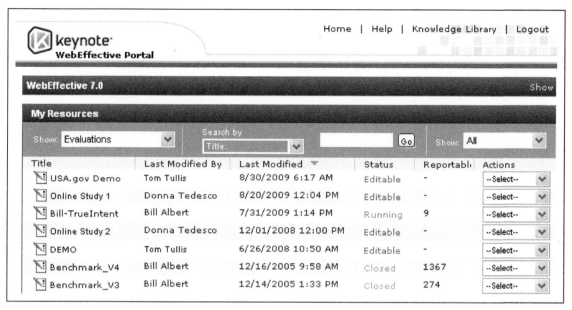

FIGURE 7.28
The WebEffective Portal. Copyright © 2009 Keynote Systems, Inc. All rights reserved.

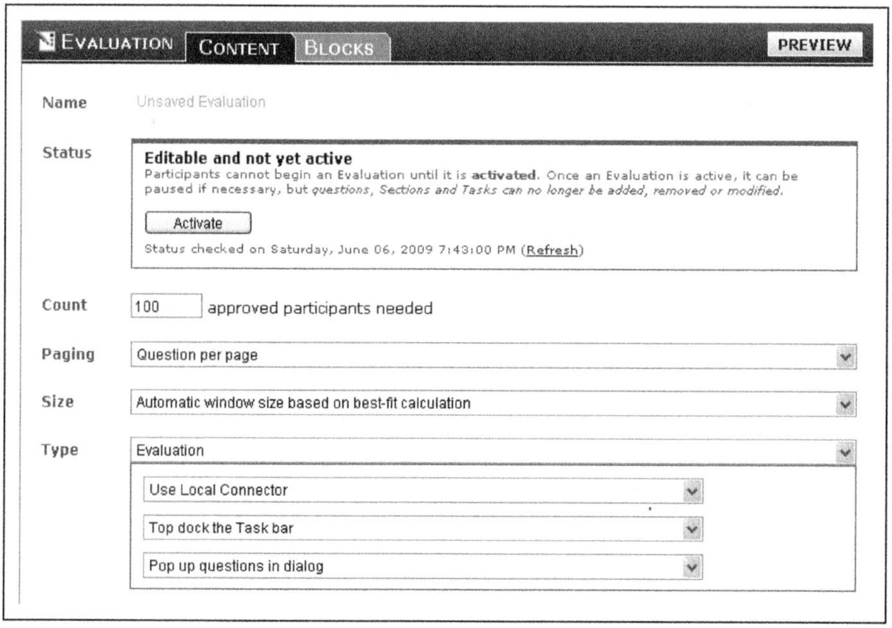

FIGURE 7.29
Initial setup screen for a new online study in WebEffective. Copyright © 2009 Keynote Systems, Inc. All rights reserved.

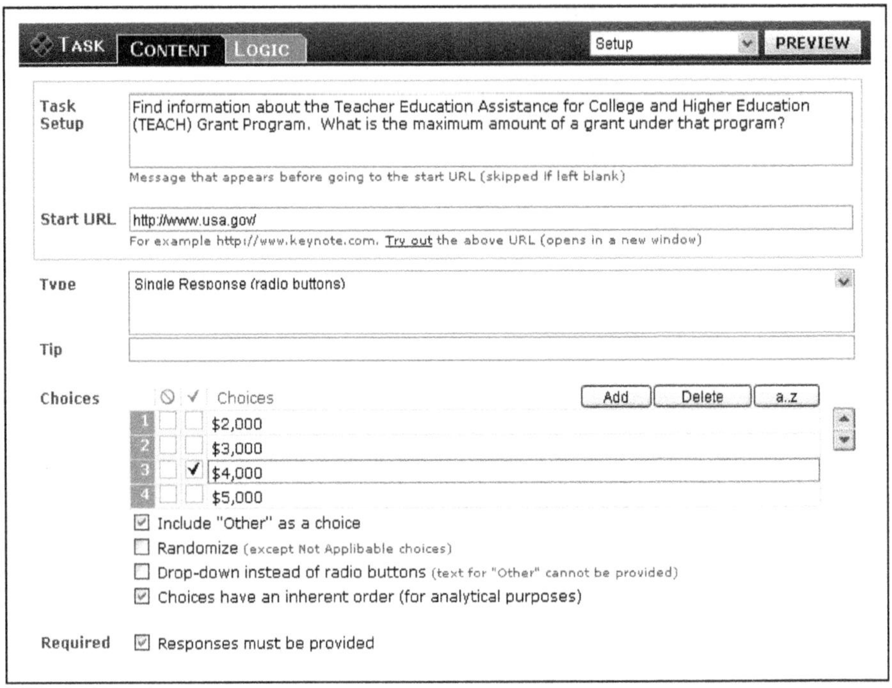

FIGURE 7.30
Editing a task in WebEffective. Copyright © 2009 Keynote Systems, Inc. All rights reserved.

study is Active, you can no longer make changes to the tasks or questions. You can then email the study link to prospective participants or provide it as an invitation on your Web site. WebEffective also maintains a large panel of potential participants if you wish to use them.

7.4.2 From the participant's perspective

When participants go to the study, they would typically be shown an introduction to the study and then an explanation of the "Connector," which is an ActiveX control that is downloaded to the participant's computer. This is what creates the taskbar and handles all of the data collection, including clickstream data. (Studies can be done without the Connector, but no clickstream data would be available.) This would usually be followed by some initial demographic questions or other preliminary questions.

When the tasks begin, each task is generally presented by itself (Figure 7.32), and then the task is repeated in the toolbar while the Web site is presented (Figure 7.33).

After the participant answers the task question, any follow-up questions are then shown, as illustrated in Figure 7.34.

This process continues through all of the tasks and then any final questions and rating scales.

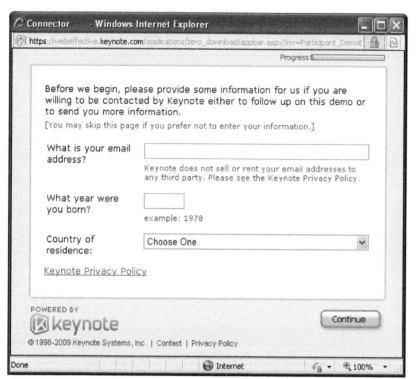

(Continued)

**FIGURE 7.31—
CONT'D**

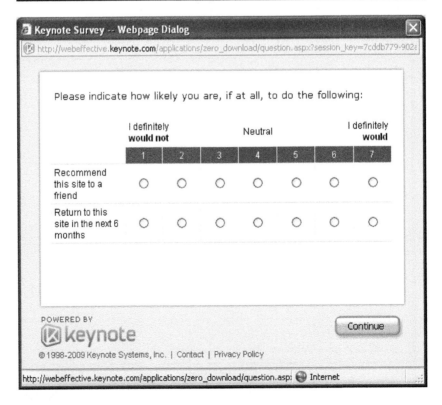

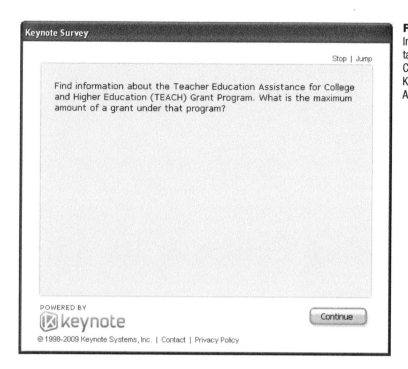

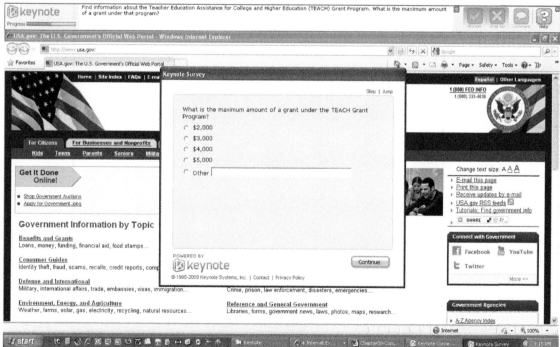

FIGURE 7.33
Subsequent presentation of a task in Keynote along with the Web site. In this example, the participant has clicked on the "Answer" button in the toolbar, which popped up the window for choosing an answer. Copyright © 2009 Keynote Systems, Inc. All rights reserved.

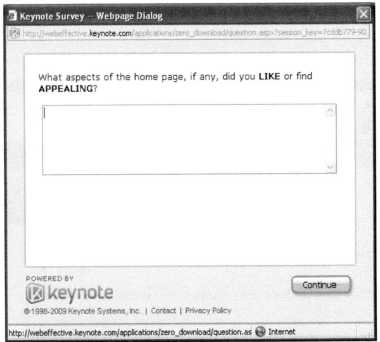

FIGURE 7.34

Sample follow-up questions to a task in WebEffective. Copyright © 2009 Keynote Systems, Inc. All rights reserved.

(Continued)

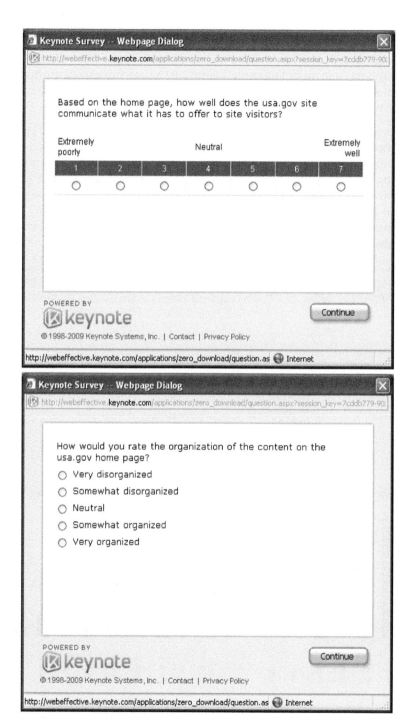

FIGURE 7.34—CONT'D

7.4.3 Data analysis

WebEffective lets you create a wide variety of reports for analyzing and displaying data from an online study. Figure 7.35 shows just one of the high-level views of the results from a study, in this case showing task completion status and task times for each of eight tasks in an online study.

In addition, you can create a wide variety of detailed reports and graphs, such as the graphs of participant demographics shown in Figure 7.36. WebEffective also provides a number of tools for analyzing and visualizing clickstream data, including a mechanism for choosing URLs to include or exclude and for visualizing how participants navigated a site in comparison to optimum paths. An example of a thumbnail view of clickstream data is shown in Figure 7.37. Options for exporting data in a variety of formats (e.g., Excel, SPSS, Word, PowerPoint) are also provided.

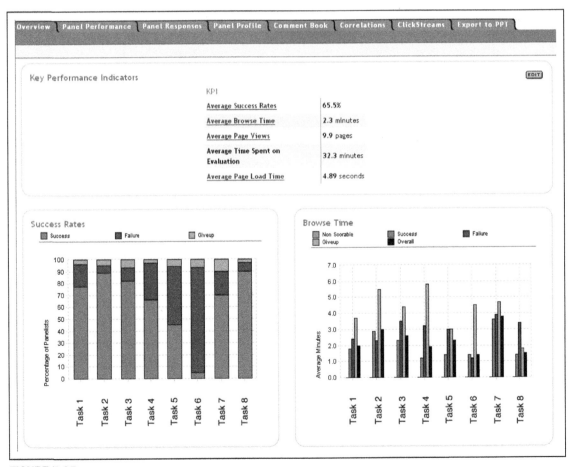

FIGURE 7.35

Sample display of data from an online study in WebEffective. In addition to summary data at the top, success rates are shown on the left for each task and times on the right. Copyright © 2009 Keynote Systems, Inc. All rights reserved.

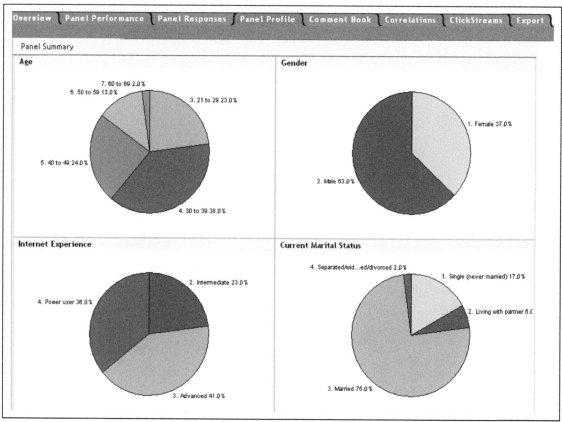

FIGURE 7.36
Sample participant demographics from a WebEffective study. Copyright © 2009 Keynote Systems, Inc. All rights reserved.

7.4.4 Summary of strengths and limitations

WebEffective is a highly flexible tool that lets you create a wide variety of online usability studies. It can be used to conduct baseline usability studies of live Web sites and competitive sites. Multiple tasks of various types can be presented to participants, as can a variety of questions and rating scales. WebEffective supports the collection of most of the kinds of data covered in this book, including task success, task times, self-reported data, and clickstream data. One potential limitation is that use of the Connector requires installation of an ActiveX control, which some users may be unwilling to do or unable to do because of restrictions on their computer. But that is only required for one of the methods supported for collecting clickstream data; an alternative proxy-based method that does not require a download is also supported. The wide range of features available in creating your online study could also be a little overwhelming to a first-timer.

FIGURE 7.37
An example of visual clickstream analysis in WebEffective using thumbnail images of the pages visited. Copyright © 2009 Keynote Systems, Inc. All rights reserved.

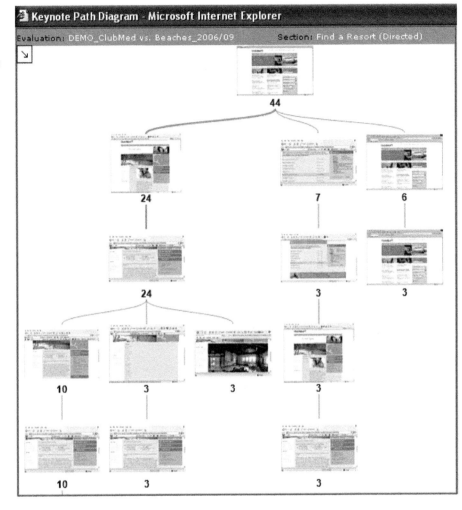

7.5 CHECKLIST OF QUESTIONS

To help you choose a commercial tool that's right for your situation, we've created the following checklist of questions. These are questions that you should consider asking any online study tool vendor you're evaluating. Not all questions will be relevant to every situation, but many will. You can also download this checklist from our Web site.

1. Cost
    a. What is the cost per study?
    b. Is there a cost per participant?
    c. Are there any extra charges for certain data (e.g., clickstream data)?
    d. Do you offer a subscription model (e.g., for unlimited studies or participants within a time period)?

2. Participants and recruiting
    a. How do you normally handle recruiting of participants?
    b. Do you have your own panel of potential participants? If so, what are the charges for using it? How large is it?
    c. Will you work with other panel providers?
    d. How does recruiting work if we provide our own participants?
3. The product being tested
    a. Are there any restrictions on what can be tested?
    b. Can you test live sites as well as prototypes?
    c. Does the test require any code or other changes to the site?
    d. Can the site be inside a firewall (e.g., an intranet site)?
    e. Can the test just deliver tasks and questions and have the user testing something else (e.g., a phone-based system)?
4. The online study tool—for the researcher
    a. Is a Web site provided for setting up the study and accessing data?
    b. Are there limits on the number of studies you can have at one time?
    c. Can different users be set up to use the online tool? Can they have different roles or permissions?
    d. Is it possible to save a study as a template for reuse? Is it possible to copy a previous study's design?
    e. Does the tool support multiple languages?
    f. Is it possible to easily preview or pilot the study?
    g. Once the study is live, is it possible to make any changes?
5. The online study tool—for the participant
    a. Does the tool require the participants to download anything to their computer? Can they still participate without downloading it?
    b. If anything is downloaded, what is done with it after the study is over (e.g., is it removed)?
    c. Does the tool provide a progress indicator?
    d. What browsers and versions does the tool support? Has it been tested on all of them?
    e. Does the tool require a minimum screen resolution?
    f. Does the tool work on mobile devices (e.g., iPhone)?
    g. Can participants access the study instructions again any time during the study (e.g., via a link in the taskbar)?
6. Study setup
    a. Do you provide assistance in setting up a study? Are there extra charges?
    b. Can the order of answer options for a multiple-choice question be randomized?
    c. Can logic be used to skip questions depending on previous answers?
    d. Are there limits on the number of tasks or questions?
    e. Is there flexibility in the placement of the taskbar?
    f. Can "welcome" and "thank you" messages be fully customized?
    g. Can participants be redirected to a custom URL after the study?
    h. Can parameters (e.g., a participant ID) be passed to the study or from the study to a follow-up URL (e.g., for an additional survey)?

    i. Can rules be set up to fill participant quotas based on screening criteria (e.g., if you want an equal mix of men and women, to stop accepting one if the quota is met)?

7. Tasks

    a. Can task order be randomized? Can one or more tasks be fixed (e.g., at the beginning or end)?

    b. Are user-generated tasks supported (where the participant defines the task)?

    c. Can the participant see the task description and the site at the same time?

    d. How does the participant indicate task completion?

    e. Is an option for giving up on the task provided?

    f. Can the task answer be either multiple choice or open ended? If multiple choice, is an "Other" option, with an input field, provided?

    g. Can tasks be chosen based on answers provided by the participant (e.g., about areas of the site they do or don't use)?

    h. Can tasks be selected randomly for each participant from a larger set?

8. Task data collected

    a. How is task success determined (e.g., by reaching one or more pre-defined URLs, by the answer to a question)?

    b. Is task time collected? If so, what all does it include (e.g., time to read the task, answer the task question)?

    c. Can the participant provide comments on any task?

    d. Are rating scales or other questions supported for each task? How many and what questions can be asked before or after each task?

    e. Are clickstream data collected and tied to specific tasks?

9. Self-reported data collected

    a. What kinds of rating scales are supported (e.g., Likert scales, semantic differential)?

    b. Are standard sets of questions supported (e.g., the System Usability Scale)?

    c. Can the number of scale values on a rating scale be controlled?

    d. What types of questions are supported (e.g., single-choice radio buttons, multiple-choice check boxes, drop-down lists, open response fields)?

10. Data analysis

    a. Is an online tool provided for analysis of data?

    b. Is it possible to access data while the study is still "live" or does the study have to be closed?

    c. Can all data be exported or downloaded? What formats are supported (e.g., Excel, Word)?

    d. Are data time-stamped (e.g., in case the site changes midstudy and you need to segment data appropriately)?

    e. What visualizations are provided for task success data, task times, and self-reported data (e.g., bar graphs)?

f. Are cross-tabs supported (e.g., looking at the task success data split by younger vs older participants)?

g. If clickstream data are supported, what visualizations and other analysis methods are provided for it (e.g., click heatmaps, analysis of most successful pages)?

h. Are mechanisms provided for easily filtering out data for participants who weren't really trying (e.g., "speeders" and "cheaters")?

7.6 SUMMARY

Each of the tools discussed in this chapter lets you create, manage, and analyze data from various kinds of online usability studies. Each has it own unique approach to designing a study and analyzing data. Each differs in exactly how a study is presented to the participants. We've tried to summarize some of the key features of these tools, highlighting some of their differences, in Table 7.1.

In addition, our Web site contains narrated demos of these tools.

Table 7.1   Summary of the Features of Four Commercial Tools for Building Online Usability Studies.

	Loop11	Relevant-View	User-Zoom	Web-Effective
Approximate Cost per Study(1)	$	$$–$$$	$$	$$$
Study Design				
Scripting or Skip Logic	No	Yes	Yes	Yes
Randomize Order of Tasks	No	Yes	Yes	Yes
Custom Control Download	No	No	Depends (4)	Depends (5)
Taskbar Placement	Top	Top or Left	Bottom	Top, Left, or Overlay
Data Collected				
Task Success	Yes	Inferred (2)	Yes	Yes
Task Time	Yes	Indirect (3)	Yes	Yes
Clickstream	Yes	Yes	Yes	Yes
Questions & Ratings	Yes	Yes	Yes	Yes
Analysis & Reporting				
Crosstab Analysis	No	Yes	Yes	Yes
Export	Yes	Yes	Yes	Yes

Notes:
1. Key: $ = Up to $600, $$ = Up to $6,000, $$$ = Up to $12,000.
2. Task success can be inferred from the answers to task questions.
3. Task time can be calculated from clickstream data.
4. Either requires a custom control download or one line of JavaScript added to the site.
5. Depends upon the method chosen for clickstream data collection.

CHAPTER 8
Discount Approaches to Building an Online Study

This chapter is for "do-it-yourselfers" who want to try to build their own online studies using discount or even free methods. If you would rather let other people worry about the mechanics of the study, then go back to Chapter 7, which describes some of the commercial tools available. But if you're willing to get your hands a little bit dirty and want to try at least some basic online usability testing techniques, read on.

The approach we're going to take is to start simple and work up from there. Data you can get from the simpler approaches will be limited but still potentially very useful. Adding more features, such as task timing, will broaden the data that can be collected. Eventually we will reach the point where you can collect a rich variety of data with surprisingly simple techniques. We'll present some basic techniques for building online studies that don't require knowledge of HTML or any other Web development languages. Some of the more sophisticated techniques, such as task timing or manipulating the placement of windows for the online study, will involve simple HTML and JavaScript, but we will show you everything you need to know.

What kind of data can you expect to collect using a "discount" approach to online usability studies? We describe techniques that allow you to collect task success data, task times, task-based ratings and comments, and post-task ratings and comments, including ratings using the System Usability Scale (SUS). The main thing you won't be able to collect using these techniques are clickstream data. For that you need to use one of the vendor tools outlined in Chapter 7.

8.1 THE BASIC APPROACH

Most of the rest of what we discuss in this chapter makes use of online survey tools to create the foundation you will build upon for your online usability test. There are many of these tools and new ones are coming out all the time; a Web search on "online survey tool" will yield a long list. Most of these tools have multiple pricing or licensing options, often based on the number of survey responses allowed per month. Most provide a free or trial option. For example, SurveyGizmo's free version allows 250 responses per month, whereas SurveyMonkey's free version allows 100 responses per month. Some also limit the number of questions per survey with the free version.

ONLINE SURVEY TOOLS

Here are some online survey tools that we're familiar with. Links to these and more can be found on our Web site.

- Checkbox Survey (www.checkbox.com)
- eSurveysPro (www.esurveyspro.com)
- Google Docs Spreadsheets in forms mode (spreadsheets.google.com)
- Infopoll Designer (www.infopoll.com)
- QuestionPro (www.questionpro.com)
- SuperSurvey (www.supersurvey.com)
- SurveyGizmo (www.surveygizmo.com)
- SurveyGold (www.surveygold.com)
- SurveyMonkey (www.surveymonkey.com)
- SurveyWriter (www.surveywriter.com)
- Zoomerang (www.zoomerang.com)

We show how you can use online surveys to collect the following types of data:

- Task success
- Task-based ratings
- Conditional comments or explanations
- Task times

Then we will go a little further and show how you can

- Randomize task order
- Position the task and site windows
- Randomly assign participants to conditions

TOTALLY HOMEGROWN TECHNIQUES FOR THE ADVENTUROUS

What if you know some HTML and JavaScript and want to try building your own online studies from scratch, without using an online survey tool? It's certainly possible and not really all that difficult. But because of the HTML and JavaScript knowledge required, it's a bit much to describe here. We will, however, give you a few pointers to help you get started and provide a complete example on our Web site that you can copy and customize. Here's an outline of the basic technique.

- One of the easiest ways to build an online study is using one long page containing all tasks, answer fields, and rating scales. This can be done using any Web-authoring tool such as Dreamweaver or FrontPage. Even though it's one long page technically, it's not going to look that way to the participant.
- Form controls are used as needed for drop-down menus of answers, text input fields, radio buttons for rating scales, and so on. A Submit button is at the very end.
- A handy trick to enable timing of each task is to size the window in such a way that only one task is shown at a time and then provide a "Next" button to jump to an anchor tag on the next task. This allows you to know when the user starts and finishes each task. (JavaScript for task timing is provided on our Web site.)
- Finally, data in the form fields and other variables must be saved in some manner when the user submits the page. There's no direct way to do this using just HTML and JavaScript, but one relatively simple way is to use a third-party service to email data to you. An example of using a "FormMail" service to do this is provided on our Web site.

8.2 MEASURING TASK SUCCESS

Simple online survey tools can be used to present tasks to users which they perform using the product, Web site, or prototype. The participants provide responses to the tasks to show whether they actually accomplished them. Figure 8.1 shows what this might look like. In this example, the link to the site being tested is shown at the beginning, opening in a new window.

HOW DO YOU MAKE A LINK OPEN IN A NEW WINDOW?

Figure 8.1 shows a link to NASA's Apollo Program Site that opens in a new window. This is done by imbedding a small snippet of HTML into the online survey. Most of the survey tools allow you to do this. Here's what that snippet looks like:

```
Please answer the following questions using
<a href="http://www.nasa.gov/mission_pages/apollo/index.html"
target="_blank">NASA's Apollo Program Site</a>.
```

The "a href=" part gives the URL of the site that the link will go to, and "target=_blank" indicates to open it in a new window. The remaining text, before the closing "</a>", is what gets shown as the link.

The participant then opens the site being evaluated and finds the answers to the questions, returning to the survey window to answer each one. Most online survey tools allow you to either present the questions all on one page or

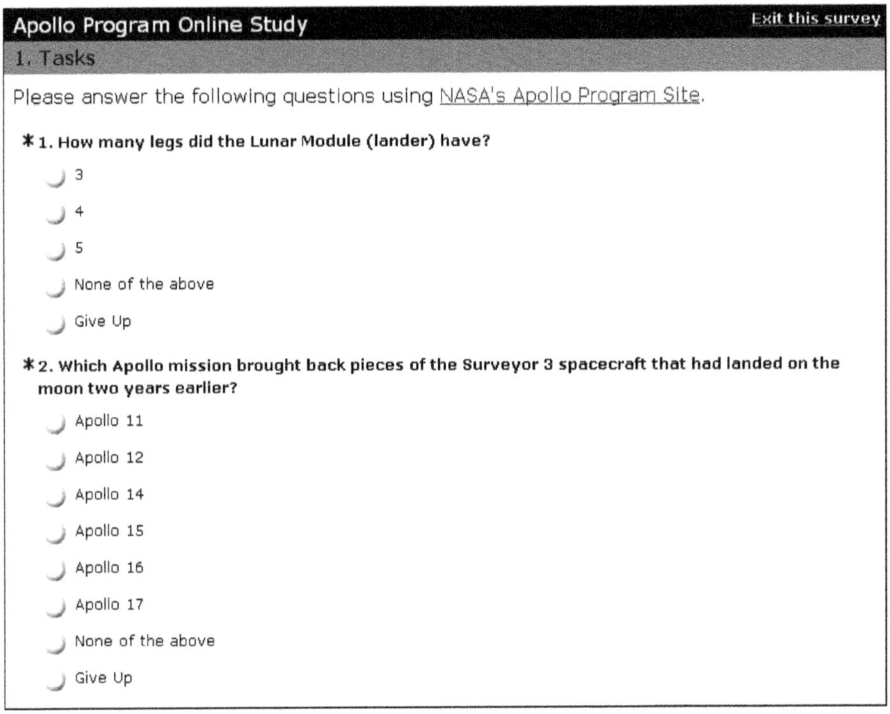

FIGURE 8.1
An example of tasks from the Apollo Program online study presented using SurveyMonkey.

present each on its own page. Presenting each on its own page would minimize the chances of the participants skipping around among the tasks, if that's a concern.

A LOW-TECH ALTERNATIVE TO ONLINE SURVEYS

Of course you could also just administer the tasks using a printed survey instead of doing it online. One advantage of this technique is that the participants don't have to deal with the window-management issues of switching between the online survey and the site being evaluated. Disadvantages include the challenges of distributing the survey, collecting the responses, and entering the data. You could get around some of those disadvantages by emailing a spreadsheet, document, or PDF containing the survey to the participants and asking them to email it back completed.

The beauty of most of the online survey tools is that they give you online access to real-time results. For example, Figure 8.2 shows results of an online study after 10 participants completed the first two tasks. In this example, the correct answers to the first two tasks are "Four" and "Apollo 12." Note that 70% of participants so far got the right answer to Task 1 but only 40% got the right answer to Task 2, indicating they are having more trouble with Task 2.

1. How many legs did the Lunar Module (lander) have?

	Response Percent	Response Count
3	20.0%	2
4	70.0%	7
5	10.0%	1
None of the above	0.0%	0
Give Up	0.0%	0
answered question		10
skipped question		0

2. Which Apollo mission brought back pieces of the Surveyor 3 spacecraft?

	Response Percent	Response Count
Apollo 11	30.0%	3
Apollo 12	40.0%	4
Apollo 14	20.0%	2
Apollo 15	10.0%	1

FIGURE 8.2
Results of sample study, viewed in SurveyMonkey, after 10 participants completed the first two tasks.

FIGURE 8.3
Task success data from sample study created by downloading data to a spreadsheet.

Most of the online survey tools also allow you to download data to a spreadsheet, although that may only be supported with a paid subscription. You could then download data for all the questions (tasks) and create an overall graph of task success, as shown in Figure 8.3.

Most online survey tools also provide various ways of customizing the questions that can be helpful. For example, some of the tools allow you to randomize the order of answer options, which can be helpful if you're concerned about participants being biased toward certain answer positions (e.g., more likely to choose the first answer in a list). Of course, this doesn't work very well when there's a natural order to the answer options (e.g., "Apollo 11," "Apollo 12," "Apollo 13") or when you're including options such as "None of the above" or "Give up." Some tools also allow you to add an optional comment field to each question. This is illustrated in Figure 8.4.

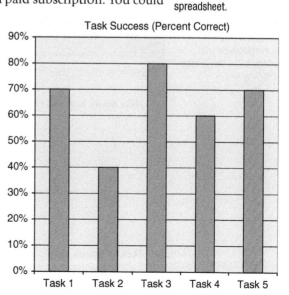

Task Success (Percent Correct)

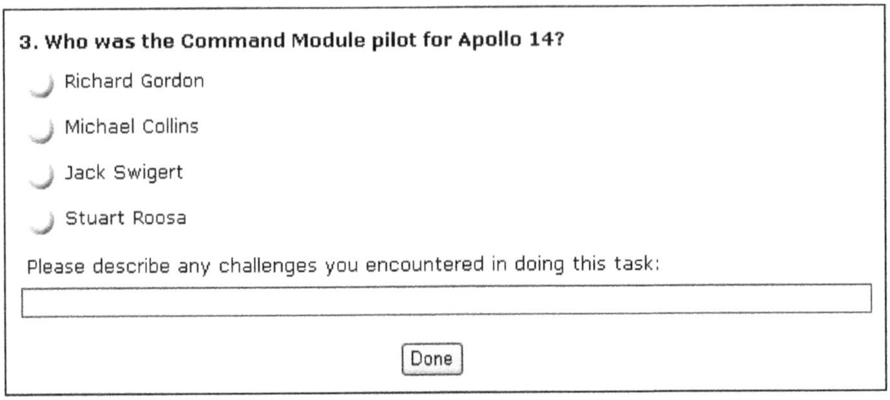

FIGURE 8.4
An example from
SurveyMonkey of a
task where the answer
options are presented
in random order to
each participant and an
optional comment field
has been added.

3. Who was the Command Module pilot for Apollo 14?

◡ Richard Gordon

◡ Michael Collins

◡ Jack Swigert

◡ Stuart Roosa

Please describe any challenges you encountered in doing this task:

[   ]

[Done]

8.3 RATINGS FOR EACH TASK

As discussed in Chapter 3, it's helpful to include rating scales or other kinds of self-reported data for each task. A common technique is a single rating scale of task difficulty or perhaps confidence that they got the right answer. Of course, multiple scales could also be used. These are easy to add to an online survey, as illustrated in Figure 8.5.

"TRICKING" ONLINE SURVEY TOOLS

Many online survey tools require that a piece of text be associated with each answer option in a multiple-choice question, which makes it difficult to create a line of radio buttons with labels only at the two ends, as used commonly in Likert and semantic differential scales. In the example of the task difficulty

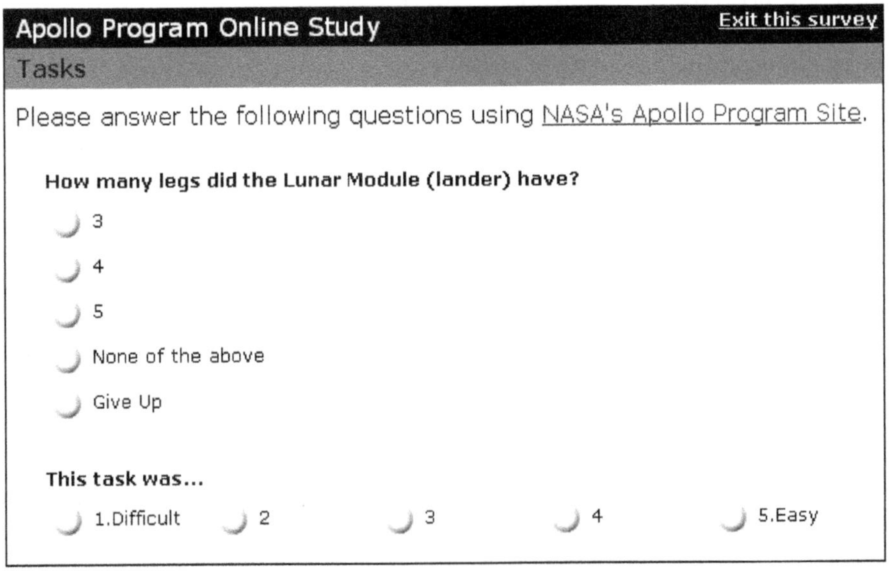

FIGURE 8.5
Sample task in
SurveyMonkey with
addition of a single task
difficulty rating.

Apollo Program Online Study   Exit this survey

Tasks

Please answer the following questions using NASA's Apollo Program Site.

   How many legs did the Lunar Module (lander) have?

   ◡ 3

   ◡ 4

   ◡ 5

   ◡ None of the above

   ◡ Give Up

   This task was...

   ◡ 1.Difficult   ◡ 2   ◡ 3   ◡ 4   ◡ 5.Easy rating shown in Figure 8.5, we were able to get around that problem by simply adding numbers for each of the answer options, plus labels for the two end points. If you didn't want numbers to appear, you could try "tricking" the tool by using the magic code " " (without the quotes) for each answer option that you want to be blank. (That's the special HTML code for a blank space.) If you do this, however, make sure that the data you get back for the responses allows you to distinguish between these various unlabeled data points.

8.4 CONDITIONAL LOGIC FOR A COMMENT OR EXPLANATION

While you could certainly include an optional comment field for each task (as shown in Figure 8.4) or for each rating, you could also prompt for comments or an explanation based on the participant's answer to the task or the rating scale. (See Section 3.5) For example, Tasks 1 and 2 shown in Figure 8.1 both include a "Give up" option. It could be very useful to add some conditional logic prompting participants who give up on the task to explain why they are giving up. This is illustrated in Figure 8.6. Most of the survey tools support this kind of logic,

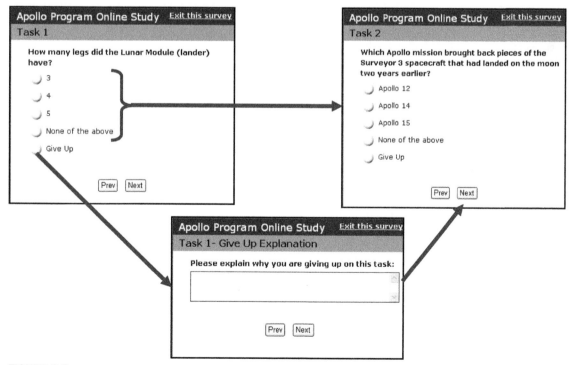

FIGURE 8.6

Illustration of conditional logic on the answer to Task 1: When users choose any of the first four answers, they are taken directly to Task 2, but if they choose "Give Up," they are taken first to a page asking for an explanation.

but it may only be with a paid subscription. It's often called "skip logic" or "conditional logic" associated with a question. In this example, conditional logic for the answer to Task 1 instructs the tool to skip the next question (which asks for a "give up" explanation) if the participant chose any response other than "Give up." That's why this functionality is often called "skip logic"—because it's usually limited to instructing the tool to jump directly to a later question, skipping over one or more intervening questions. It's common for a response to this kind of conditional comment field to be required.

Figure 8.7 illustrates what the conditional logic for the Task 1 answer looks like in SurveyMonkey. Conditions needed to be defined for each of the first four answer options to cause them to skip the question asking for an explanation, as that's the next question in the survey. But no condition is needed for the "Give Up" option because it will default to the next question in the survey.

In addition to providing useful information when a participant truly gets stuck on a task and eventually has to give up, these kinds of comment fields can also reduce the number of participants who are simply trying to "fly through" the study (by choosing "Give up" for each task) to get the incentive.

This same technique can also be used to prompt participants who give a poor task rating (e.g., a "1" or "2" on a five-point scale of "Difficult" to "Easy") to

FIGURE 8.7
An example from SurveyMonkey of conditional logic for the answer to Task 1.

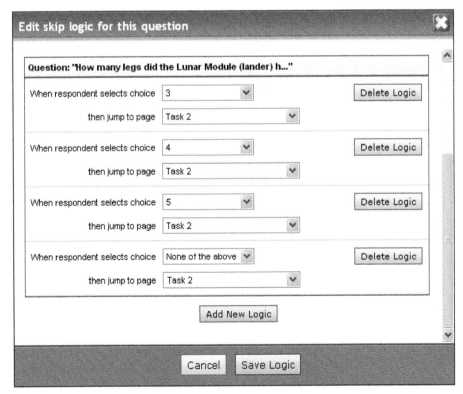

explain what they found difficult about the task. Using the rating scale shown earlier in Figure 8.5, conditional logic for a rating of "3," "4," or "5" would cause the tool to jump over the next question, which would be the question asking for an explanation of what was difficult about the task.

8.5 TASK TIMING

The data we've discussed so far in this chapter—task success, task ratings, and conditional comments—can be collected using most online survey tools. But now we're going to venture into territory where not all of the tools will work. The timing of individual tasks (questions) is a feature that only certain online survey tools support. Some of the tools we are aware of that support this feature are Checkbox Survey, SurveyGizmo, and SurveyWriter. We illustrate the basic technique of task timing using SurveyGizmo.

In order to time tasks, each needs to be presented on its own page. That way you can identify when each task is shown to the participant and when it is answered. Then an elapsed time variable needs to be associated with each of those task pages. In SurveyGizmo, this is done by first adding an "Action" to the page, indicating that it is a "Hidden Value" to be added, giving the value a name, and then choosing the "Advanced Value" of "Time spent on Survey page." This is illustrated in Figure 8.8. The exact mechanism will, of course, vary from one survey tool to another. Look for options that allow you to add a predefined value or variable, or a hidden value.

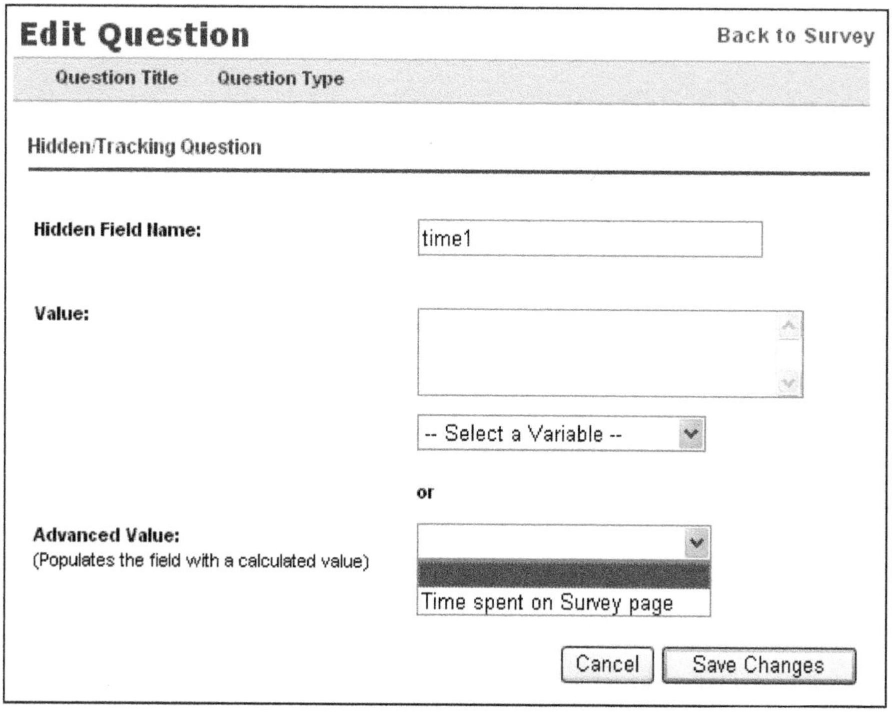

Edit Question   Back to Survey

Question Title	Question Type

Hidden/Tracking Question

Hidden Field Name: time1

Value:

-- Select a Variable --

or

Advanced Value:
(Populates the field with a calculated value)

Time spent on Survey page

Cancel   Save Changes

FIGURE 8.8
The process of adding a "Hidden Value" in SurveyGizmo to time a task.

FIGURE 8.9
The question editing mode, in SurveyGizmo, after a timing variable has been added to Task 1.

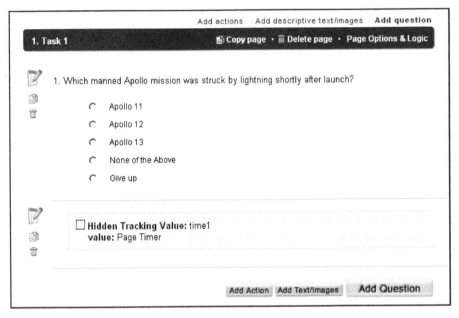

Figure 8.9 shows what this looks like in the question editing mode after a time value has been added to Task 1.

The easiest way to add this timing variable to each task is to create the first task page with the timer on it, copy that page to create the other task pages, and then modify those copied pages to include the new task and answer choices.

AN EASIER SOLUTION...

If the process of setting up a study to include task timing sounds a bit confusing, there's an easier solution: just copy the template we've provided for an online study built using SurveyGizmo. It includes task timing; all you have to do is modify the task questions and possible answers. Directions for accessing it are on our Web site.

Getting at task time data after the study is "live" may require that you download raw data, as time data may not be a part of the standard reports that are available online. In SurveyGizmo, this is done by downloading raw data to a CSV file, which can be opened with Excel. Table 8.1 shows what this looks like for three tasks and four participants. Task times are shown in seconds.

8.6 RANDOMIZING TASK ORDER

As described in Chapter 3 (Section 3.4.7), it's often helpful to randomize the order of tasks in an online study. With a fixed task order, the first task usually takes a significant performance "hit" relative to the later tasks. A few of the online survey tools, including SurveyGizmo and QuestionPro, allow you to randomize

Table 8.1		Sample data for four participants, including task times, downloaded to a CSV file from SurveyGizmo. In addition to answers given for each of the three tasks, the time to find those answers (in seconds) is also shown.					
Date started	Date finished	Task 1	time1	Task 2	time2	Task 3	time3
3/1/2009 1:00	3/1/2009 1:07	Apollo 12	75	Richard Gordon	82	Cernan and Schmitt	68
3/2/2009 9:05	3/2/2009 9:09	Apollo 13	64	Michael Collins	61	Conrad and Bean	90
3/3/2009 11:06	3/3/2009 11:12	Apollo 12	89	Stuart Roosa	98	Cernan and Schmitt	92
3/4/2009 3:06	3/3/2009 3:14	Apollo 12	104	Stuart Roosa	110	Armstrong and Aldrin	115

the order of the questions or pages in your survey. Figure 8.10 illustrates the use of this feature in QuestionPro. This is generally a feature provided only with paid subscriptions. If you have one question per task (i.e., just the answer to the task), then randomizing the order of the questions should work for you. If you have more than one question per task (e.g., the answer plus a rating), then you may need to put each set of questions for a given task on its own page and randomize the pages. Some survey tools may also let you define a set of questions as a "block" and then randomize the blocks.

Options for randomizing the order of questions or pages might be provided under something such as "Advanced Features" or "Randomization Options." If the survey tool you're using doesn't support randomization of questions or pages, then you might want to consider having the first task be a "throw-away" task whose results you don't count.

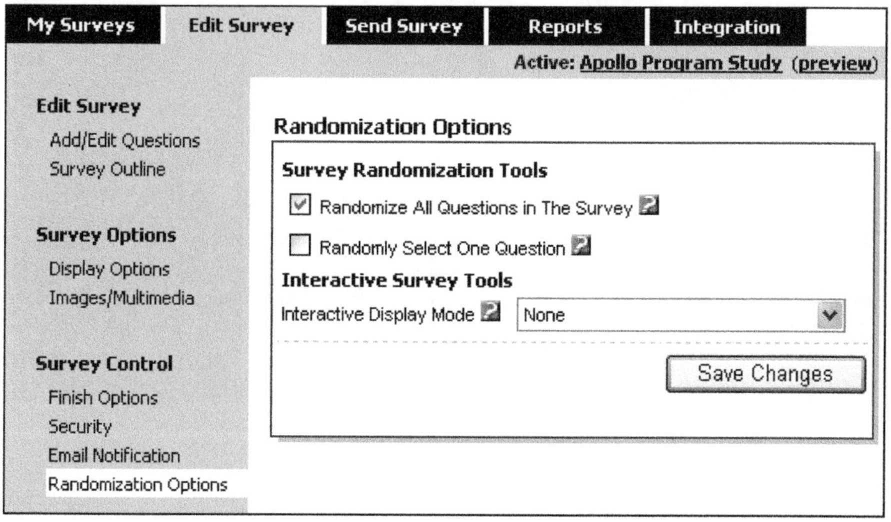

FIGURE 8.10
Question randomization feature in QuestionPro.

8.7 POSITIONING OF WINDOWS

Up to this point we've let the participant deal with the window management issues of having two separate windows: one for the study (the tasks) and another for the site or prototype being evaluated. For some participants, especially those with less expertise in the use of windowing systems, this can be rather challenging and perhaps too much to ask of them. But we can set up those windows for them using some basic HTML and JavaScript.

The two most common window arrangements for online usability studies, as illustrated in Figure 8.11, are with the task window on the top or on the left. In both cases, the larger window is used for the site or prototype being tested.

In both approaches, you try to design the task window as small as possible, leaving the majority of the screen for the main window. You also try to design the task window so that it presents just one task or question per page and avoids or minimizes the need for any scrolling within it.

We know that most users are frustrated by the need for horizontal scrolling to see all of a page, so the goal should always be to avoid that whenever possible for the main window. However, most users are quite comfortable with vertical scrolling. The decision about which arrangement to use should be based partly on what you know about the "target resolution" of the site being evaluated and partly on the resolutions that your participants are likely to be running in. The "target resolution"

FIGURE 8.11
Two different arrangements for task and site windows.

(Continued)

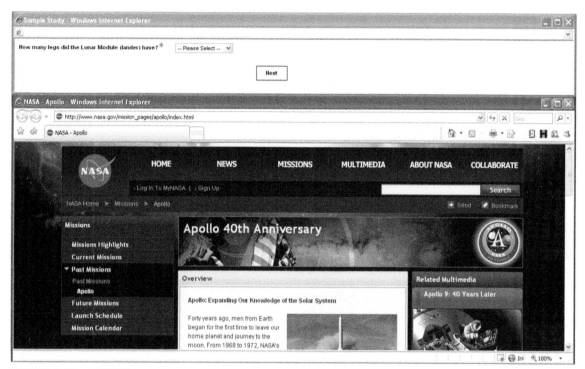

FIGURE 8.11—CONT'D

of a site is the minimum page width that it will support without horizontal scrolling. For NASA's Apollo Program site, for example, that minimum width is about 950 pixels. The minimum workable width for the tasks window (when placed on the left side) is about 200 pixels, yielding a combined width of 1150 pixels.

Now the question turns to what resolutions your candidate participants are likely to be running in or, more specifically, what *horizontal* resolution they're likely to be running in. You should try to find out what screen resolutions they're currently using. If you're working on the redesign of an existing site, it's quite possible that data are available about the resolutions being used by the visitors to the site. Screen resolution data are commonly collected by some of the Web analytics tools (e.g., Google Analytics). If those data aren't available, then you can try some of the general sources available on the Web about screen resolutions.

The stats for general Web users indicate that about 36% of them are running in 1024×768 or lower resolution (as of now), meaning they have 1024 pixels or fewer available horizontally. Consequently, if you were to use the side-by-side arrangement of the task and site windows for the online study, their combined width of 1150 pixels would exceed the available screen width (1024 pixels) for just over a third of the general Web users. That would mean horizontal scrolling of the main site window for those users. In that case, it would probably be better

SCREEN RESOLUTIONS OF GENERAL WEB USERS

One of the sources we like for data about screen resolutions of Web users is W3Counter (http://www.w3counter.com/globalstats.php). Their data are updated monthly and are derived from a wide variety of sites worldwide that are using their page-hit counter. For the latest month that data are available as we write this (August 2009), their stats are shown in Table 8.2.

Table 8.2	Frequencies of different screen resolutions.
Resolution	**Percent**
1024×768	31%
1280×800	20%
1280×1024	12%
1440×900	9%
1680×1050	6%
800×600	5%
1152×864	3%
1920×1200	2%
1366×768	2%
1280×768	2%

to use the arrangement where the two windows are on top of each other. One of the last things you want is your participants telling you that they don't like the site because they despise horizontal scrolling.

We've used the top-and-bottom arrangement of the windows more often than the side-by-side arrangement, mainly because of the numbers we just outlined. But if the site being tested has a target minimum resolution of 800 pixels (as some still do), then the combined width of the task and site windows would only be 1000 pixels. Because only about 5% of users are running in 800 × 600 or lower (at this moment), a side-by-side arrangement might be acceptable. Similarly, with the advent of widescreen TVs and monitors, screen resolutions, especially horizontal resolution, continue to get higher. In the future it might be more common to use the side-by-side arrangement of the windows. It's also helpful to capture the screen resolution of each participant. So, if a participant is running at 800 × 600, you will be able to analyze their data separately in the case of horizontal scrolling.

Opening and positioning the two windows of the study (the task window and the main site window) will require a bit of HTML and JavaScript. Although it could be done a number of different ways, we'll show you one that we think is the simplest. First, we start with an "instructions" page or a "launch" page, as shown in Figure 8.12.

WHAT ABOUT THE SIZE OF THE SCREEN?

You may be wondering why we've only been talking about screen *resolution* and not actual screen *size*. The only thing that actually matters is how many pixels are being used to display the Web page, which is determined by the screen resolution. If 17″ and 22″ screens are being run at the same resolution, then the same number of pixels are being used by both. It's just that the pixels are larger on the 22″ screen, creating an image that's physically larger. The reason many people get screen resolution and screen size confused is that larger screens are generally designed to be run at higher resolutions. But they don't have to be.

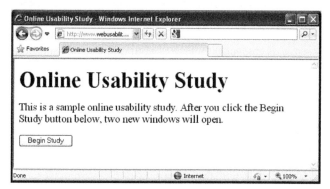

FIGURE 8.12
Sample "instructions" or "launch" page.

This is the page that contains the code for opening the other two windows when the user clicks on the "Begin Study" button. For this example, we're going to assume that we're doing an online usability study of the USA.gov Web site and that we're using a survey built using SurveyGizmo. Because the USA.gov Web site has a target resolution less than 800 pixels wide, we're going to use a side-by-side arrangement of the two windows.

Figure 8.13 shows the code for the "instructions" or "launch" page. If you're not familiar with JavaScript, note that comments follow the "//" characters.

The most important part of the code is the function near the top that says "Open_Windows()". That's the JavaScript function that opens the two windows of the study. Briefly, here's a summary of what it does.

- Two parameters are passed to the function when it is called: win1 is the address of the online survey and win2 is the address of the site or prototype being tested.
- Checks the height and width of the user's screen (screen.height and screen.width) in pixels.
- Sets w1 to the desired width of the task window (240 pixels).

TIP
This code is available to download from our Web site. Another version that positions the two windows one above the other is also available.

```
<html>
<head>
<title>Online Usability Study</title>
<SCRIPT language="JavaScript1.2">
function Open_Windows(win1,win2) { //win1 is the task window, win2 is the main site
        w = screen.width //screen width
        w1 = 240 //width for task window
        w2 = w-w1-30 //width for main window
        h = screen.height //screen height
        h1 = h-70 //height for task window
        h2 = h-140 //height for main window
        var TaskWin = window.open(win1,
            'MyTaskWin','width='+w1+',height='+h1+',left=0,top=0,\
            location=no,resizable=no,scrollbars=no,toolbar=no,menubar=no,status=no');
        var MainWin = window.open(win2,
            'MyMainWin', 'width='+w2+',height='+h2+',left=260,top=0,\
            location=yes,resizable=yes,scrollbars=yes,toolbar=yes,menubar=yes,status=yes');
}
</SCRIPT>
</head>
<body bgcolor="#FFFFFF" text="#000000">
<h1>Online Usability Study</h1>
This is a sample online usability study. After you click the Begin Study button
below, two new windows will open.
<form>
    <input type=button value="Begin Study"
        onClick="Open_Windows('http://www.surveygizmo.com/s/108637/example/',
    'http://www.USA.gov')">
</form>
</body>
</html>
```

Replace this with the address of your online study questions.

Replace this with the address of the site being tested.

FIGURE 8.13
Code for opening, sizing, and positioning the two study windows.

- Sets w2 to the desired width of the main window, which is the screen width minus the width of the task window and minus an additional 30 pixels (to account for the scroll bar of the main window).
- Sets h1 and h2 to the desired heights of the task and main windows. In both cases, some amount is subtracted from the screen height to allow for the various toolbars of the windows.
- Opens the task window using the "window.open" JavaScript function. The first parameter specifies the URL for the online survey (win1). Additional parameters specify the height, width, and location of the window. The final parameters specify that we want it to be a fixed size, with no scrollbars, and no toolbars or other "window dressing."
- Opens the main window using the "window.open" JavaScript function. The first parameter specifies the URL for the main window (win2). Additional parameters specify the height, width, and location of the window. The final parameters specify that we want it to be a normal resizable window with the usual "window dressing."

FINDING A WEB HOST

To use the technique shown in Figure 8.13, you'll need to host the page containing that code somewhere on the Web. If you don't already have some space you can use, you'll need to find a Web hosting service. There are easily hundreds of them available. A key consideration is that the service must support JavaScript in the pages that you want to host there. Some of the free services, including Google Sites, do not allow you to include JavaScript in your pages. Other free services may put ads on your pages, which you may not want for the page launching your online study. Our Web site includes links to some hosting services that you might want to consider.

Feel free to experiment with these various parameters, such as the height and width of the two windows. The main body of this page would then contain any instructions that you want to give to the participants at the beginning of your study. Finally, the last part of the code creates the "Begin Study" button, which when clicked calls the "Open_Windows" function, passing the addresses of the online survey (http://www.surveygizmo.com/s/108637/example/) and the site being tested (http://www.USA.gov) as parameters. Figure 8.14 shows what the screen looks like after the two windows are opened. In this example, the first question for the participant is to provide an email address. (Note that many of the online survey tools, including SurveyGizmo, provide for basic validation that the user has entered an appropriately formatted email address.) Control of the online

WOULDN'T IT BE EASIER TO JUST USE FRAMES?

The astute reader who is familiar with HTML may be wondering why we don't just use frames for the two windows instead of two separate browser windows. Well, we've tried it and there's one significant problem: the "Back" button. In most online usability studies, you want the participant to be able to use the Back button freely when navigating around the site being evaluated. However, you commonly want to disable the Back button for the tasks. (In most cases, you don't want to allow the user to go back to an earlier task. It messes up task times and other data.) The problem with frames is that they all share the same Back button. So, for example, let's assume a participant is working on Task 2 of a study and merrily navigating around the site when he starts clicking the Back button multiple times to get back to some earlier page in the site. If he happens to click the Back button too many times, he will then suddenly be taken back to Task 1. That's because the Back "history" is shared between all frames in the same browser window. And we've never figured out a way around that problem, except to have them as separate windows.

FIGURE 8.14
Configuration of the two windows after the user clicks "Begin Study."

study now passes to the online survey (in the task window), which does all of the data collection.

This example has used a side-by-side arrangement of the two windows, but with some minor modifications it can be used for the top-and-bottom arrangement. It's just a matter of changing the sizes and locations of the two windows. You can find that modified code on our Web site.

8.8 RANDOM ASSIGNMENT OF PARTICIPANTS TO CONDITIONS

One thing we really like about online studies is that they make it easy to compare alternative designs by randomly assigning participants to the various designs or conditions. These might be different design approaches you're considering for a site, a current design vs a new design, or perhaps even different competitors' Web sites. So how can you randomly assign participants to different conditions? Again, it's not hard with a little bit of HTML and JavaScript.

Let's assume that you want to do an online study comparing the Google and Yahoo Web sites. You want the participants to be assigned randomly to one site or the other. You've developed the tasks for the online study using SurveyGizmo. In order for the survey tool to "know" which site is being tested, the easiest thing to do is to make an exact copy of the survey under another name. One version will be used for Google and the other for Yahoo. We're now going to build on the code shown in the last section for opening the windows of the study. The additional feature is that the code needs to randomly select which site will be shown. Figure 8.15 shows what the new code looks like.

```html
<html>
<head>
<title>Online Usability Study</title>
<SCRIPT language="JavaScript1.2">
function Open_Windows (win1a,win1b,win2a,win2b) {
            w = screen.width //screen width
            w1 = 240 //width for task window
            w2 = w-w1-30 //width for main window
            h = screen.height //screen height
            h1 = h-70 //height for task window
            h2 = h-140 //height for main window
            var r = Math.random() ; //generates a random number between 0 and 1
            if (r < .5) {
                        var r1 = win1a;
                        var r2 = win1b;
            }
            else {
                        var r1 = win2a;
                        var r2 = win2b;
            }
            var TaskWin = window.open(r1,
                'MyTaskWin', 'width='+w1+',height='+h1+',left=0,top=0,\
                location=no,resizable=no,scrollbars=no,toolbar=no,menubar=no,status=no');
            var MainWin = window.open(r2,
                'MyMainWin', 'width='+w2+',height='+h2+',left=260,top=0,\
                location=yes,resizable=yes,scrollbars=yes,toolbar=yes,menubar=yes,status=yes');
}
</SCRIPT>
</head>
<body bgcolor="#FFFFFF" text="#000000">
<h1>Online Usability Study</h1>
This is a sample online usability study. After you click the Begin Study button
below, two new windows will open.
<form>
    <input type=button value="Begin Study"
            onClick="Open_Windows ('http://www.surveygizmo.com/s/108637/google/',
            'http://www.google.com/',
            'http://www.surveygizmo.com/s/108637/yahoo/',
            'http://www.yahoo.com')">
</form>
</body>
</html>
```

> New code for randomly picking one of the two sites.

> Replace these URLs with the addresses of the two surveys and two sites being tested.

FIGURE 8.15
Code from Figure 8.13 modified to include random selection of the site to be tested from two possible sites (Google and Yahoo in this example).

As before, this code can be downloaded from our Web site. Bolded areas are parts that have changed or are new. Here's a summary of the changes.

- There are now four parameters passed to the "Open_Windows" function: online survey #1 and the site that goes with it, and online survey #2 and the site that goes with it.
- The "Math.random()" function is used to generate a random number between 0 and 1. If that number is less than .5 (which it will be half the time), then the first pair of addresses is used. Otherwise the second pair of addresses is used.
- In the OnClick event for the button to start the study, the four addresses are passed to the Open_Windows function. The first two represent addresses for the Google study and the second two for the Yahoo study.

This basic technique could be extended to randomly choose among more than just two conditions. For each new condition, a new pair of addresses would be introduced and the IF statement following the Math.random function would be modified accordingly [e.g., using "if (r < .33)" for three conditions].

8.9 PULLING IT ALL TOGETHER

We hope that these examples have inspired you to try some of these discount approaches to building an online usability study. A variety of different examples of these kinds of studies are provided on our Web site. We've also built some additional online study "components" that you can make use of. For example, we provide a complete SUS survey that you can copy and use in your own online study. We also provide an example of a complete online study built using the discount techniques outlined in this chapter that includes the following.

- Random assignment of participants to conditions
- Opening and positioning of the study windows
- A variety of tasks, with the following data collected for each:
  - Task success
  - Task time
  - Subjective rating of task difficulty
  - Conditional comment field if the user gives a poor rating
- Two open-ended comment fields at the end of the study:
  - Features that the user found particularly intuitive
  - Features that the user found particularly confusing
- The SUS, consisting of 10 rating scales

We also provide information about how you can copy our online surveys and customize them for your own needs.

8.10 SUMMARY

This chapter outlined how you can build your own online usability studies using standard online survey tools and a little bit of HTML and JavaScript. Some of the key takeaways are as follows.

- Online survey tools can be used to present tasks to participants and collect their answers, allowing you to capture task success data.
- You can easily add rating scales to the online survey to collect task-based ratings, such as how easy or difficult each task was.
- You can use conditional logic in an online survey to collect comments or explanations related to the tasks (e.g., why they gave up on a task or rated it as being very difficult).
- Using certain online survey tools, you can add a variable to each task that allows you to capture task time.
- Certain online survey tools also allow you to randomize the order of your tasks.
- With a little bit of HTML and JavaScript, you can position the task window (containing the survey) and the main window (containing the site or prototype being evaluated) so that the participant can work with both of them easily.
- Finally, with a little more HTML and JavaScript, you can randomly assign participants to different conditions or prototypes.

CHAPTER 9
Case Studies

This chapter presents seven case studies. These case studies describe how online usability testing has been used to evaluate a wide variety of products, utilizing various tools and numbers of participants (see Table 9.1). The contributors are from industry and consulting and were selected based on their diverse set of experiences in online usability testing. It is hoped that you find these case studies helpful in understanding how online usability studies are carried out in a variety of professional settings. We thank the following case study contributors for sharing their experiences: Kristen Peters and Robert Schumacher; Michelle Cooper and Betsy Comstock; Charles Mauro, Allison O'Keefe-Wright, and Cianna Timbers; Nate Bolt, Tony Tulathimutte, and Alana Pechon; Melanie Baran, Kavita Appachu, and Alex Genov; Tyson Stokes; and Heather Fox.

Table 9.1 Case study summaries.

Case Study	Product Evaluated	Tool	Number of Participants
9.1	Public Health Records (Microsoft Vault vs. Google)	Task Access Survey	41
9.2	Lotus Notes	In house tool	24
9.3	MTV.com	Keynote's WebEffective	300
9.4	UCSF hospital web site	UserZoom	100
9.5	Tax software	Keynote's WebEffective	134 and 268
9.6	Familysearch.org	Inhouse tool and ClickTale	24
9.7	Authentication and identity management system for Dupont	Vividence eXpress (now part of Keynote)	200

9.1 ACCESS-TASK SURVEYS: A LOW-COST METHOD FOR EVALUATING THE EFFICACY OF SOFTWARE USER INTERFACES

Kirsten Peters and Robert M. Schumacher User Centric, Inc.

Today there are a variety of tools for conducting online, remote usability tests. WebEffective™, LEOtrace®[1], and UserZoom® are sophisticated tools for task- or intercept-based automated usability testing. They often provide the "missing DNA" between in-person lab-based testing and Web analytics. One of the strengths of these tools is that they allow for collecting data from large numbers of participants across a wide area and over time. While these tools are very valuable, they are often overkill; they can be laborious to construct and data can be complex to analyze. Sometimes what is needed is something much simpler and less formal, especially in more formative stages of research and design. We present here a case study of a tool (called the "Access Task Survey") used to evaluate the efficacy of two personal health records (PHRs).

9.1.1 Background

In order to understand which usability-related issues may support or limit PHRs from being accepted, we compared the outcomes of a classical usability test and the Access Task Survey. We conducted both studies using two PHRs visible in the marketplace: Google Health and Microsoft HealthVault.[2]

In the usability study, 30 participants completed key tasks using each PHR application and provided qualitative feedback, ratings, and preference data on five specific dimensions: usability, utility, security, privacy, and trust. Overall, participants reported that they found Google Health more usable because navigation and data entry of health information was easier than on Microsoft HealthVault. Participants also liked that Google Health used more familiar terminology than Microsoft HealthVault and provided a persistent health information profile summary.

9.1.2 Access Task Survey tool

Based on results from the comparative usability study, we wanted to see if these findings would extend to a larger user group using a low-cost methodology. It is fair to assume that initial impressions of the visual design of a Web page can have a measurable impact on perceived usability; we wanted a tool that enabled us to look at how self-evident some of the features were. We considered one of the sophisticated tools mentioned previously; however, our needs were simpler. We wanted to know: What is a user's first instinct? In other words, when given a goal, where would users click to get to an answer? We call these "access tasks" because they are the supposed first point of contact for this type of goal. To capture these data, we constructed a tool called the "Access Task Survey."

---

[1]LEOtrace is a registered trademark of SirValUse GmbH, UserZoom is a registered trademark of Xperience Consulting, and WebEffective is a trademark of Keynote Systems.
[2]Neither Google nor Microsoft commissioned or participated in these studies.

The Access Task Survey had two objectives. First, we wanted a tool with high face validity—one that would tell us about the designs with realistic user goals and questions. The Access Task Survey data needed to be able to be used to validate and augment the page layout and terminology findings from the usability study. Second, we needed a low-cost and simple tool that could be used to reach large, dispersed, and diverse participant pools.

The Access Task Survey tool was built to register the page coordinates (i.e., X, Y) of each participant's click, as well as their individual responses to a number of rating questions. The output of the Access Task Survey allowed us to validate that users' common and critical goals could be achieved by the proposed design.

While we collected a substantial amount of data from the usability study, we focus on the methodology, findings, and conclusions from the Access Task Survey of the online PHR applications.

9.1.3 Methodology

Each participant received eight trials, which consisted of a task (described later) presented at the top of the screen and the Web page displayed in Figure 9.1. The participant was instructed to read the task and then click on the location of the

FIGURE 9.1
Home pages of Google Health (above) and Microsoft HealthVault (next page).

(Continued)

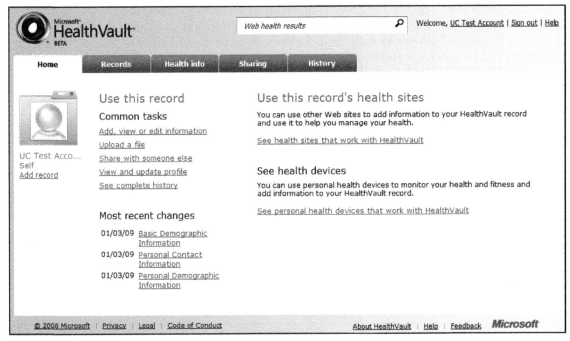

FIGURE 9.1—CONT'D

screen image that best fit where they would click to satisfy the goal. Participants were not told if their click was on the correct location. It is important to note that the participants never actually used the PHR. Once the participant clicked on the Web page they were asked two rating questions.

All participants completed the same tasks on each PHRs. The order of PHRs and the order of tasks were counterbalanced across users. Each participant saw the same task order for each PHR. These particular tasks were selected because they were high-frequency tasks and matched the usability tasks enabling comparison with the earlier study. The following task scenarios were used.

Task 1: Imagine that you have a child and you would like to store her information in your PHR so that it is easy to find. Where would you click first to do this?

Task 2: Where would you click first if you wanted to find out if the two medications you are currently taking have any negative side effects when taken together?

Task 3: Your physician also uses an online PHR. She uses it to keep track of your information as a patient. You are interested in linking your medical history from your doctor's PHR into your personal PHR profile. Where would you click first to do this?

Task 4: Imagine that you have been feeling ill lately. You went to the doctor yesterday, who told you that you had the stomach flu. Where would you click first to update your profile with this information?

After participants completed each access task, they were asked two seven-point rating questions about their perceptions of "ease of use" of the page and "confidence" that their selection was correct.

After completing all tasks with each PHR, participants answered three additional rating questions about each PHR. These questions assessed participants' overall impression of the PHR's page design, ease of use, and perception of security. Finally, participants were asked to select which PHR they preferred overall and on each of three dimensions—usability, security, and trust.

Forty-one participants completed the access test survey. None participated in the usability test, and none had prior interaction with either of the PHR Web sites tested; most (37/40) did not keep any personal health information in a PHR.

9.1.4 Results

The Access Task Survey generated a number of preliminary findings about participants' expectations of where to find information within each of the two PHRs. Click data from the access tasks will first be presented, followed by post-task data.

Access Task 1: Add a child's medical information

In this task, participants were asked to locate the link that would allow them to create a second file for an additional family member (i.e., "profile" on Google Health or "record" on Microsoft HealthVault).

In Google Health, users can create a profile for an additional person by clicking on the "Create a new profile" link located at the bottom of the navigation menu. Only a few participants clicked the correct link (7/41, 17%) on this hPHR (see Figure 9.2). Most participants instead selected one of the "Add to this profile" links. However, clicking this link would not create a separate file for the child, but only add health data to the current profile.

In Microsoft HealthVault, a new file could be created by clicking in one of two places: the "Add Record" link located on the left side of the screen or the "Record" tab located in the top row of navigation tabs. While the success rate for this task on this PHR was still low (15/41, 37%), more participants were successful at this task in Microsoft HealthVault (37%) than in Google Health (17%). Similar to Google Health, most other participants clicked on the "Add, view or edit information" link located in the "Use this record" section.

Access Task 2: Drug interactions feature

The usability study revealed that this feature is highly desired. Participants were asked to indicate where they expected to access information about possible negative side effects of medications they were currently taking. Google Health offered this feature but Microsoft HealthVault did not. This task then allows us to ask a "what if" question: If Microsoft HealthVault had this feature, where would users click?

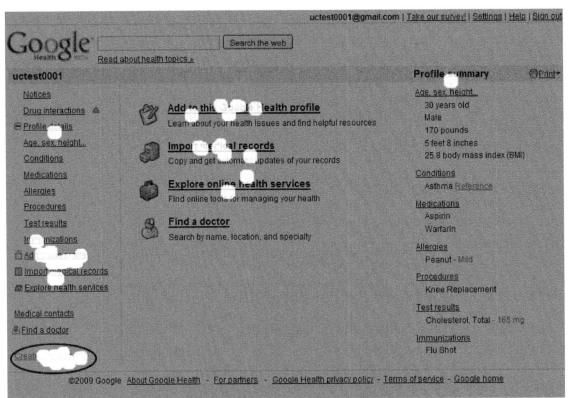

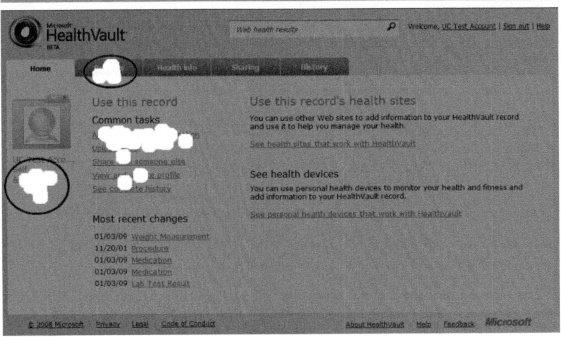

FIGURE 9.2
Results for Task 1: Add a Child's Medical Information.

In Google Health, the "Drug Interactions" link was located near the top of the left navigation menu and most participants were able to locate this link easily (33/41, 80%), which was located in a highly visible location, near the top of the navigation menu. The majority of the other participants clicked on one of the two "Medications" links. However, Google Health did not include an additional link to the drug interactions feature from the Medications pages.

In Microsoft HealthVault, most participants indicated they would expect to access negative side effect information by clicking on the "Health Info" tab (26/41, 63%). Other participants expected to view this information by clicking the "Medication" link under the Most Recent Changes section (7/41, 17%), similar to Google Health.

Since we assume that satisfaction of user goals is reflected in where they click, then looking at the relative affinity users have to specific labels can reveal strengths and weaknesses in the information architecture, even when a particular case is not embedded (e.g., finding out about drug interactions). Knowledge of strong label affinities to goals (e.g., "Health Info") might suggest placing content underneath such labels. Had the selections been more diffused, an interaction designer might consider providing an additional or a better label on the Web page.

Access Task 3: Access doctor's electronic health information

Participants were asked where they would click to link the medical history from their doctor to their personal PHR profile. The correct Google Health link, labeled "Import medical records," was presented in the main area of the screen and on the lower left navigation area. As shown in Figure 9.3, almost all participants were successful at locating the correct link (37/41, 90%). This implies that the link was well labeled as it was easily identifiable by most participants.

The appropriate page can be accessed in Microsoft HealthVault by clicking the "See health sites that work with HealthVault" link presented on the left side of the main screen.

Less than one-third of the participants chose a correct link (12/41, 29%) in Microsoft HealthVault. Many participants instead chose to click on the "Share with someone else" link. These participants may have believed the "someone else" could have been their doctor. However, this link would only lead the user to set up the account to give someone else read and write access to the Microsoft HealthVault PHR profile.

Access Task 4: Update PHR profile

Participants were asked to indicate where they would click to update their PHR profile with a recent illness. In the Google Health PHR, updates to a PHR profile can be made by clicking on the "Add to this Profile" link in the left navigation menu or the "Add to this Google Health profile" in the main body area.

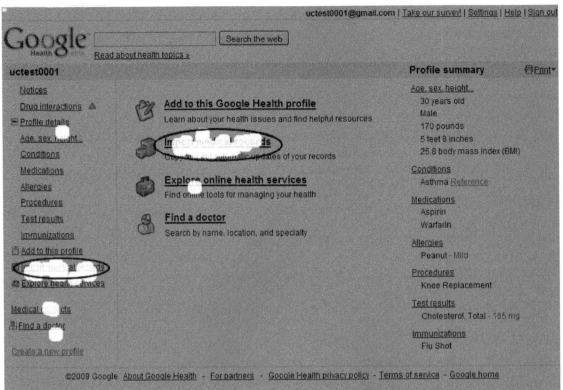

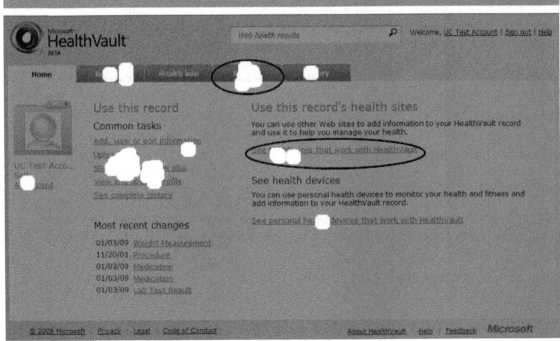

FIGURE 9.3
Google Health and Microsoft HealthVault Access Task results for Task 3: Access Doctor's PHR Information.

Almost all participants clicked on one of the four correct links to add a condition (37/41, 90%) using Google Health. Most participants chose to click on the links in the left navigation menu; however, some participants also chose to click on the "Add to this Google Health profile" in the center of the screen.

In Microsoft HealthVault, additional health information, such as having the stomach flu, can be added to the PHR by clicking on the "Health Info" tab in the top row of navigation tabs or the "Add, view or edit information" link located under the Use this Record section.

For this task, a little over half of the participants clicked on one of the two correct links (22/41, 54%) of Microsoft HealthVault. Many of the other participants clicked on the "View and update profile" link and may have interpreted "profile" as the place where their health data are stored. However, in Microsoft HealthVault, the users "profile" is where they can update personal information, such as name and email address.

Post-task ratings, post-PHR ratings questions, and final PHR selections

Following the completion of each task, participants were asked to rate, on a seven-point Likert scale, how easy they believed the task was (Ease of Use, 7=very easy) and how confident they were that they clicked the correct link (Confidence, 7=very confident). Table 9.2 shows the average ratings of each question for each task, as well as the overall access task success rates.

Upon inspecting Table 9.2, there were some conflicts between success rates and average Ease of Use or Confidence ratings. For example, although participants were more successful during Task 4 using Google Health, the average Ease of Use and Confidence ratings for Task 4 were slightly higher for Microsoft HealthVault. Additionally, although participants were less successful at Task 3 using Microsoft

Table 9.2 Access task success rates and averages for post-task ratings questions.

Task	PHR	Success rate (%)	Average ratings (out of 7.0)	
			Ease of use	Confidence
1 (Add child's medical info)	Google Health	17	3.8	4.0
	Microsoft HealthVault	37	4.9	4.6
2 (Drug interactions)	Google Health	80	5.5	5.9
	Microsoft HealthVault	NA	3.0	2.8
3 (Access doctor PHR)	Google Health	90	4.9	4.7
	Microsoft HealthVault	29	4.8	4.6
4 (Update PHR profile)	Google Health	90	4.9	4.5
	Microsoft HealthVault	54	5.1	5.0

HealthVault, participants gave similar Ease of Use and Confidence ratings for both PHR applications. Task 2 garnered the highest and lowest ratings for both Ease of Use and Confidence. The lack of a clear label on HealthVault (vis-à-vis Google Health) seemed, at least on face value, to have an effect on rating data. However, because we did not do a full statistical analysis, it is hard to know if this is important. What is more to the point for this case study is that the combination of success rates for click data can be put side by side with rating data, which enables further insight than simply success data alone.

Post-PHR ratings questions

After completing all tasks on each PHR, participants were asked to rate each PHR's overall page design, ease of use, and perceived security of their personal data. Table 9.3 shows the average ratings for each dimension (based on a seven-point Likert scale, 7=high).

On all three dimensions, participants favored Google Health over Microsoft HealthVault. However, the greatest difference between the ratings for the two PHRs was on the dimension of Ease of Use. This is slightly different than the individual task Ease of Use ratings, where participants only rated Google Health clearly higher during Task 2. In fact, during Task 1, participants rated Microsoft HealthVault easier to use than Google Health. However, the overall preference for Google Health may have been attributed by the fact that participants were generally more successful in the survey tasks with this PHR. Another interpretation might be that—barring task 2—that HealthVault might have been slightly easier to use, but this technique shows how important page design/visual appeal is to the user; if it falls short in visual appeal, the perception is that it may not work as well. All this is speculation though. The point is that, with usability data and the Access Task Survey, we can ask and answer interesting questions.

Final PHR selections

After all tasks had been completed on both PHRs, participants were asked which PHR application they preferred overall and on each of the dimensions: ease of use, security, and trust. Table 9.4 shows the selection results for each PHR.

Google Health was preferred by participants to Microsoft HealthVault on all three dimensions and overall. Similar to post-PHR ratings, the greatest difference was on the dimension of Ease of Use.

Table 9.3	Average ratings for post-PHR questions.	
Dimension	**PHR**	
	Google Health	**Microsoft HealthVault**
Page design	4.3	3.9
Ease of use	4.4	3.6
Security	4.5	4.2

Table 9.4 Percentage who preferred each PHR on three key dimensions and overall.

Dimension	PHR	
	Google Health	**Microsoft HealthVault**
Ease of use	82%	18%
Security	67%	33%
Trust	76%	24%
Overall preference	72%	28%

9.1.5 Discussion and conclusions

Our findings suggest that participants responded better to the layout, terminology, and overall design of the Google Health home page. Participants were more successful at selecting the correct links and gave more positive ratings for Google Health than Microsoft HealthVault.

Google Health's consistent left navigation menu may have aided participants with many of the tasks. Microsoft HealthVault used a more general top-level navigation structure that created fewer initial options for the participant to choose from. In addition, the navigation tabs had labeling that could be considered to be more general, which may have led participants to be less confident in their selection. In contrast, Google Health displayed all of the functions and features of the PHR in a single left navigation menu. Google Health may have had an advantage in this survey because the features and functions of the PHR application were accessible from this one location.

The Access Task Survey tool allowed us to gain a better understanding of which aspects of labeling, layout, and design of a PHR home page were best received by participants. The click portion of the Access Task Survey allowed us to understand the efficacy of certain labels to common goals and helped us differentiate between two functionally similar Web sites.

While the study was valuable in collecting participants' initial expectations for specific tasks, the custom online Access Task Survey tool did limit the type of data that could be collected. Because participants completed the survey online, we did not collect any qualitative feedback. Had participants been able to describe why they selected certain links or gave certain ratings, researchers may have been able to better understand the user experience of each home page.

However, because this study included very similar tasks to those used in the previous usability study, we were able to compare, augment, and extend the findings using this Access Task Survey. When viewed in contrast to traditional usability techniques, this low-cost, fast-to-implement tool can be useful when (a) trying to tease apart different designs and/or (b) ensuring high "hit" rates to key user goals early in the design process. One other benefit of this tool is that it can be used with a large number of participants from multiple user groups at lower costs.

There are certainly many additions that can be made, such as adding an open-ended "Comments" field for participants to elaborate on their selections and ratings. However, we will resist the urge to complicate this too much as part of what makes this a good tool is that it sits in a nice niche between full-featured tools and other usability methods.

Biographies

- Kirsten Peters is a user experience specialist at User Centric, Inc., a user experience consulting firm based in the greater Chicago area. Kirsten holds a B.S. in industrial engineering from Iowa State University and an M.S. in human factors and ergonomics from San Jose State University.
- Robert Schumacher is managing director at User Centric, Inc. He has been in human factors and user experience since the mid-1980s. He is the editor of the "Handbook of Global User Research" (2009). Bob has a Ph.D. in cognitive psychology from the University of Illinois at Urbana Champaign.

9.2 USING SELF-GUIDED USABILITY TESTS DURING THE REDESIGN OF IBM LOTUS NOTES

Michelle L. Cooper and Elizabeth M. Comstock, IBM Lotus Software Group

The purpose of this case study was to describe one of the methods used to gather feedback from users during a redesign of IBM[3] Lotus Notes®. Lotus Notes is a groupware product that provides applications such as mail, calendar, contacts, and integrated instant messaging. Lotus Notes also provides several other customizable applications, such as databases, discussion forums, and team rooms. All of these different types of applications are assembled together into one integrated collaboration framework. Lotus Notes was first introduced in 1989. Today, over 10,000 IBM® Business Partners worldwide provide integrated solutions running on Lotus Notes. Lotus Notes is used by over 140 million users in over 46,000 medium and large organizations worldwide.

In the middle of 2005, IBM announced that there was to be a complete overhaul of the Lotus Notes interface. To accomplish such an overhaul, the Lotus Notes User Experience team employed many different methods to bring user feedback into the design and development of Lotus Notes 8. For the full set of methods, see Comstock et al. (2009). This case study describes one of those methods in more detail: self-guided usability tests.

We designed self-guided usability tests to complement the other user feedback methods used for Lotus Notes 8. We wanted the tests to be particularly strong in getting feedback from Lotus Notes 8 early adopters who were using the product to perform their own work. Because Lotus Notes is a collaborative system, we also wanted to test in an environment that fostered collaboration, not just operating the user interface. The goal was for the test participants to use their

---

[3]IBM and Lotus Notes are trademarks of International Business Machines.

own mail files and collaborate with colleagues as they typically would in their own work environment.

The self-guided usability test allowed users to give feedback on their own time and allowed them to choose tasks that were most important to them. It was also a way for the users to walk through some of the new features being introduced in Lotus Notes 8.

Compared to other methods we used, self-guided usability testing was strong in many ways. It reached participants in a wider set of locations and was more realistic than usability testing in a lab. It was also more flexible for participants because they could participate when they wanted and complete only the sections they wanted. It was more hands-on than a survey. Unlike unsolicited and general discussion forum customer feedback, participants were not just motivated to report problems during usage, but instead were more task oriented in their feedback.

9.2.1 Methodology

For self-guided usability testing, we tested Lotus Notes 8 beta—an early version of the code, available only to companies participating in the beta program.

Tasks

We developed a series of tasks around six main areas of Lotus Notes, areas that saw the largest feature changes. The tasks walked the participants through end-user features of Lotus Notes and then asked for specific feedback about those tasks. The tasks focused on the highest priority issues in each area. Our intention was that each set of tasks would take about a half hour to complete. The breakdown of each task set and number of tasks are shown in Table 9.5.

For each task we asked for detailed comments on what worked well and what didn't, as well as an overall satisfaction rating for the specific task. Some tasks also included additional feedback or usage questions specific to the task. We made a special effort to encourage participants to enter any other comments in the topic area that they liked (see Figure 9.4).

At the end of each of the six task sets was a final set of questions that asked the participant to give an overall quality assessment of the new Lotus Notes UI. The feedback was to be based on completing the previous tasks as a whole and the participants' experiences with the beta (see Figure 9.5).

Table 9.5 Task sets.

Task set	Number of tasks
Overall Lotus notes framework	7
General mail	7
Mail threads	7
Calendar	13
Contacts, part 1	5
Contacts, part 2	8

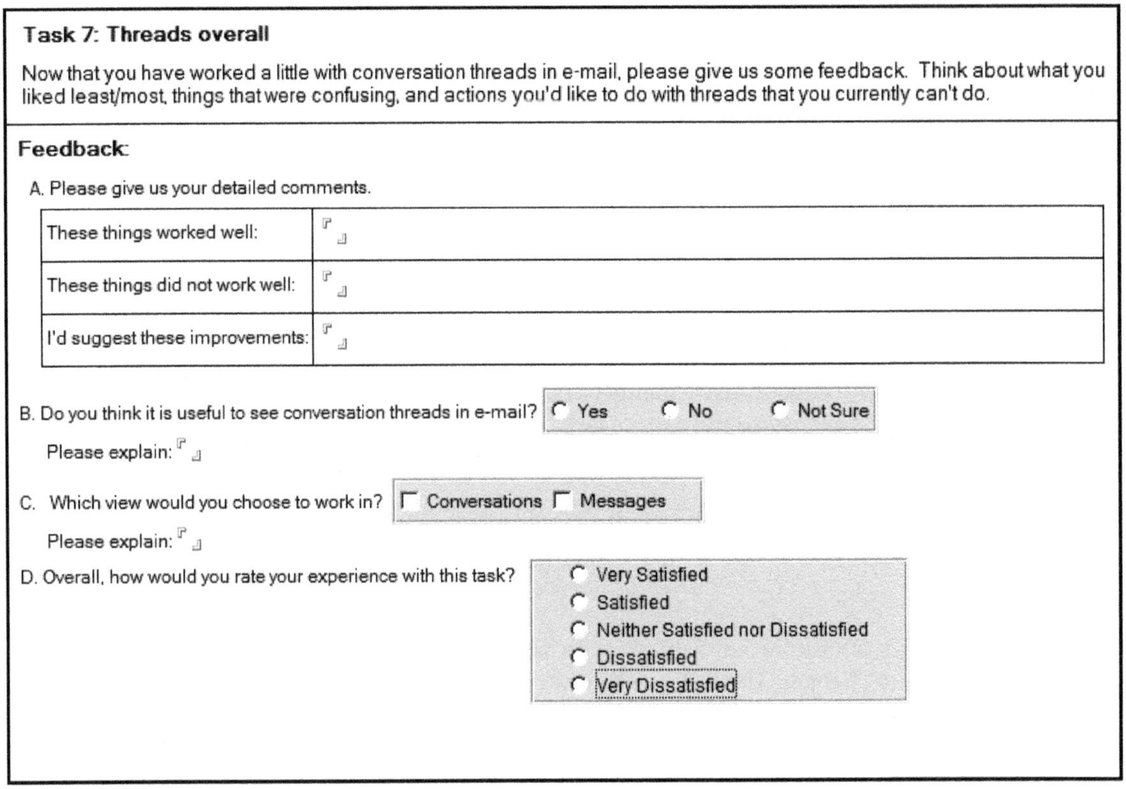

Task 7: Threads overall

Now that you have worked a little with conversation threads in e-mail, please give us some feedback. Think about what you liked least/most, things that were confusing, and actions you'd like to do with threads that you currently can't do.

Feedback:

A. Please give us your detailed comments.

These things worked well:	⌐ ⌐
These things did not work well:	⌐ ⌐
I'd suggest these improvements:	⌐ ⌐

B. Do you think it is useful to see conversation threads in e-mail? ⌐ Yes   ⌐ No   ⌐ Not Sure

   Please explain: ⌐ ⌐

C. Which view would you choose to work in?   ☐ Conversations ☐ Messages

   Please explain: ⌐ ⌐

D. Overall, how would you rate your experience with this task?
   ⌐ Very Satisfied
   ⌐ Satisfied
   ⌐ Neither Satisfied nor Dissatisfied
   ⌐ Dissatisfied
   ⌐ Very Dissatisfied

FIGURE 9.4
Example of a task with additional questions.

After verifying that the tasks were clear and that they covered the desired features to test, we posted them in a dedicated view in the beta program discussion forums, along with details for how the users could participate.

Participants

We targeted participants at the sites that we knew had deployed Lotus Notes 8 beta code. At the time, beta code was available to a managed beta program, design partners, and a select group of invitation-only internal IBM beta users. There were approximately 220 companies who had already joined the managed beta and design partner programs, downloaded the beta, and were a "ready" audience for the self-guided usability tests. Each of these groups already had their own established Lotus Notes discussion forum that was well known by the beta participants and frequently used to ask questions and give feedback about Lotus Notes 8. We were able to create a special entry in each of those forums to access the task sets. This was also the only way we could ensure that all security, nondisclosure, and user account and password procedures were followed. Nondisclosure was especially important because some of the new features had not been made public yet.

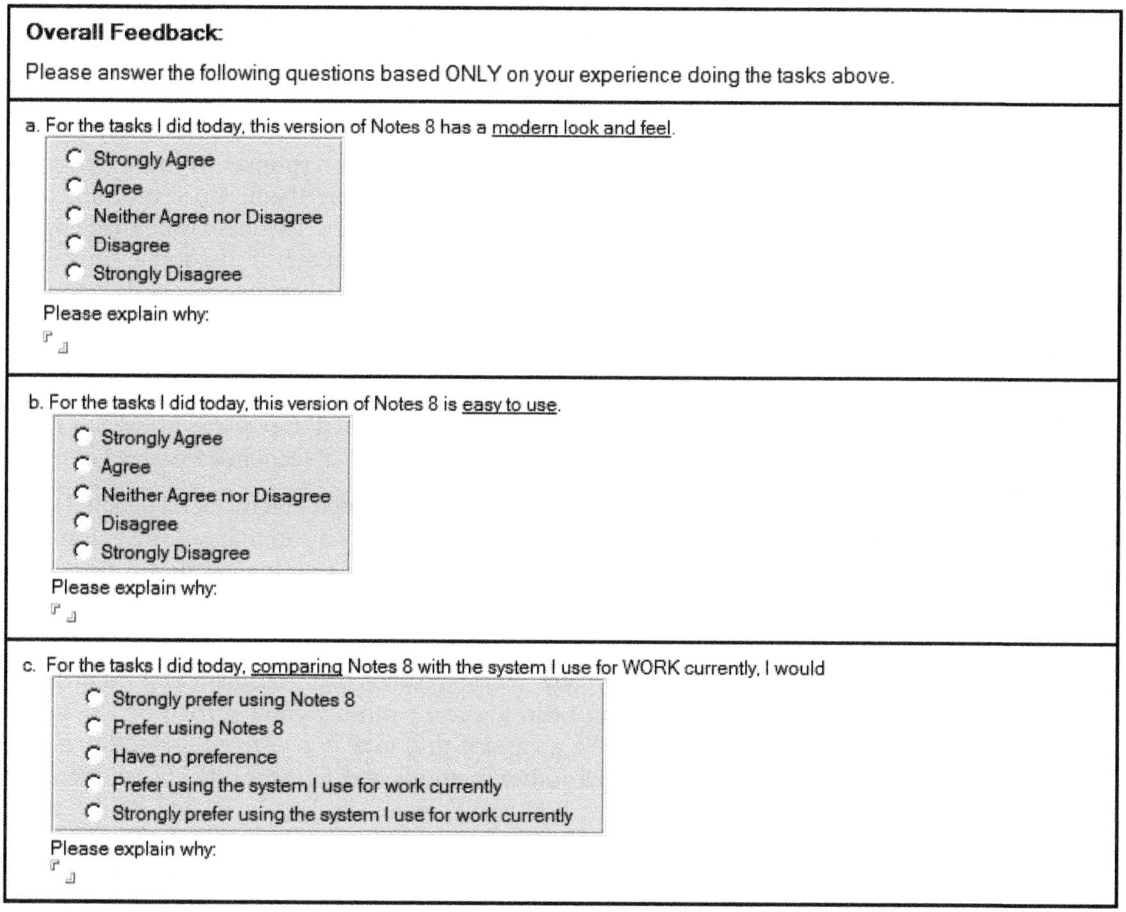

Overall Feedback:

Please answer the following questions based ONLY on your experience doing the tasks above.

a. For the tasks I did today, this version of Notes 8 has a <u>modern look and feel</u>.

- ○ Strongly Agree
- ○ Agree
- ○ Neither Agree nor Disagree
- ○ Disagree
- ○ Strongly Disagree

Please explain why:

b. For the tasks I did today, this version of Notes 8 is <u>easy to use</u>.

- ○ Strongly Agree
- ○ Agree
- ○ Neither Agree nor Disagree
- ○ Disagree
- ○ Strongly Disagree

Please explain why:

c. For the tasks I did today, <u>comparing</u> Notes 8 with the system I use for WORK currently, I would

- ○ Strongly prefer using Notes 8
- ○ Prefer using Notes 8
- ○ Have no preference
- ○ Prefer using the system I use for work currently
- ○ Strongly prefer using the system I use for work currently

Please explain why:

FIGURE 9.5
Example of the Overall Experience questions.

Companies participating in the Lotus Notes 8 beta had agreed to install and deploy Lotus Notes 8 client software and an IBM Lotus Domino®[4] 8 server in a test environment similar to their production environment. In addition, because we weren't sending sample mail files or giving participants a sample environment to use, companies set up a fully functioning collaborative environment that enabled users to use their own mail files to perform tasks with Lotus Notes 8 Mail, Contacts, and Calendar.

Once we had posted the tasks, we invited beta users to participate in the self-guided usability tests. We did this through two means, via an invitation in the discussion forums and by announcing the program at one of the regularly scheduled weekly Lotus Notes beta meetings.

Users who wanted to participate in the self-guided usability test were instructed to use the Lotus Notes 8 beta code that they'd installed in test environments at

---

[4]Domino is a trademark of International Business Machines.

their own companies. Participants could access the tasks and answer the questions in the beta discussion forums either directly through their Lotus Notes client or by using a Web browser. This method enabled participants to view the tasks and Lotus Notes 8 on their screen at the same time.

Users could work on any set of tasks, save their responses as draft, and then return to their responses at any time to complete them. Once they felt they were finished, they submitted their final responses. The tasks were made available for 2 months. Any responses that were still in draft form at that time were considered complete and were included in the final results.

9.2.2 Results

The design of the results database was such that we could immediately see responses that were saved or completed. We collated responses on a weekly basis to get snapshots and a "temperature" of the kind of feedback we were getting.

At the end of the 2 months, a final report was created that included detailed findings from each of the individual tasks, as well as a summary of the comments made by participants. The self-guided usability test generated 100 responses from 24 different participants; 13 identified themselves as end users and 12 said they were in more technical, IT roles.

This self-guided usability test method succeeded in identifying additional usability issues that hadn't been found by other means. A total of 131 issues were recorded across the six areas. Of that total, 72 were new usability issues that we hadn't seen through other methods and 59 were added as supporting evidence to issues that we had seen previously, largely in one of the three laboratory usability tests. Each usability issue that was uncovered was tracked in our internal usability issues database and was used to recommend solutions and to influence decisions about which issues were most important to fix.

Although the purpose of the self-guided usability tests was to find usability issues, some participants also recorded bugs or performance issues. We passed those items along to the proper channels within the development organization.

9.2.3 Self-guided usability testing: Discussion and conclusions

In general, we were pleased with the results we obtained using self-guided usability testing. It complemented our other methods, allowing us to collect in-use feedback from early adopters on critical new areas of Lotus Notes 8. We succeeded in getting useful feedback from 24 additional people and identifying 72 usability issues that we hadn't seen before.

It's useful to compare self-guided usability testing to more traditional lab testing. When we test Lotus Notes in the lab, we have one setup and one way that the participant's Lotus Notes system is configured. We use fictional materials designed to mimic a realistic corporate use of Lotus Notes. Participants play the role of an employee at that company. However, no matter how realistic we try to make the sample mail messages, contacts, and calendar entries, they do not look to users like their own mail messages, contacts, and calendar entries.

With self-guided usability testing, participants used their own mail messages, contacts, and calendar entries. They could collaborate using Lotus Notes 8 as they normally would in their jobs. This allowed participants to focus on the details of the tasks and the new user experience in a more realistic way.

Participant comments supported our impression that this method of using participants' own mail files and not our generic test data was more meaningful, and we gained more opportunistic feedback that we might not have otherwise learned.

Another useful comparison is with the satisfaction ratings. At the end of every pre-beta lab usability test, we had asked participants to rate their overall satisfaction on three questions. We also asked those same rating scale questions of the participants in the self-guided usability tests. Figure 9.6 shows that the ratings were comparable among the lab tests, a less formal test at a large IBM Lotus customer conference, Lotusphere 2007, and these self-guided usability tests.

Limitations

Although self-guided usability testing worked well, we did find certain limitations. First, although we targeted a select group of companies, we didn't have good control over who the actual participants were. Even those who identified

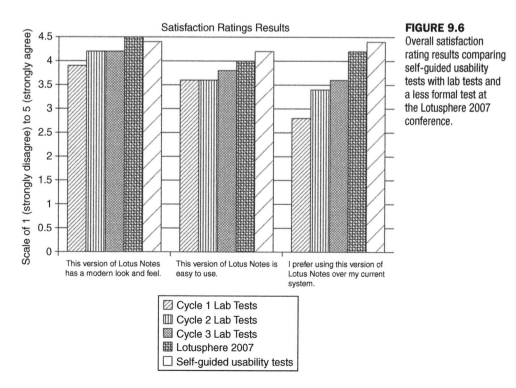

FIGURE 9.6
Overall satisfaction rating results comparing self-guided usability tests with lab tests and a less formal test at the Lotusphere 2007 conference.

themselves as end users were likely more technical than the average end user, as beta code generally isn't deployed to nontechnical end users. We also had no way of knowing how many people had access to the invitation to participate in the study, and thus we had no way of calculating a response rate.

A second drawback is inherent in the unattended nature of this self-guided testing. We don't know exactly what the participants were doing, what they saw and experienced, or if the software wasn't working well. In a lab test, the moderator can see if the participants are struggling and whether they are working in the intended area of the UI, but during a self-guided usability test, we were unable to tell from their responses if they misinterpreted the question or were just answering about something else they had experienced and needed an avenue to comment.

In many cases, answers participants gave were brief or incomplete, were difficult to interpret, and didn't paint a picture of what they had been doing. We specifically wanted people to collaborate using Lotus Notes 8 during the tests, but we had no way of knowing if they actually did. None of the respondents recorded any information to allude to this.

A final set of limitations concerned the discussion forum technology. Although using the Lotus Notes discussion forums had many advantages, including the ease of connecting to a database and the ease of receiving and viewing responses, we found that the overall setup of our self-guided usability testing was more difficult and took much longer than expected. The major difficulty was creating tasks that worked properly within the limitations of the Lotus Notes discussion forums we used. For example, it was difficult to control form layout and difficult to provide the ability for participants to paste screenshots in line with the tasks they were doing at the time. We accepted these difficulties because using these forums allowed us access to the users we wanted to reach. In the future, however, we'd like to explore other tools that are aimed at making it easier to set up testing like this.

Lessons learned

In addition to investigating other tools, there are at least two main things we'll do differently next time. First, we need better ways to motivate participation. Fewer people chose to participate in this study than we had hoped. The ones who did were spotty in the way they filled them out, and the actual responses were often very brief. There was no incentive other than the chance to influence the design of Lotus Notes 8 and the tasks may have been too long. Our task sets may have included too many tasks and relied on the participant to enter too much text for each task. In any future attempt we would change the tasks sets to be shorter and more narrow in scope. We'd also like to offer something more concrete as a gift for those who participate fully.

A second lesson (and another way to shorten the task sets) is to eliminate all of the per-task satisfaction ratings. The overall satisfaction ratings were somewhat useful in showing that self-guided testing gave consistent ratings to lab testing and that participants' satisfaction was improving as Lotus Notes 8 neared completion. However, the per-task ratings proved to not be useful for us.

We collected ratings about the satisfaction of each task, but they differed little and didn't turn out to be useful in guiding design.

In conclusion, we found self-guided usability testing to be a useful complement to other user feedback methods. It uncovered issues we did not find using other methods. The experience described here set a foundation for future self-guided usability tests with other Lotus products.

Acknowledgments

The authors gratefully acknowledge the many people who helped make this self-guided usability testing a success. We particularly thank IBM employees Christopher Baker, Sheri Branco, Roger Didio, Jan Kenney, Christine Kergaravat, Andrew Lafleur, Craig Lordan, Deborah Maurer, and Cara Viktorov. Finally, the largest thank you goes to the all the early adopters who took the time to participate in this study.

Reference

Comstock, E. M., Raven, M., Branco, S. F., Cooper, M. L., & Maurer, D. E. (2009). Open by design: How IBM partnered with the user community in the redesign of Lotus Notes. In *Proceedings of the 27th International Conference Extended Abstracts on Human Factors in Computing Systems* (pp. 2931–2944). CHI EA '09. New York: ACM.

Biographies

- Betsy Comstock is a senior user researcher with IBM Lotus Software. After receiving her Ph.D. in psychology from the University of Massachusetts, she worked in a variety of companies, including Digital Equipment Corporation and Polycom, helping to make products good for the people who use them.
- Michelle Cooper is a user researcher at IBM. She is responsible for helping improve the user experience in the Lotus software division. Michelle holds a bachelor's degree in elementary education from Butler University and a master's degree in information science from Indiana University.

9.3 LONGITUDINAL USABILITY AND USER ENGAGEMENT TESTING FOR THE COMPLEX WEB SITE REDESIGN OF MTV.COM

Charles L. Mauro, MauroNewMedia; Allison O'Keefe-Wright, MTV; and Cianna Timbers, MauroNewMedia

Traditionally, usability testing has been focused on testing single points in time to reveal a snapshot of the overall usability and user engagement performance of a Web site or other interface. A major benefit of longitudinal testing is that it provides series of interrelated ratings of a user experience extended over a significant period of time. These ratings provide very detailed direction for the enhancement of user experience design on both tactical and strategic levels. When employed in an AGILE[5]-like manner where studies are integrated into development "Sprints," longitudinal testing provides the development team with rapid and highly actionable feedback on the impact that changes made during development "Sprints" are having on the user's experience. In the future, online longitudinal usability and user engagement studies will become a critical component of producing robust user experiences by tightly integrating formal usability testing methods directly into the product development process models. This case study presents a complex online longitudinal usability testing study for a large media Web site undergoing major structural and user interface development changes and updates. The authors present a discussion of key issues related to the longitudinal study design through the use of robust online behavior tracking and survey technology[6] and a series of compelling examples documenting the types of data such studies provide, followed by a brief discussion of business impact.

9.3.1 Project background

This longitudinal usability and user engagement research effort was designed to aid MTV executives and development teams in the creation of a Web-based user experience that would meet the changing media consumption behaviors of its core viewers and would directly influence the design of new Web-based services and media delivery systems that would maintain and expand MTV's success in the youth media market.

9.3.2 Why a longitudinal study design

MTV faced a complex development problem, which included the need to deliver numerous major media content categories within a rapidly changing youth media landscape. The multisegment, longitudinal testing model was felt to be the most effective way for aiding in the development and testing of user experience design solutions that would improve engagement objectively. The longitudinal methodology would also provide understanding on how media consumption behaviors were changing during the development process to determine how to best maintain and expand the MTV brand in core viewer segments.

At the start of the research effort MTV had in place a "Flash-based" Web site, which was benchmarked on a core set of user engagement metrics. The remaining testing segments measured the progress of the design across the same user engagement metrics. This approach provided highly structured and repeatable performance metrics for measuring the progressive success of the new development effort. The study was undertaken in concert with internal MTV market research efforts. Each longitudinal study segment followed an AGILE Sprint development cycle, providing iterative feedback to the development team on variables known to influence user engagement and business performance.

---

[5]The term "AGILE" refers to a type of iterative development methodology that focuses on adapting the interface as it goes through rapid cycles shifting between development and review of the changes made.
[6]This article is based on the use of Keynote WebEffective. Please note that the concepts discussed in this chapter may not apply to other online systems of less functionality.

9.3.3 Task structure

The Web interface undergoing development delivered multiple business-critical media content categories. The complexity of the site and the breadth of research needs required the development of a complex, logic-based study design that included several hundred questions and four to seven task-based behavior tracking modules. Due to the large size of the survey, a randomized matrix sampling technique[7] was employed to gather the large amount of usability data required without overburdening individual respondents and sacrificing the study completion rate (Grizzle and Raghunathan, 1995). The task sequence was structured to evaluate the ability of the Web site to support the four behavioral modes users undertake when using Web-based interfaces of this complexity: Unconditioned viewing, Conditioned viewing, Informal search, and Formal search (Choo et al., 2000). The information-seeking behavior task structure provided an important measure of overall Web site usability measuring the ability of the Web site design to meet support users searching and using MTV media content.

9.3.4 Data gathering technology and process

Subjective responses were gathered using Keynote WebEffective technology and objective behaviors were tracked using Keynote "Connector" data gathering methodology.[8] Keynote WebEffective was chosen as the appropriate technology for several reasons.

1. The tool itself allows for the development of a very large number of questions and offers sophisticated section randomization techniques not available in less robust tools.
2. Keynote WebEffective is especially powerful at screening out respondents that attempt to game a survey to reap the rewards.
3. Keynote "Connector" technology provides robust microlevel behavior tracking data not available in most online tools.
4. Keynote also offers extensive professional recruiting and respondent tracking services that ensure appropriate sampling and respondent screening.

9.3.5 Respondent recruiting and incentives

The entire study included several hundred respondents prescreened to meet the target youth profile and additional criteria. Two separate participant panels were constructed. One panel contained users familiar with the MTV Web site and the second contained users who were unfamiliar with the MTV Web site. The research design incorporated an extensive psychodemographic screening component that allowed for detailed user segmentation of data. An MTV content viewing question set tracked changes in MTV viewer media consumption behaviors, technology utilization ratings, and social networking behaviors.

For the online study launch, respondents were invited to participate through uniquely tagged email invitations that allowed for a post-study segmentation of

---

[7]Matrix sampling randomly assigns separate question sets or task segments to different respondents.
[8]Keynote "Connector" data gathering technology was not yet available during the launch of Longitudinal Study Segment 1 and therefore was only employed for Longitudinal Study Segments 2 and 3.

respondents. All respondents received a $35 Amazon gift certificate in return for appropriate execution of the study as determined through WebEffective motivation tracking technology. Study complexity, clarity, and length were tracked in follow-up questions to all respondents who completed a study sequence successfully. Ratings on these variables were found to be strong positives on all key scales.

9.3.6 Lab study and online data gathering methodology verification

Prior to launching each major longitudinal testing segment, the entire online survey was verified through execution of a 2-day lab-based study. Participant behaviors were recorded and analyzed later using Morae behavior tracking software. Survey data from the small-scale lab verification studies were analyzed separately from the large sample of online participants to avoid bias due to survey mode administration (Christian et al., 2009). Administering a lab study prior to launch of a large-scale study has several highly valuable benefits. First, lab study data provide valuable information related to the frequency, type, and severity of critical usability issues and offer professionally observed behavior data that are difficult to detect reliably during online testing (Tullis and Albert, 2008). Second, the lab study provides preliminary data that allow the team to generate a hypothesis that can be evaluated through the large sample quantitative study. Third, most Web site design glitches are discovered prior to launching the more expensive large sample study. Finally, the lab-based study verifies the online study logic and uncovers any tasks or question sets that are too complex for participants to understand, minimizing the likelihood of participant confusion.

9.3.7 Data analysis

Data were verified and then segmented using Keynote WebEffective tools and exported into Excel and an advanced statistical software program (Stata) for analysis. In addition, an optimal pathway analysis was performed on behavioral data gathered through the Keynote behavior tracking software to track navigational performance of the site and produce large sample objective task success/fail data. Due to large samples sizes, tests of significance were possible, thus providing a measure of confidence in the impact that progressive updates in the site design were having on actual user engagement and usability.

9.3.8 Results and discussion

The value of findings from the longitudinal study was largely derived from the longitudinal study design's ability to track the progress of the Web site design across each design implementation phase. The longitudinal study design was further used to uncover innovations for enhancing the user experience of core media categories delivered by the Web site. Results of the longitudinal study provided detailed insight along research avenues unique to each individual study segment. Additionally, the longitudinal segments provided comparison data between consecutive segments, as well as longitudinally, across all three study segments. Critical results from the longitudinal research effort are discussed here in more detail.

Nomenclature analysis findings

During Longitudinal Study Segments 1 and 2, a nomenclature analysis was undertaken in an effort to improve the navigation and clarity of the early stage Web site redesign. The first study segment employed a nomenclature comprehension analysis to determine nomenclature changes that would improve the existing design. Based on findings from Study Segment 1, three high-level navigation menu labels were modified as follows: "Think" was changed to "Activism," "On TV" to "Shows," and "Main" to "Home." High-level navigation labels were then retested during Study Segment 2. A comparison of comprehension levels before and after nomenclature changes were implemented as shown in Figure 9.7. The longitudinal analysis of Web site nomenclature showed marked improvement in nomenclature comprehension. For example, findings clearly indicated an increase in understanding from when nomenclature originally labeled "Think" was changed to a more widely understood label, "Activism." Both the nomenclature redesign replacing "On TV" with "Shows" and "Main" with "Home" also demonstrated improved comprehension levels. Another interesting finding from the analysis was the increase in understanding of the nomenclature "Mobile," despite having not changed this label. This finding suggested an increasing

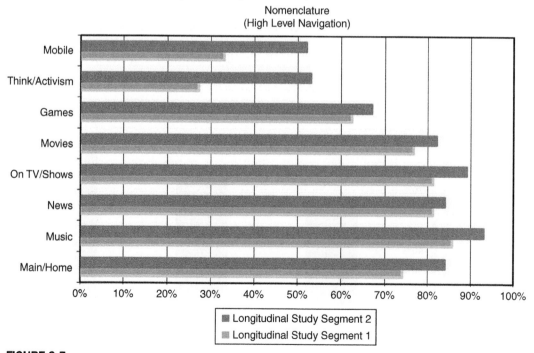

Comparison of nomenclature understanding ratings for Study Segment 1 vs. Study Segment 2 (plot = % rated "Totally Clear/Totally Understand")

Nomenclature
(High Level Navigation)

FIGURE 9.7

Comparison of high-level nomenclature comprehension ratings from Longitudinal Study Segments 1 and 2. Copyright © MauroNewMedia, 2009. All rights reserved.

awareness of mobile content and mobile usage. Additionally, it is likely that the position of the "Mobile" menu item on the navigation bar had some affect on the participant ratings. The "Mobile" label was located directly to the right of the new "Activism" label, and the improved clarity of the "Activism" term is likely to have affected the perceived clarity of the surrounding navigation labels.

Content, features, and functions

Each study segment (1, 2, and 3) was utilized to identify and prioritize which areas of content, features, and functions were critical for driving deeper levels of engagement with the Web site and would most improve the experience of MTV.com users. One of the important findings from content exploration was that over the course of the study the delivery of online video content was rapidly becoming more important to MTV.com users (see Figure 9.8). In response to the dramatically shifting set of user needs, the MTV development team made a strategic decision to focus on improving the MTV.com online video experience by redesigning the video player and objectively exploring how users search and discover the Web site's video content to develop a navigation structure that supports this model. A comparison analysis of the MTV.com video player with a video player of a significant competitive site was employed to benchmark the proposed video player redesign and related navigation with that of existing competitive video players. Results of an optimal pathway clickstream (Keynote behavior tracking) analysis identified critical areas of improvement that would be most likely to improve the ease of accessing MTV.com's online video content. The improvements identified during the clickstream analysis were incorporated into the subsequent Web site redesign and in the design of the new video player. Subjective ratings of the core user profile indicated that the new video player design was much preferred to the competitive Web site's design.

FIGURE 9.8
Findings from longitudinal analysis of the importance of video content to study participants who visit MTV.com. Copyright © MauroNewMedia, 2009. All rights reserved.

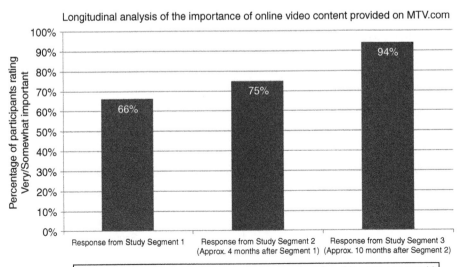

Longitudinal analysis of the importance of online video content provided on MTV.com

■ % saying Very/Somewhat important: Video content (anything you can watch)

It is interesting to note that this dramatic increase in the importance of viewing video content coincided with the rapid rise in the presentation of video content through sites such as YouTube and others. By employing longitudinal methodology it was possible to track changes carefully and reliably in content consumption behaviors for key user profiles. This made it possible for development teams to prioritize user interface design functions in a meaningful manner that focused the combined design and research efforts on the most beneficial content areas for user experience improvement.

Imagery analysis findings

Because MTV.com is the Web-based representation of a popular youth media brand known for being cutting edge and innovative, the visual design of the Web site was a critical focus for the redesign project. Utilizing a longitudinal study design provided the ability to measure the visual impact of design changes executed during each design phase. Findings showed that the visual design changes implemented over the course of the study continuously improved the visual impact of the Web site on several key attributes, such as "Fun," "Engaging," and "Interesting." Longitudinal analysis of imagery ratings further demonstrated that the redesign phase that changed the Web site from Flash based to HTML based significantly decreased the negative imagery attributes of "Too Flashy," "Complex," and "Confusing." Overall, the redesign had a powerful impact on the imagery ratings for MTV.com. A subset of findings from the imagery analysis is shown in Figure 9.9.

Interactive quality findings

One of the standardized question sets applied across all study segments measured the interactive quality attributes of the Web site after each development cycle. A critical finding from Segment 1 is that after the first AGILE release the new site had achieved significant improvements in interactive quality but had not achieved nearly as significant an improvement in visual design, a factor known to be vitally important to the MTV brand. Based on data from Segment 1, the MTV development team focused major effort on improving the visual design of the MTV.com user experience. As can be seen from data covering segments 2–3, the visual design rose to a high level and came in line with the other three interactive quality ratings. The important insight from this view of data is that a dramatic improvement in visual design did not have a negative impact on the other interactive quality ratings. In other words, the MTV.com development team had improved the visual design of the user experience dramatically while maintaining high levels of usability. This is rarely the case. By viewing all testing segments together in this manner it was possible to verify that the new version of MTV.com had achieved high levels of objective improvements on all four interactive quality ratings. MTV brand imagery ratings also tested during each phase exactly traced the changes in interactive quality shown here. When viewed in summary form in Figure 9.10, the key finding of the longitudinal research approach is that the new MTV.com site offered users a highly balanced user experience that gave equal weight to usability, simplicity, and visual design.

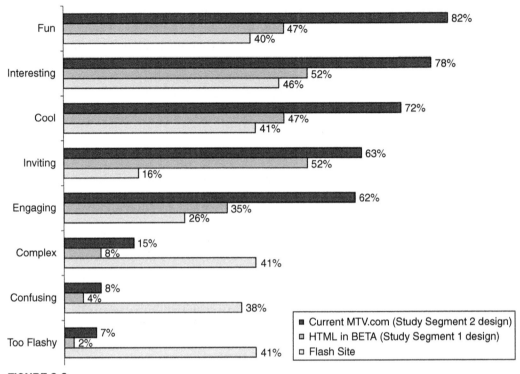

FIGURE 9.9
Results of imagery analysis comparing the original Flash-based Web site to Web site redesigns. Copyright © MauroNewMedia, 2009. All rights reserved.

9.3.9 Conclusion

For MTV, tracking the user response across study segments delivered a robust set of findings that provided rapid confirmation that the design iterations were consistently making improvements to the user experience across core user profiles. In addition to confirming that the Web site design was improving consistently, the longitudinal study offered critical insight into the underlying cognitive models of how its core user profiles think about the online media consumption tasks that they undertake and which new Web site functions and characteristics objectively build increasing levels of Web site and brand engagement. The case study discussed previously illustrates how a robust longitudinal study design can complement an iterative AGILE design process utilizing usability science as a tactical and strategic asset to increase customer acquisition, retention, and migration rates while producing dramatic reductions in downstream interface redesign costs (Mauro, 2005).

The strength of utilizing a longitudinal study design is that it ensures that critical usability and user engagement issues are prevented early in the design phase, reducing downstream development costs while developing a robust, high-quality user experience. Currently, structured longitudinal studies are not applied rou-

Overall comparison of Interactive Quality attributes (Original Flash site/Segment 1/Segment 2/Segment 3)
(Chart displays percentage of participants giving an Excellent rating for corresponding Interactive Quality attribute)

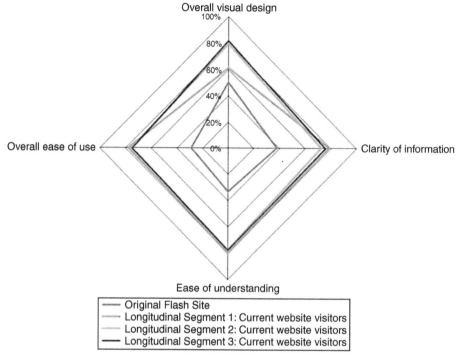

- —— Original Flash Site
- —— Longitudinal Segment 1: Current website visitors
- —— Longitudinal Segment 2: Current website visitors
- —— Longitudinal Segment 3: Current website visitors

FIGURE 9.10
Interactive quality attributes ratings for current Web site visitors across all longitudinal study segments. The semantic differential scale depicted is copyright of MauroNewMedia, 2009. All rights reserved.

tinely as a methodology for incorporating usability science into Web site interface design. The primary reasons for infrequent application of such methods can be traced to a combination of assumed high costs and a paucity of reliable online data gathering tools. However, recent developments in online data gathering technology, combined with the application of professional study design, have made online longitudinal usability studies possible and cost-effective. When executed properly, online longitudinal studies are vastly more powerful than traditional lab-based testing or even online snapshot studies using similar online data gathering tools and methods. In the future, online longitudinal usability studies such as the one discussed earlier will become a critical component of the market research and product development process for complex Web site development.

References

Choo, C. W., Detlor, B., & Turnbull, D. (2000). *Web Work: Information Seeking and Knowledge Work on the World Wide Web*. Dordrecht: Kluwer Academic Publishers.

Christian, L. M., Dillman, D. A., & Smyth, J. D. (2009). *Internet, Mail, and Mixed-Mode Surveys: The Tailored Design Method* (3rd ed.). Hoboken, NJ: John Wiley & Sons.

Grizzle, J. E., & Raghunathan, T. E. (1995). A split questionnaire survey design. *Journal of the American Statistical Association*, 90(429), 54–63.

Mauro, C. L. (2005). Usability science: Tactical and strategic cost justifications in large corporate applications. In R. Bias & Mayhew (Eds.), *Cost-Justifying Usability* (pp. 265–296). San Francisco, CA: Morgan Kaufmann Publishers.

Tullis, T., & Albert, B. (2008). *Measuring the User Experience: Collecting, Analyzing, and Presenting Usability Metrics*. Burlington, MA: Morgan Kaufmann Publishers.

Biographies

- Charles L Mauro CHFP is CEO of MauroNewMedia (MNM), a New York-based consulting firm offering services in usability testing, formal user-centered design, and high performance user interface design. He holds a masters degree in human factors/ergonomics from New York University (NYU). Mr. Mauro's experience spans more than 35 years and includes consumer, commercial, military, and aerospace applications. He has received the Alexander C. Williams Award from the Human Factors and Ergonomics Society and citations from NASA and the Association of Computing Machines.

- As Vice President of Strategic Insights and Research at MTV, Allison O'Keefe Wright is responsible for spearheading initiatives in large-scale consumer life-style investigations, brand and buzz tracking, program testing, website usability, and other consumer insight initiatives for MTV, MTV2, and mtvU across all screens. Allison is the author of the book D_Code 5, an investigation of leading edge youth culture and marketing across the globe. Her research and insight have been featured on television and radio programs worldwide, including CNN and BBC, and highlighted by magazines/newspapers across the globe, including The Economist and Brand Republic, among others.

- Cianna Timbers serves as a research associate for MauroNewMedia (MNM), a consulting firm focused on providing services in usability testing, user interface design, and new media strategy. As a research associate at MNM she works in concert with clients on a wide range of product and user interface design issues developing and conducting complex usability and user experience optimization research and analysis. Cianna holds dual undergraduate degrees in Chemistry and Industrial Engineering and is a graduate of Columbia University Department of Industrial Engineering where she focused on human factors engineering and systems analysis.

9.4 AN AUTOMATED STUDY OF THE UCSF WEB SITE

Nate Bolt, Tony Tulathimutte, and Alana Pechon, Bolt | Peters

In 2007 a study of the UCSF Medical Center Web site and the UCSF Children's Hospital Web site was performed using the automated online usability testing tool UserZoom. The study had three goals: (1) to validate results from a round of qualitative studies performed earlier in the year, (2) to identify the points in the Web site where users were most likely to stop using the UCSF site and seek help elsewhere, and (3) to provide quantitative data to support usability recommendations that could be used to inform an IA redesign in case a redesign was found to be necessary. Automated online testing afforded a quick way to recruit a large sample and gauge their task performance on the real UCSF Web site, addressing the goal of corroborating earlier small sample qualitative findings.

9.4.1 Methodology

This study consisted of 100 unmoderated usability evaluations, each covering five tasks on UCSF Web sites relating to typical searching and gathering medical information. Testing was conducted remotely, with users participating from their own workstations using the automated online research tool UserZoom. Participants were recruited from the ucsfhealth.org Web site using Ethnio, a Web-based tool that displays a pop-up DHTML recruiting screener to a portion of the site's visitors. As an incentive to participate, the visitors were offered a 1-in-10 chance of receiving a $75 Amazon.com gift certificate.

The target audience for this study was identified as "patients, both prospective and current" who

1. Have used the Internet in the past to find health information
2. Are the decision makers regarding health care for themselves (if single) or for their family
3. Have health insurance (excluding Medi-Cal and Kaiser)

In order to qualify the survey respondents as recruits, the following data were gathered from each recruiting survey respondent:

1. Purpose of visit to UCSF Web site
2. Health insurance carrier
3. Status as a patient, decision maker, and relative of patient

Qualified respondents who agreed to participate in the study were sent an email upon receipt of their survey responses, directing them to a Web address where they were greeted with a set of participation instructions. First they were to answer a series of Likert questions, indicating how much they agreed/disagreed with the following statements:

1. UCSF has a reputation as one of the top medical centers in the US.
2. I would expect to receive excellent care if I were a patient at UCSF.
3. My most recent visit to ucsfhealth.org was successful. (I got the information I went there for.)
4. The ucsfhealth.org home page reflects a reputation of a top medical center.

They were then prompted to download the UserZoom browser bar application and then perform a series of tasks as directed by the application. Each task was followed by multiple-choice questions to evaluate the outcome of their task performance, whether or not they were able to complete the task successfully.

The five tasks were as follows.

1. For this question, please assume you or a loved one has been diagnosed with a brain tumor. After seeking treatments at various medical centers, you have decided to pursue a Gamma Knife procedure at UCSF Medical Center. You have made an appointment to have the procedure. Your task is to **find information about how to prepare for a Gamma Knife procedure**.

2. You are a parent whose child has an abnormal heartbeat. You have been advised by your pediatrician to make an appointment with a specialist. Because you live in the Bay Area, you would like to start with a local physician. Your task is to **make an appointment with a pediatric arrhythmia specialist at UCSF Children's Hospital**.

3. Imagine that you injured your knee several months ago during a sporting event. You have been receiving physical therapy at UCSF Medical Center after a successful surgery. In the process of filling out insurance forms, you find that you need some additional information. Your task is to **find the address of the Sports Medicine Center**.

4. For this task, please assume that your child has been successfully treated for a brain aneurysm. (A brain aneurysm is a balloon- or bubble-like growth usually located on an artery at the base of the brain.) It is time to make a follow-up appointment. Your task is to **find the phone number for returning pediatric cerebrovascular patients to call for an appointment**.

5. Assume you have just come home from a visit to your primary care physician. She has told you that she suspects that the cause of your recent severe weight loss and difficulty swallowing may be cancer. You have written down the type she mentioned, and when you come home, you visit the ucsfhealth.org Web site to begin learning more about it. Your task is to **find information on the diagnosis of esophageal cancer**.

The last sentence of each set of task instructions was displayed in the browser bar framing the actual Web site (see Figure 9.11.) As they went about performing tasks, users were also prompted to memorize or write down the information ("not using copy-paste commands") once they found it so that they would be able to answer a verification question relating to the information later.

After each task, users were given statements about any problems they encountered over the course of performing tasks and were asked to check all of these statements that applied to them:

1. It was difficult to know what steps or paths to take to find the correct information.
2. I didn't find the information in the place I was expecting to find it.
3. Links didn't take me to the information/section I was expecting.
4. The links were unclear.

5. The information, options, or menus were difficult to understand.
6. The information presented was not clear.
7. Search results didn't meet my expectations.
8. The information presented was incomplete.
9. I couldn't figure out what to search for.
10. I had trouble spelling or typing something I wanted to search for.

They were also asked to evaluate the task on a Likert scale for several values:

1. Overall rating of the ease of the task
2. It was clear how to start searching
3. Finding the procedure preparation information was easy
4. I felt satisfied with my results at the end of this task
5. Doing this task increased my confidence in the UCSF Medical Center
6. This task took a reasonable amount of time to complete

FIGURE 9.11
An example of how the browser bar containing task instructions is positioned below the Web site.

After completing all five tasks, users filled out a final questionnaire, including open-ended questions about what they would improve, what the best and worst things about the site were, and a final set of Likert scale questions asking users to agree or disagree with the following statements about the site:

1. Graphic design is good
2. Easy to navigate
3. Accurately reflects UCSF's reputation
4. Easy to find info on the site
5. Makes me more likely to come to UCSF as a patient
6. Never felt lost while navigating through it
7. Overall good quality of the site

9.4.2 Results and discussion

These results surprised us: the success and completion rates seemed relatively high in light of the low success rate from the previous qualitative study and some of the open-ended comments from this study, which expressed frustration and confusion about the navigation (see Table 9.6).

Examining the results further, we determined that there was a large discrepancy between users who used the search function on the site versus users who did not (see Table 9.7). We also found that the proportion of users who employed search during this study was far higher than average, which led us to conclude that, due to our own oversight, users were significantly assisted in their tasks because the tasks and search terms were explicitly shown to them in the UserZoom browser bar. For instance, users were assisted in finding the phone number for returning pediatric cerebrovascular patients simply because the term was right there in front of them, complete with perfect spelling, whereas in normal usage they might not have this exact term to search for and may be forced to navigate the site manually, leading to a lower success rate.

Table 9.6 Average success and ratings for all five tasks.

5-Task Average: All Users (Scale of 1–7)

	Success	Error/Abandon
Task Success Rate	76% *(avg time 1:33)*	24%
Ratings	**Weighted for All Users**	
Overall Task	**4.3**	*(Successful users only: 5.4)*
"It was clear how to start searching"	**4.2**	*(Successful users only: 5.2)*
"Finding x information was easy"	**4.2**	*(Successful users only: 5.2)*
"Satisfied with results"	**4.8**	*(Successful users only: 6.0)*
"Increased my confidence in the UCSF Medical Center"	**4**	*(Successful users only: 5.0)*
"Task took a reasonable amount of time"	**4.3**	*(Successful users only: 5.3)*

Table 9.7   Average success and ratings for all five tasks for those users who did not use the search functionality.

5-Task Average: Users Who Never Used Search (Scale of 1–7)		
	Success	**Error/Abandon**
Task Success Rate	52% *(avg time 1:35)*	48%
Ratings	**Weighted for All Users**	
Overall Task	3.1	*(Successful users only: 4.9)*
"It was clear how to start searching"	3	*(Successful users only: 4.7)*
"Finding x information was easy"	3	*(Successful users only: 4.5)*
"Satisfied with results"	3.3	*(Successful users only: 5.1)*
"Increased my confidence in the UCSF Medical Center"	2.6	*(Successful users only: 4.0)*
"Task took a reasonable amount of time"	3.1	*(Successful users only: 4.8)*

The fact that a significant percentage of users (even successful ones) reported difficulties with browsing- and navigation-related activities corroborated our suspicion that search inflated the success rate artificially.

9.4.3 Conclusions

With the findings from this study, along with results of the previous qualitative study, the UCSF Medical Center was able to use the findings to convince the board that the cost of a major redesign was justified. The redesign is still in process and has not yet been implemented.

In this study we encountered obstacles that speak to the major challenges of designing and analyzing the findings of an automated user study. Many of the challenges faced in conducting this study arose from the limitations of the UserZoom testing apparatus; having the search terms appear in the browser bar alongside the browser frame has the potential to skew results, as it does not reflect typical usage. Also, the requirement that users refrain from using copy/paste to answer the questions—a consequence of including multiple-choice verification questions—may be an unnatural constraint for users who are accustomed to using copy/paste. Finally, evaluating the success of the users' task performance with a multiple-choice question isn't ideal, as there is the slight possibility that users might have found the correct information, but mistakenly entered the wrong multiple choice response, for whatever reason.

Because of these shortcomings, it was very important to interpret the findings properly; we managed to obtain useful data by noticing the skew in the raw findings, but these might have been easily overlooked had they not conflicted with our previous qualitative findings and open-ended qualitative survey questions.

To mitigate these issues, researchers should strive to design tasks that draw out users' behaviors without explicitly naming what they need to look for and to use open-ended questions to provide insight and context to the quantitative findings. If possible, supplementing the study with moderated qualitative research can be of great help in interpreting the numbers properly.

Biographies

- After directing the UX department at Clear Ink in 1999, Nate Bolt cofounded Bolt | Peters. He now serves as the CEO, overseeing hundreds of user research studies for Sony, Oracle, HP, Greenpeace, Electronic Arts, and others. Beginning in 2003, he led the creation of the first moderated remote user research software, Ethnio. Nate regularly gives presentations on native environment research methods and is coauthoring Remote Research, a book on remote testing (Rosenfeld Media, late 2009).
- Tony Tulathimutte is a UX writer/researcher for Bolt | Peters, specializing in remote user research over the Web and native environment research. Tony has worked with Autodesk, AAA, HP, and Harvard Business Review; he was the lead researcher on the player experience studies for EA's Spore. He is currently coauthoring a remote research book with Nate Bolt.
- Alana Pechon is a UX researcher for Bolt | Peters, where she has worked with a wide variety of clients, including Sony, Esurance, and Autodesk. She was the lead researcher for the UCSF study discussed here.

9.5 ONLINE USABILITY TESTING OF TAX PREPARATION SOFTWARE

Melanie Baran, Kavita Appachu, and Alex Genov, Intuit

The goal of this study was to understand how participants shop for online tax software and evaluate the tax preparation experience. Key research questions include the following: How long did customers take, on average, to complete their tax returns? What areas took the longest to complete? Was the tax preparation experience perceived as easy or difficult? To answer these questions, an online study was conducted.

An online study is a useful methodology to use when evaluating tax preparation because tax preparation can take hours and can occur across days, weeks, or months. Furthermore, tax preparation is most often a seasonal process where the forms are not available all year and tax documents often arrive piecemeal over a few weeks. Tax preparation involves sharing personal information and details about one's finances. Preparing one's taxes is often done in the comfort of one's home, at various times of day. For a process that is seasonal, it can be difficult to gather an adequate data sample.

This case study discusses the application of automated remote usability testing of an SSL Web application for do-it-yourself tax preparation.

9.5.1 Methodology

In this study, multiple online tax software applications were evaluated. Multiple recruiting firms recruited participants from across the United States via email invitations. A total of 268 participants completed the shopping portion of the study, while 134 participants completed both shopping and tax preparation portions of the study. Study participation required use of a computer with Internet access.

Participant compensation was $15 for the shopping portion of the study and $50 to $75 for the tax preparation portion of the study, depending on the complexity of the participant's taxes. The cost for the tax software was not covered; participants paid for the software on their own. This study required a time commitment of more than an hour for the majority of participants. For something as personal as tax preparation, a financially sensitive topic that involves the use of personally identifying information such as social security numbers, prediction and planning for incidence rates were essential to the success of the study.

The online tool Keynote was used. There are various online tools available, and the authors of the study do not endorse any particular tool. The online tool worked by tracking information about each screen the participant viewed, along with time spent on each screen. Participants were prompted at various predefined points during their tax preparation. When prompted, survey questions were presented, which the participant would respond to and then continue on with their main task of tax preparation. Once tax preparation was completed, the participant would click a button to indicate they had finished their task. An online tool was chosen because it tracks behavior (i.e., screens viewed/navigation path), along with the ability to present survey questions at predefined points during tax preparation.

Because some of the screens included in the study did not contain unique URLs, there was some difficulty distinguishing between screens viewed by each participant. As a result, it was necessary to perform a manual analysis of screen views for some screens. The additional time required to perform such analysis was factored into the study timeline.

Data captured included duration and number of times participants used the software before finishing their tax returns. This information was used to better understand how participants complete their tax returns while using software.

9.5.2 Results and discussion

This is the second year this study was conducted. The first-year pilot provided some key insights to help us identify areas of the experience to focus on to help meet a business priority for the next year.

We realized the time to complete taxes with Product A took much longer than Product B (the two comparable products) and Product C took much longer than Product D (the two comparable products)(see Table 9.8). This was related to slightly higher exit rates. Customers of Product A and Product C had also reported in the past that the software was thorough and complete and we

Table 9.8	Comparison of average task completion time for tax preparation in year 1 of the study.		
Average Time and Linger Rates			
	Average total time (hours)	**Average linger time/ page (seconds)**	***n***
Product A	2:14	63	42
Product B	1:34	37	40
Product C	3:46	80	38
Product D	2:58	72	23

believed that would be a more compelling reason for people to use Products A and C to prepare their taxes over other available choices.

Data gathered from the pilot (year 1) helped us draw the following conclusions.

> While people want to be confident that their taxes are accurate, not everyone likes to walk through every tax code (i.e., things that may not apply to them).
>
> Preparation of an accurate and complete tax return is important. It is equally important to do so as efficiently as possible, that is, in the least amount of time.

While Products A and C were easy to use, Products B and D were rated equally easy to use. This was an important learning as the brand and key positioning of Products A and C in the market include ease. Behavioral data helped us identify key areas of opportunity for Products A and C along with an understanding of areas of strength for Products B and D.

For instance, it was easy for people to shop for and select the right tax preparation product on the various product Web sites. By tracking people's product selection behavior—pages visited and information accessed along with their self-reported data—we were able to determine how Products A and C compared with Products B and D. In addition, exit rates from the sites of Product B and D and respective in-product tax preparation experiences were lower than Products A and C, even though Products A and C had higher volume. We were also able to identify key areas within the site and product that led to higher exit rates for Products A and C compared with Products B and D.

In year 2, we conducted the same study to gather data on the impact of changes made to the product based on learnings from year 1. Given the success of the pilot, the organization decided to broaden the scope of the study from four products to six products: the same four products from year 1 (Products A–D) plus additional Products E and F. Products A, B, and E were comparable, and Products C, D, and F were in the other category.

Data gathered from the year 2 study helped us draw the following conclusions (see Table 9.9). While completion times for Products A and C were faster than the other products, Products A and C were still perceived to take the same time as the other

Table 9.9	Comparison of average task completion time for tax preparation in year 2 of the study.		
Average Time and Linger Rates			
	Average total time	**Average linger time/page**	***n***
Product A	1:14	32	67
Product B	1:45	35	48
Product C	1:53	29	73
Product D	1:52	37	23
Product E	1:12	31	21
Product F	1:52	28	37

products. Because we had access to users' click streams for all six products, we were also able to identify the root cause of this perception. Even though users saw fewer screens in Products A and C, these products had loops that contributed to this perception. Products B, D, E, and F, however, followed a linear wizard-like path.

Products A and C also did not move the needle on ease. They may have improved the ease of use but so did the other products. We were also able to quickly do a deep dive into the experience of multiple users to further identify the areas where people found Products A and C not as easy to use as other products. Figure 9.12 represents how Products A and C compare on ease with other products during various sections of the product. We used this to further assess specific parts within each of the sections of the products to identify areas for improvement by understanding the behavior of users to identify what worked and what did not compared to other products on the market.

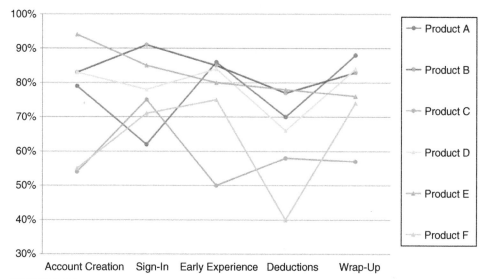

FIGURE 9.12
Comparison of ease of use over time for tax preparation in year 2 of the study.

These insights are important for tenured products such as Product A and C. It allows them to stay ahead of the competition.

9.5.3 Advantages and challenges

In terms of the study approach, there were quite a few advantages along with some challenges. Advantages of using this online approach include the following.

- It allows us to observe the users' real experience. People prepare their taxes in the privacy of their homes, the way they would were they not participating in this study. We do not capture any personal identification data, which helps alleviate privacy concerns.
- Users prepare their taxes over as many sessions as they normally would. While it is possible to do so when we invite them to the lab, it is not practical or cost-effective.
- We are able to observe a larger sample size than we would in a lab study with a good geographical spread that better represents the market segments for each brand.
- It is extremely cost-effective. It costs a third of a lab study with the same number of participants.

Some of the challenges with this approach include the following.

- We rely on the participants for a good faith effort to prepare their taxes with their real data for that year and file with the IRS. To ensure validity of data, we do go through our log files to eliminate any users that do not seem to have used the tax software to prepare their tax return. Given the tax code, it is not easy for people to make up numbers and produce a legitimate tax return.
- It is hard to recruit people, as taxes contain sensitive personal information. Even though we do not capture any personal information, some people are not comfortable participating in the study.
- Tax software is a seasonal product and we have a small window of opportunity to conduct research. There is also the aspect of time, where one segment of our users uses the product early in tax season and the other segment tends to use it toward the latter half of the tax season. We have to be very efficient in planning and executing our research.

In reflecting upon both advantages and challenges of the online study approach we utilized, the following can be noted.

- This approach helps us capture users' clickstream data, that is, the path they follow in the tax software. This applies to the use of our product and competitor's products and Web sites.
- Web analytics methods such as the automatic logging of user behavior online (beaconing) allow us to capture metrics, such as screens viewed, completion times, and linger rates within our own product. The online study approach described here allows us to expand our gathering of data for the same metrics on our competitors as well.

9.5.4 Conclusions

The online study findings were well received. Having a larger sample size than qualitative research provides was a factor. In addition, having a quantitative comparison across online applications at various points of the tax preparation experience was both insightful and useful and was a nice complement to qualitative research conducted previously. Additional studies were conducted to complement this study. Lab studies were conducted to gather richer observational data. Data were then triangulated across methods (quantitative, qualitative).

The study findings were used in a variety of ways. First, the findings were used as a guide to planning the product for next year. Second, the study findings informed strategy development. Third, the findings were used as a benchmark. Going forward, future learnings can be compared against the findings presented in this study (e.g., benchmarking).

The difficulties of finding sufficient participants for each participant profile and keeping the duration of the study and number of follow-up questions reasonable were challenges. Time was important, and it was not possible to run the study for more than a few months due to limitations in cost and the duration of the tax season.

Overall, utilizing an online study methodology makes sense for tax preparation, which can be a lengthy and personal task where getting the best possible tax refund is important. It is generally easier to encourage participation in a study when participants can engage on their own time, in their own way, using their own computers, for this once-a-year task that is required of the population.

Biographies

- Melanie Baran is a human factors engineer at Intuit where she conducts generative and evaluative design research for online financial services and software. Her prior work includes research on the impact of interruptions on primary–secondary task performance, the design of mobile interfaces for ordering medical tests, and the use of voice-over Internet protocol (VoIP) in a Web casting application for e-learning. Melanie's research interests include emotional design, eye tracking, and curiosity about the future of ubiquitous computing.
- Kavita Appachu is a human factors engineer at Intuit where she conducts generative and evaluative research for financial services and software. Her past experience includes working at AOL where she was involved with conducting research on AOL products, including Netscape and AIM. She also worked at Qwest Communications researching and developing B2B applications and e-commerce sites. Kavita's research interests include interfaces for resource discovery and information retrieval, impact of culture on cognition, and semantic networks and knowledge representation.
- Alex Genov is responsible for customer research and usability of TurboTax's products and services. He received his Ph.D. in experimental social psychology from Clark University. Areas of research include emotions,

individual differences, nonverbal measures of emotion, and usability. During his academic career, Alex developed and taught courses in research methods, statistics, and psychology.

9.6 ONLINE USABILITY TESTING: FAMILYSEARCH. ORG

Tyson Stokes, FamilySearch.org

This case study is an evaluation of a new registration flow for FamilySearch.org. FamilySearch.org is a suite of family history Web sites provided by the Church of Jesus Christ of Latter-Day Saints. This suite of Web sites provides access to millions of records such as birth, death, and census; the ability to search a database of hundreds of millions of individuals; access to research guidance to help locate ancestors; and connection to the largest genealogical library in the world.

FamilySearch.org is currently in the process of bringing the suite of Web sites together into a unified experience. In order to create a single user experience it will be necessary to create a registration process suitable for all Web sites. Initially the registration flow was a step-by-step flow. More feedback was needed to determine the feasibility of the step-by-step flow for a broader audience. In the future we hope to attract a broader demographic audience from around the world. A second design of a single page flow was developed to try and reduce the time it took to register. An A/B test was set up to compare the two design options.

This case study illustrates the methods used, such as who was tested, how they were recruited, tools used, how the design was measured, and how data were collected. The case study looks at data itself and examines the patterns identified. Finally, the case study talks about how the results were presented to stakeholders and what was done to help integrate findings into new design changes.

9.6.1 Study goals

The main goal of the study was to find the best design option for registering. To accomplish this goal, we compared two different designs to determine which option was faster, had the highest satisfaction, and was the most preferred by the audience. Satisfaction addressed how the individual feels, and preference will talk to their behavior. Each option represented a different approach to registration, as shown in Figure 9.13. The goals were operationalized into several smaller test goals. The first test goal was to determine the time on task that establishes the faster option. The second test goal was to measure satisfaction using the System Usability Scale (SUS) to help establish perceived easiness and user approval. Finally, we were interested in learning registration preferences by asking a set of questions at the end of the test.

9.6.2 Why online usability testing?

This test was a good candidate for unmoderated online usability testing for several reasons. (1) Registration uses a linear flow. There is only one way through the registration process. The complexity of the interaction is reduced greatly, which decreases the likelihood of a participant needing assistance during the evaluation. (2) Registration is a private activity where users enter sensitive user name and password information; unmoderated online usability testing allows the participants to be on their own computers and in their own environments. (3) Family Search has a broad demographic and geographic representation of users. This broad representation ensures a better sampling of a worldwide audience. (4) Online testing is a cost-effective testing approach to reach a broad demographic and geographic audience, saving both time and money.

9.6.3 Methodology

Recruiting

FamilySearch.org is a nonprofit organization that has a long history of involvement in family history. This involvement has resulted in a network of thousands of volunteer family history consultants around the world. The recruiting process consisted of sending a message in a biweekly newsletter sent to all the consultants asking them to post an attached flyer (shown in Figure 9.14) in family history centers in their area. There are more than 4500 family history centers

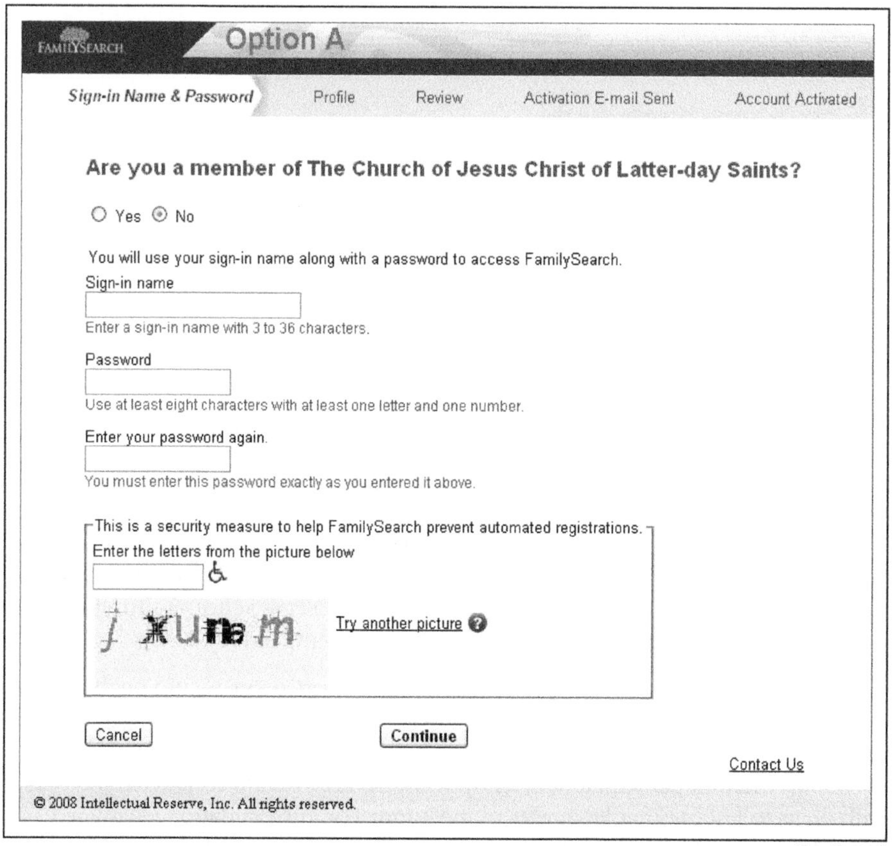

FIGURE 9.13
FamilySearch registration design Options A (step by step) and B (single page).

(Continued)

**FIGURE
9.13—CONT'D**

worldwide. Centers are designed to help individuals identify their ancestors through research help from the staff, provide training classes, and offer referrals to other libraries or archives. Most centers are located in meetinghouses of the Church of Jesus Christ of Latter-Day Saints. Anyone is welcome to visit the centers and use their resources. The flyer included a link sending individuals to a Web page that walks individuals through a screening survey.

Because many of the individuals likely to sign up to participate would be those with high levels of interest and family history experience, we made a special plea in the message for the family history consultants to reach out to less experienced individuals to encourage them to participate. Currently, most evaluations are conducted in English with plans to test in other languages in the future. For this evaluation we invited 148 individuals and 24 completed the evaluation as illustrated in Table 9.11.

Request for Evaluators of the New FamilySearch.org Web Site

The Church of Jesus Christ of Latter-day Saints is developing a new version of the FamilySearch.org website. This new website will help individuals identify ancestors, link them to families, and will help members perform temple ordinances.

Can you volunteer an hour of time to help evaluate this new website? Do you know someone else who might be interested? We need feedback to make the final website as easy and enjoyable to use as possible. **We are especially interested in feedback from individuals who are new to family history.**

Anyone over age 18 interested in participating in this evaluation should go to the following internet address to sign-up:

http://labs.familysearch.org/temple/static/signup.htm (tear away address below to take with you)

Thank you for your interest and enthusiasm. We greatly value your time and opinion.

Sincerely,
The FamilySearch User Experience Evaluation Team
Family History Department
The Church of Jesus Christ of Latter-day Saints

FAMILYSEARCH.

(Cut along dashed lines and tear away internet address for your convenience)

http://labs.familysearch.org/temple/static/signup.htm

FIGURE 9.14
Participant recruiting request flyer.

Compensation

One of the advantages of being a nonprofit organization—producing a Web site that provides free access to records and databases of individuals—is that people are willing to participate in our evaluations for free. Individuals participate for the chance of helping us improve FamilySearch and are eager to have an early look at our designs.

Study mechanics

After selecting individuals from the user pool by their different levels of family history and computer experience, email messages were sent with instructions and a link to the evaluation. Based on previous response rates, shown in Table 9.10, we sent out varying amounts of invitations to each of the three categories of family history experience: high, medium, and low as illustrated in Table 9.11. This response rate prediction method is not always accurate, as only 24 individuals of the expected 42 participated in the study. Keeping a record of the response rate of each study has been very helpful in creating an accurate response expectation.

Table 9.10	Rate of return calculation for unmoderated usability tests of individuals with high family history experience.		
Evaluation date	Invited	Completed	% Complete
07.20.07	30	14	47
08.10.07	11	5	45
08.31.07	8	6	75
11.14.07	15	13	87
12.03.07	22	8	36
01.21.08	812	318	39
02.20.09	64	20	31
03.30.09	125	37	30
07.20.07	30	14	47

Table 9.11	Invited versus completed based on family history experience.			
	High family history experience (1:2.5)	Medium family history experience (1:3)	Low family history experience (1:5)	Totals
Number of invitations sent out	35	42	71	148
Number of users expected to complete the evaluation	14	14	14	42
Number of users who completed the evaluation	8	16	0	24

The largest numbers of invitations were sent to those with lower family history experience, as this demographic has shown the least amount of interest in the past. They are less likely to participate than those with more experience. Data were collected, and the information was processed the day after the deadline date that was given.

Tools

A variety of tools were used for our test. Tools included an online survey, image and HTML editing software, server hosting for prototypes, remote video capture of user's screens, and a spreadsheet for data organization. These tools were a combination of both commercial and customized in-house resources.

Limitations

This study was restricted by the type of data our tools were able to collect. Because many of the tools used in the study came with a small price, the tools also came with limited flexibility in the type of data that could be collected.

We faced a limitation from our in-house tool that facilitated the survey questions. The tool had no capability to ask open-ended or multiple-select questions. All the questions had to be asked in the form of a single select, multiple choice. General comments and thoughts were not captured. In our experience, it helped to ask open-ended questions during unmoderated online usability testing to better understand context and feelings.

9.6.4 Metrics and data

As the goals were to determine registration speed, measure satisfaction, and learn individual preferences, three measurements were administered. We captured time on task to establish speed, the satisfaction metric was captured using the System Usability Scale, and individual preferences were measured by asking survey questions at the end of the evaluation. Time on task and SUS results are shown in Table 9.12, and three of five of the preference questions are shown in Tables 9.13, 9.14, and 9.15, respectively. We broke out the responses by high and low computer experience to illustrate that there was a different perspective of the registration flow based on levels of computer experience.

Table 9.12   Time on task and satisfaction scores.

	Step by step (Option A)	Single page (Option B)
Average time to complete registration:	4 min 19 sec	2 min 37 sec
SUS score	88	87

Table 9.13   QUESTION: Which of the two options did you find easiest?

	Average %	High computer experience %	Low computer experience %
Step by step (Option A)	12.5	0	0
Single page (Option B)	37.5	**60**	0
Either option, both are the same	**50**	40	**100**
None of the above	0	0	0

Table 9.14   QUESTION: Which of the two options did you find to be the fastest?

	Average %	High computer experience %	Low computer experience %
Step by step (Option A)	16.7	20	20
Single page (Option B)	**45.8**	**80**	0
Either option, both are the same	37.5	0	**80**
None of the above	0	0	0

Table 9.15	QUESTION: If you had to choose one option over the other, which one would you select?		
	Average %	**High computer experience %**	**Low computer experience %**
Step by step (Option A)	25	20	40
Single page (Option B)	**46**	**80**	0
Either option, both are the same	29	0	**60**
None of the above	0	0	0

9.6.5 Results and discussion

Data indicate that general satisfaction (the SUS score) was one point higher for the step-by-step option. This single point difference is not a statistically significant difference. When asked to choose a preferred option, the majority on average selected the single page option. Even though the step-by-step option took twice as long to complete as the single page option, the step by step had a slightly higher satisfaction rating. In the three questions shown in Tables 9.12, 9.13, and 9.14, the majority of the audience with high computer experience selected the single page option. The majority of those with low computer experience selected "Either option, both are the same." Individuals with lower computer experience either find both options equally acceptable or they do not discern a difference.

9.6.6 Data and user experience

It is interesting to note that even though the SUS scores were nearly identical for both options, preference for the single page option, when averaged across all levels of computer experience, was nearly 2 to 1. The differences between satisfaction and preference are not clear in this case and would likely be better understood in a moderated usability test. In our experience, unmoderated online usability testing does not do a very good job of telling us the mood and perception of the participant. The inherent factors of an unmoderated online usability test, such as the physical space the individual is in, or external factors, such as sounds or visual distractions, can influence the behavior of the user at the time of the test. When moderating a test face to face, we have a better sense of the participant's mood and can probe to determine if the product itself is affecting the user or if it is something unrelated.

9.6.7 Getting results heard and integrated

Because our organization has moved to agile development cycles, we have created a page on our intranet Web site where we can post the findings quickly. The agile development model encourages reducing written reports and replacing it with more verbal dialog to communicate changes. We use intranet postings as a way to reduce our reporting footprint. We also have a list of all the key stakeholders in the organization to whom we send an email highlighting the study findings. The email shows a summary of the findings from the evaluation, as well as a link to the intranet Web site showing the complete results. The summary email includes a thumbs up/thumbs down chart indicating success or failure of each individual user experience testing goal; a screenshot of the main page tested; quotes from users (if captured); highlights of designs that are working well; highlights of issues found; and an outline of the demographics of those tested. We have received feedback that the summary email provides valuable levels of feedback without overwhelming the reader.

9.6.8 Conclusions

When presenting usability findings, we always hope for the best, but there is never a guarantee that the information will cause a change for the better. The findings from this study were presented, and two key factors helped the product manager make a design decision. The first factor is that nearly twice as many people on average chose the single page option over the step by step as their preferred option. The second factor is that the single page option was nearly twice as fast to complete as the step by step. These factors helped them select the single page option to implement in the registration process. These results were shared with senior level management as a way to show progress and provide data to support the decisions made.

9.6.9 Lessons learned

The most valuable lesson learned from this study was that our unmoderated online usability test left us with some unanswered questions about differences in satisfaction and preferences. We would have been benefited by supplementing the study with a moderated usability test. It would have been valuable to validate what was found, and it would have helped us feel more confident that the unmoderated study did not affect the user in any unintended way. Another lesson learned was to find another way to provide open-ended questions for participant feedback. Even a single question would have provided broader feedback for any unusual edge cases, as well as added depth to the single select survey responses.

Biography

- Tyson Stokes conducts user research at FamilySearch.org. He collaborates with design and development teams to improve the user experience. Tyson holds a bachelor's degree in psychology from the University of Utah and a master's degree in human factors and applied cognition from George Mason University.

9.7 USING ONLINE USABILITY TESTING EARLY IN APPLICATION DEVELOPMENT: BUILDING USABILITY IN FROM THE START

Heather Fox, Phena Partners

In 2001, Phena Partners LLC was engaged by the DuPont Company's Information Security organization to lead the redesign efforts of their E-Pass Administrative Application, an enterprise-wide, two-factor authentication/identity management system that was proving to be expensive and difficult to both use and maintain. Working with the client, we interviewed and surveyed a set of global stakeholders (information security officers, IT vendors, IT managers, and a representative set of application end users) and held global virtual sessions to elicit future state requirements. With a comprehensive set of business and user requirements in hand, we developed a detailed technical specification that documented key business processes, application functions/features, use cases, and the required system architecture. We held global workshops to validate the specifications, review personas, review process maps, and application wire frames.

After client signoff on the specifications, we developed an online prototype of the future-state system based on the approved wire frames and process maps, complete with a realistic data set and a brand-compliant user interface. The following case study focuses on the online usability test we performed on the E-Pass prototype in December 2002.

9.7.1 Project background

Several issues converged to compel Phena's client to redesign its E-Pass application.

- The application's code was difficult and costly to maintain.
- End users of the application were not able to perform basic support tasks without calling the help desk or their application sponsor, who vouched for that user's ability to access the client's networks and protected applications via the authentication application.
- The application's user interface was application/function-centric; users were able to select functions that they did not have the privileges needed to use. Users could start a transaction and would find only at the end of the transaction that it was a task they could not perform.

The goals of the redesign effort were to:

- Improve customer satisfaction
  - Address ease-of-use issues—simplify tasks and provide a user-centered experience
  - Support efficient and effective business processes
- Reduce the cost of support of the application
  - Enable self-service support where appropriate, secure, and safe
  - Increase the efficiency of traditional support services (help desk or the "sponsor" user type)
- Improve the application's maintainability
  - Employ generic models
  - Fully document the application code
  - Practice good partitioning and reuse of coding modules

Prior to the start of the redesign project, the client commissioned a customer satisfaction survey; key users of the application identified several new functions they'd like to see in the application, along with requests for improved user interface ease of use, additional context-sensitive online help at both the page and the field level, and, in general, more troubleshooting information that would

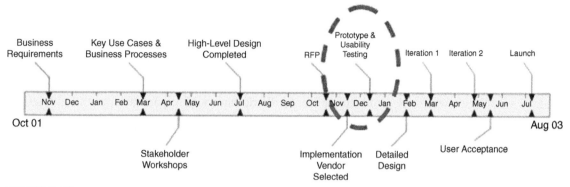

FIGURE 9.15
Project timeline.

help users cope with the issues they could perhaps solve themselves. Customer satisfaction survey data were key input into the definition phase of the project, which spanned November 2001 through December 2002.

Application-detailed design was completed in February 2003, and the application was ready for rollout at the end of 2003, but due to business conditions was rolled out the following March.

This case study focuses on the part of the project timeline highlighted in Figure 9.15.

9.7.2 Creating the usability study environment

To test the redesigned application prior to the start of the development cycle, we developed a working prototype of the application that presented the new business processes and user tasks as structured, consistently-designed transactions that included:

- transaction summary pages
- confirmation steps before submitting final changes
- explicit summary screens confirming the completion of a transaction

Within the prototype we signaled where a user could turn for help, other than to one's sponsor, by providing context-sensitive help at the page and field level when appropriate. All application training materials were embedded into the home page, accessible to the user without their logging into the application.

We created a testing environment that served to engage the sponsor user community in new application training; a key goal of the usability study was to get our first read on how "ready" sponsors would be to embrace redesigned business processes and tasks, both for themselves and for the users they supported. Data on how effectively and efficiently they performed the testing tasks, along with their anecdotal comments about the testing tasks and their satisfaction ratings of the tasks and the system in general, would give us insight into user readiness for the redesigned application and its rollout.

From both a cost perspective and a testing cohort perspective, online usability testing, as opposed to lab, field, or paper prototype testing, seemed to be our best choice to validate the definition and design phases of the software development life cycle. Using an online tool allowed us to gather a global group of users and streamlined our data gathering efforts. Because we had a limited amount of time (1 month) prior to completion of the application's detailed design document in which we could gather user feedback that could impact the application's design, our choice of tool needed to focus on how we could get good data gathered and organized quickly to analyze the prototype's effectiveness.

Taking the application to the field using a third-party online/remote usability tool also signaled a willingness to gather feedback in a nonbias or less-biased way, as opposed to having the firm designing the application (Phena) administer the usability test. We were able to step away from administration of the testing process via the use of an online usability tool.

9.7.3 Study goals

The usability study of the prototype application focused on the following high-level goals.

1. Confirm that new business processes and user tasks could be understood and navigated by users.
2. Identify the places in which users get "stuck."
3. Gather insight into how to roll out the redesigned application to its key user base.
4. Identify where it was clear that requirements were in place and design choices were sound, but ease of use still suffered (i.e., requirements for training intervention and/or readiness coaching).
5. Confirm that we had elicited all essential requirements for authentication administration.

The redesigned application radically changed how end users and sponsors use the application, and the way sponsors perform their authentication administration tasks was changed dramatically. Key changes we wanted the usability study to expose to the sponsors included:

- How a sponsor finds a user he/she sponsors within the system
- How end users could now perform limited self-service support tasks themselves, without relying on any help/support from the sponsor
- How sponsors were related to one another, or not, within the system and how they could use new functionality to help one another support their users

9.7.4 Methodology

Using Vividence's eXpress scripting/site evaluation tool (now part of the Keynote suite of Internet test and measurement tools), we created a 30-minute evaluation of the key transactions. Our test script featured a structured tour of the system, starting with a review of the new home page, progressing to logging into the application, and then completing a series of tasks that sponsors perform routinely.

The study was set up to gather quantitative performance data on how efficiently, consistently, and correctly users could complete the transactions in question, along with a qualitative satisfaction rating for performing the transactions and questions on changes or improvements users would suggest.

The study had 15 sections, each corresponding to the exploration of a page, feature, or task; one section was reserved for demographics. In each section the test participant was asked to perform a task, with a follow-on series of questions about performing the task that measured task understanding and satisfaction. For some tasks, test participants were probed for additional detail about performing the task successfully or were asked for opinions on what might be missing or misrepresented.

If a test participant gave up on a task, he/she was asked to explain why. If a test participant left a section and its questions idle for more than 5 minutes, the test protocol presented an intercept question to confirm that the test participant was still working the test and gave them an option to give up on the task. This type of question should have also probed for whether the test participant was interrupted; however, we did not ask, thus "give up" data did not differentiate between being stymied versus being interrupted.

We selected the sponsor user type as the focus of our prototype usability study, as this user performs 90% of the application tasks on at least a weekly basis. The customer support and administrative user populations were limited (50 or less users for each group) and none of these users used the system as often and as intensely as the sponsor user type. We took the global user database list of the sponsor users and sent a recruiting email to the 2000 sponsors across the globe, asking for 200 testers. Within 2 days after requesting participants, we had the 200-person cohort, with the following geographies covered (see Figure 9.16).

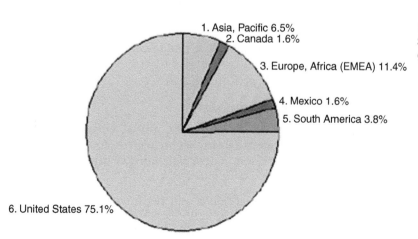

1. Asia, Pacific 6.5%
2. Canada 1.6%
3. Europe, Africa (EMEA) 11.4%
4. Mexico 1.6%
5. South America 3.8%
6. United States 75.1%

FIGURE 9.16
Study participant geographies.

We ran the test over an 8-day period (December 10–18, 2002); 185 testers completed the study during the time period.

There was no intent to compensate users for participating in the study, as we were testing an internal application used by employees. But the Vividence platform had a gift certificate feature built in to its panel management process. The idea that we could "gift" test participants created quite a stir within the client organization—many participants were leery about accepting a "gift" for what they perceived to be doing their job. We had to edit our recruiting email message to confirm that a "gift certificate" was offered for participation and that it was deemed okay by management to accept the gift. The recruitment process for the test itself seemed to demonstrate the effectiveness of the client's business ethics program!

Custom email invitations were created and sent to the list of 200 sponsors accepted from the recruitment process. The invitations contained a link to a page on the Vividence Web site where study participants could download the "Vividence Connector" and begin the E-Pass site evaluation. Testers were asked to complete the evaluation from their office computers.

The Vividence Connector is a special toolbar that works with Internet Explorer and guides participants through the evaluation process. As participants navigate the site and complete the tasks asked of them, the Connector tracks each page viewed during their visit and records the time spent on each page, navigation path, keystrokes, and a screenshot of each page. The Connector also collects testers' open feedback and responses to questions. All of the information collected was aggregated within the Vividence eXpress report.

Key data points

- Time spent performing task: target was 2 minutes or less in the test environment (which included reading the instructions and then performing the task)
- Satisfaction rate for individual task performance and for newly designed top level and landing screens (1–5 Likert scale used; answers of 4 and 5 were positive and aggregated to confirm satisfaction, agreement, and/or understanding of task)
- Polling about what was noticed in the new screen designed, what was liked and what was disliked, and what could be improved
- Tasks abandoned
- Mistakes made while performing tasks

9.7.5 Results and discussion

Overall, study results showed that the majority of sponsors in the test cohort could successfully navigate the tasks they were given and that the "newness" of the redesigned application was not overwhelming or frustrating, except in a few areas (see Table 9.16).

Study data showed that 10 of 12 tasks were performed at an 80% or greater success rate and that 84% of the study cohort was either satisfied or very satisfied with the redesigned application (see Figure 9.17).

| Table 9.16 | Study results summary. | | | | |

Task	Successful completion	Failure to complete	Gave up on task	Function/ task is useful	Key issues noted
Home page overview	84%	16%		84%	Prior system's home page was a log-in screen
Home page training topics	69%	31%		Not asked	Questions focused on whether sponsors provided training or not, as there wasn't a need to train users in the prior system
Home page trouble-shooting and help	91%	9%		91%	
Logging in	88%	9%	3%	85%	Location of the "Log In" link was problematic
Start page— waiting tasks	50%	48%	2%	87%	Concept of a "start page" was unexpected in addition to being new
Start page— process a request	91%		9%	88%	
Start page— replace an expiring token	95%		5%	99%	
Register a new user	89%		11%	64%	Prior system had users registering themselves via an email template
Navigate the "Start" page	82%	18%			
Navigate the "Manage User" page	80%	16%	4%	72%	Working with sponsored users via a profile was new and unfamiliar to sponsors
Start page— find a user's profile	80%	8%	12%	77%	
Revalidate a user	96%		4%	90%	

Question #109
Overall, how would you rate your satisfaction with the re-designed E-Pass application based on what you've seen today?
Please enter a number from 1 to 5 where:
1 = Very unsatisfied
2 = Unsatisfied
3 = Neutral
4 = Satisfied
5 = Very satisfied

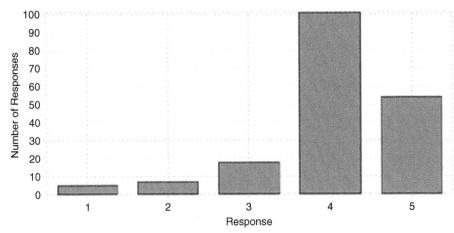

FIGURE 9.17
Satisfaction with the redesigned application.

The hot spots where satisfaction and/or successful completion were under 80% were:

- Training topics
- Start page: waiting tasks
- Register new user

All of these areas were new to study users and were not a part of the current application. The only task with high satisfaction and successful completion that nonetheless had a significant number of negative comments was the Log-in feature.

Eighty-one percent of the test cohort indicated they were not frustrated with the redesigned application. For the minority of sponsors who did find some of the tasks frustrating, Figure 9.18 shows tasks for which the sponsors wanted to give up on their completion.

All tasks completed successfully could be performed well under 2 minutes in the test environment. Two minutes per page can seem like an eternity today, but at the time of this test (December 2002), only 80% of our users were on the corporate network; network speeds outside the United States were slower overall, and we factored in a delay for users to work with the Vividence Connector, which is a browser overlay, sitting on top of the application screens, providing the test protocol and gathering feedback.

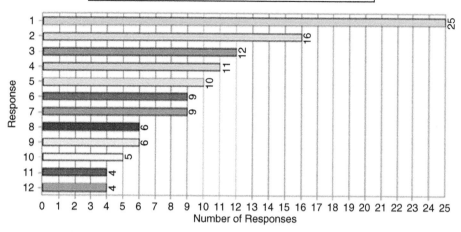

Tip: This question was triggered conditionally for some panelists. The number of answers may not equal the number of participants in the evaluation.

FIGURE 9.18
Frustrated users and the tasks on which they wanted to "Give Up."

Response	#	%
1 Registering a new user: Jose Manuel Fernandez	25	52.1
2 Revalidating Robert Hays' E-Pass	16	33.3
3 Re-assigning an E-Pass request from Barton Biggs to Jan Hooks	12	25.0
4 Figuring out how to help a user with a problem	11	22.9
5 Identifying waiting tasks on the Start page	10	20.8
6 Identifying the reports available on the Start page	9	18.8
7 Requesting a replacement for your expiring token	9	18.8
8 Reviewing the information pages: "What is E-Pass?", "Training" and "Job Aids"	6	12.5
9 Reviewing the Troubleshooting page and self-service operations	6	12.5
10 Reviewing the home page	5	10.4
11 Logging in	4	8.3
12 No Answer Given	4	8.3
Total number of respondents	48	100.0
Not Asked	137	n/a

Although 88% of the test cohort logged into the system successfully, the pointed comments received on improving the log-in process were noted and acted upon. Testers noted that the log-in function was practically invisible and that most had to really scour the page to find it.

Using an online usability testing tool gave us great insight into task performance, along with insight into significant minority cohort discomfort with tasks and features that otherwise rated high for ease of use and overall satisfaction. Data showed us what worked with the design and what aspects of the design needed to be tweaked.

9.7.6 Conclusions

Data did not indicate that any requirements or needed functionality was missing. We were confident based on the test results that the application as designed would be accepted as improved and appreciated as easy to use by the majority of users.

Test data–recommended design changes were mocked up and demonstrated with the client and key stakeholders for final review for inclusion in the detailed design document. Approved changes were updated in the requirements, prototype, and functional specification artifacts. Finally, the detailed usability findings were shared with the application development team, along with a prototype to fully ground the team in user experience expectations/needs.

Overall, key stakeholders and the client appreciated the study experience and its findings; the study confirmed the client could proceed with application development without the concern that requirements or features were missing or that the functionality as designed would not be used easily. Usability testing gained a lot of advocates in the client organization as a result of this project. The sponsor user community appreciated the involvement in front-end application design and in usability testing; high levels of sponsor participation in user acceptance testing and change management activities prior to rollout were noted.

The engagement's focus on usability and flexible/maintainable design was well worth the upfront investment. When the application went into production in March 2004, the rollout was a nonevent. Change management activities prior to rollout prepared users for the new application and change in business processes via application "tours" and cheat sheets; problems encountered while using the application were usually answerable by the online help feature. The company was able to reduce help desk call volume by 50% and the annual enhancement budget for the application was reduced by 75%.

9.7.7 Study limitations and lessons learned

The Vividence remote online testing process didn't allow for observation of actual behavior via video or keystroke logging. One of the key limitations noted was lack of detail about interruptions; we had no idea how many task "give ups" were pauses or abandonments. In the future, we'd suggest allowing a tester to specifically click a "pause" button that signals the evaluation is on hold while the tester deals with the interruption at hand.

If the design being tested was less developed and the test was being used to gather further user requirements, we would suggest using tools that include video and keystroke capture for more detailed contextual data gathering needs.

Overall, we were pleased with the Vividence tool—scripting was easy and the test environment for users was both easy for us to construct and easy for users to navigate, although it was clear in the comment logs that most of our study cohort had never participated in an online, remote usability test. The key lesson learned is that online usability helped us reach a large, global testing cohort in a limited time period and provided close-to-immediate feedback on the application's ease of use due to the testing tool's automated data gathering and analysis features.

Biography

- Heather Fox has over 20 years of computer-mediated communications experience and has held senior positions with Phena, DuPont Pharma, IBM, and the DuPont Company. She has an MSOD from the University of Pennsylvania and a BS in Biomedical Science and English from Grand Valley State University, where she was recently named a Distinguished Alumna in Residence.

CHAPTER 10

Ten Keys to Success

This chapter offers 10 keys for success when carrying out an online usability study. These keys can help you get the most out of the study, save money and time, and even enhance the reputations of you and your team. These keys are not set in stone for every researcher or for every study. They are dependent on the researcher and the situation. Furthermore, there are many other important aspects to consider that we have not included in this chapter. It is hoped that you simply use this chapter as a guideline when embarking on an online usability study.

10.1 CHOOSE THE RIGHT TOOL

In golf, choosing the right club for any particular stroke has a major impact on the outcome. Online usability testing is no different. The golf club in this case is the Web application you will use to design and administer the study. The application you choose will have a significant impact on whether your goals are met within your time frame and budget. When making a decision about which Web application to use, you will need to answer the following three important questions.

What is your budget?

The cost of running an online usability test can vary substantially. Some vendors require payment on a per-complete or per-study basis, whereas other vendors provide unlimited use after purchasing a license or subscription. It is important to consider how many online studies you will (realistically) run over the next 12 months, what type of data you need, whether there are any limitations with respect to the number of studies, recruiting costs, and other incidental costs. Chapter 7 reviews many of the issues to consider when choosing a vendor solution and provides details on four representative vendors.

What is your goal?

Choose your tool after you have set your goals. If you simply want to benchmark task success and task time on a core set of tasks against the competition or you want to better understand abandonment in an ecommerce transaction, you will need to consider different vendor solutions. In making this decision, it's helpful to think about what type of Web site issues you want to solve. You can use an out-of-the-box solution, such as Loop11, WebEffective, RelevantView, or UserZoom (see Chapter 7). These solutions will give you tremendous flexibility in how you design the study, and will also give you access to a wide range of data, most notably clickstream data. Alternatively, if you have very simple needs, perhaps you should consider building your own online study using a standard survey tool (see Chapter 8).

How much support do you need?

If you already have experience in setting up online surveys or if you have a very simple study, you may need less assistance. This might be your first foray into online usability or you simply don't have the time. Regardless, you need to determine your own role relative to the tool you chose. Luckily, the options run the gambit, from having a vendor design and carry out the study with your guidance to doing it all yourself. Obviously, your budget will also play a key role in this decision. Chapter 2 discusses some of the issues you will need to consider when deciding how much support you need.

10.2 THINK OUTSIDE OF THE (WEB) BOX

Most researchers think of online usability testing occurring with Web sites, particularly Web sites that are live or in production. Likewise, most vendor solutions are geared toward evaluating Web sites, with an emphasis on collecting clickstream and other behavioral data about the user's experience. However, this does not have to be the case. Although most of our discussion throughout this book has centered on Web sites, we argue that online usability testing can and should go beyond the Web. For example, online usability testing could easily be used to evaluate products such as mobile devices, desktop software, video games, consumer electronics, and voice response systems.

The basic premise of an online usability test using something other than a Web site involves the participant switching between the study (a Web browser) and the product they are interacting with. For example, a participant is given a task via a Web survey, they perform a series of actions with the product, and, once completed, they go back to the survey, answering a series of questions. Depending on how the survey is implemented, you can capture task success, task time, ease and confidence ratings, satisfaction, and any other self-reported metric.

Online usability tests are often far less expensive than testing Web sites in a laboratory setting. You can easily use a standard survey tool to capture most data you would be interested in. Of course, you can't collect data about actual use, but with a thoughtful set of questions, you can infer behavior quite well. You can also run a follow-up lab study to gain a better sense of actual behavior with the product. Or if you wanted to get a little fancy, and spend a little more, you could send webcams to some of the participants and record their interactions via an application such as TechSmith's UserVue or WebEx.

10.3 TEST EARLY IN THE DESIGN PHASE

We can't stress enough the importance of running online usability studies early in the design phase. Some researchers only think of online usability testing as something that should be done as part of a summative research plan, following completion of the final design. This simply is not the case. If you limit online usability testing to the end of the design phase, you're missing one of the unique strengths of this approach.

You're not just limited to testing live or fully functional Web sites. Testing partially functional prototypes or even screenshots is not only possible, but also quite easy to do. Look at the case studies (Chapter 9) for some inspiration. A participant only needs to look at a wire frame design or even a concept of a design to get a good idea of how it might work. They don't even need to interact with it. In fact, we have found that very early prototypes, in black and white, using a sketch-style font, are one of the most effective ways to communicate to the participant that the design is still very preliminary. In fact, many basic Web applications used for surveys allow you to display an image as part of the questions. Some of the tools, such as Chalkmark, also collect where on a screenshot users click, which is especially suitable for wire frames and other low-fidelity design images.

Online usability testing may also be used as part of an iterative design process. Online usability tests can be used to identify problematic tasks and pages, test look and feel aspects of the design, examine different navigation schemes, identify confusing content or terminology, and nearly any other design decision that needs to be made prior to development. In fact, sometimes it is faster and less expensive than running a 10-person lab study for each set of design questions. We have routinely run online tests that take no more than a day from start to finish. If this is a direction in which your organization would like to head, it is imperative that you have ready access to an online study tool (licensed or built in-house) and a large user base (company employees, customer lists, or panels).

10.4 COMPARE ALTERNATIVES

One of the strengths of online testing is being able to compare design alternatives. Comparing different conceptual designs is a valuable way to provide focused direction during the design process. Whatever the motivation, comparing designs is a critical part of online usability testing. Metrics, when analyzed in isolation, never provide as much meaning as when compared against one another. For example, knowing that 70% of users complete a task successfully is not as meaningful as knowing that design A has a 10% higher task success rate than design B. In the end, it is all relative.

One of the most important aspects of comparing design alternatives is to make sure that the differences are meaningful. A meaningful difference is not decided arbitrarily at the last minute before the study launches, but is based on some sort of discussion or even debate about the alternatives, with pros and cons associated with each alternative. Design alternatives could also be derived based on a set of design guidelines or even cognitive theory. Meaningful distinctions might include different visual treatments, content, or navigation structures.

We recommend keeping a broad perspective on alternatives at first and then starting to narrow down the alternatives as more data are collected. Not considering different design solutions, and simply iterating on an initial design, will probably lead to perfecting a suboptimal design. One of the problems many organizations face is committing to a design too early (Buxton, 2008). Start with at least three design alternatives, and ideally up to five or even more. Make adjustments and narrow down the list of alternatives over time. Make sure you are including as many metrics as possible so that you can tap into different aspects of the user experience. We cannot emphasize a broad perspective enough.

One of the challenges when comparing design alternatives is to understand why one design wins out over another design. The best way to do this is to play the role of an experimental psychologist by controlling as many variables as possible, while only manipulating a small number of variables. For example, if you're comparing three designs, everything might be exactly the same, except for the navigation structure. Alternatively, even a more subtle distinction may be three designs that are identical with the exception of the visual treatment of a "get started" button. In any experiment, the goal is to control the variables as much as possible so that whatever difference is observed in data can only be attributed to the variables that were manipulated in the design. In some cases, you may not be able to control all the variables, or even want to. Some designs are so different than one another that it just isn't practical to identify all the variables that may influence the results. In such cases, it is less important to understand the precise reason why one design wins out than it is to identify the best design and make decisions accordingly.

10.5 CONSIDER THE ENTIRE USER EXPERIENCE

Perhaps the greatest strength of online usability testing is gathering data about the entire user experience. If you only are focusing on traditional usability metrics, such as task completion or efficiency, you're missing out on a lot. There are many important facets of the broader user experience that you should consider tapping into. Remember that everything is connected. When someone is dissatisfied with their experience, it usually ties back to the effectiveness and efficiency of the design. When someone sees the brand as lacking an edge, it might tie back to specific aspects about their experience. However, despite this association, there is not a complete one-to-one correlation of performance data to subjective or attitudinal data, so collecting one metric does not replace the other.

Broadening the user experience is more than just including a wide range of metrics in the study. It is also about what you examine. There are many different lenses you can use to examine a design. For example, we have conducted studies that have specifically examined content, navigation, terminology, page layout, visual aesthetics, and awareness of specific functionality.

One of the most effective ways to broaden your perspective is through the use of "true intent" studies. By allowing users to interact with the product as they originally intended, you're more likely to capture a wider set of issues, as well as issues that users are going to be more passionate about (compared to performing a task that may or may not be relevant to them). Using open-ended questions, while harder to quantify the results, will ultimately prove more useful in capturing the broader user experience.

10.6 USE YOUR ENTIRE RESEARCH TOOLKIT

Online usability studies are not meant to replace other research techniques. We see online studies as a complement to many other valuable research techniques. Each user research method comes with its own strengths and limitations. Online usability studies are no exception. Chapter 1 reviewed some of the specific situations in which online usability testing works well and doesn't. Therefore, we strongly encourage you to take advantage of other methods and data such as traditional lab testing, card sorting, qualitative field research, market research studies, and heuristic evaluations, to name just a few. After all, we should never lose sight of the overall goal of developing a complete and accurate picture of how a product is or will be used and perceived. Ultimately, online usability testing is only one means to an end.

One of the perks of bringing other methods and data into a project is how your work is perceived. Not only will you have more credibility in what you are saying, but it will help establish or further enhance your expertise. Business sponsors and clients are less likely to pigeon-hole you as only providing traditional usability lab tests or running online usability tests. They will see you as a more versatile researcher who can draw upon a wide variety of techniques to answer a complex set of questions about user behaviors and preferences.

10.7 EXPLORE DATA

Data from online usability studies are incredibly rich. Not only may you have a wide range of quantitative data about the user's experience, but also demographic and psychographic data about the users, along with verbatim comments about their experience and attitudes. We like to think of each piece of data as a unique building block that can be put together in creative ways to tell a story about the overall user experience. One of the best uses of your time during any online usability study is to explore data. Look for interesting and unusual patterns and even try to answer business-critical questions that were not originally part of your goals. This is your chance to be creative.

Exploring data always starts with answering the basic questions stated in your research plan, such as what tasks are most problematic and why? How do different products or designs compare against each other? What is the overall usability of the product? How do different user groups compare? What is the abandonment rate of a key transaction and why? Take your time in answering these questions. Make sure you get it right. After all, answering these questions was presumably the entire motivation of the study and what your business sponsors/clients (and users!) ultimately care about most.

Once the basic questions are answered, we recommend you think about combining different variables together in interesting ways. For example, you might be interested in looking at the success rates for certain tasks by individuals who report tasks as easy, at how much time was spent (in pages or time) before someone abandoned a key transaction, or at how success correlates with satisfaction for different user groups. The possibilities are endless.

Create new variables. Start with aggregating data across tasks, such as average task success, average completion time, and average ease of use rating. Next, consider creating overall usability metrics, such as using the percentages method. Creating new variables can also be based on a set of conditions, for example, task completion times less than a minute with a task success or a top-2-box satisfaction rating with the number of pages visited less than five. There are so many new variables to create. All of your efforts should focus on the overall goal of understanding different aspects of the user experience.

10.8 SELL YOUR RESULTS

Selling your results is critical to the success of the project and should not be overlooked. Even when you have collected reliable, actionable data, your job is still not done. We have a few tips to help sell your results to your business partners or clients.

First, it is critical that you keep your results short and sweet. It's easy to fall into the trap of presenting each metric for every task and every user segment. This will no doubt overwhelm your audience. If you're running a comparative study, focus on the deltas—places where there is a significant difference between designs or products. Summarize those differences; even tell a story describing the differences between each of the products. If you are performing an in-depth analysis of a single product, try a usability scorecard or overall metric that represents the entire experience. Also, only focus on the most critical issues. Remember that your audience has a limited attention span and just wants to focus on the big problems and will worry about the rest later. If you need to include every detail, stick it in an appendix; no one will complain.

Another strong selling point, particularly in the current economy, is that online usability testing can be very cost-effective. To collect a comparable set of data through traditional methods would be very expensive in both out-of-pocket costs and labor. For example, to run 100 participants in 30-minute lab sessions would require 50 hours of lab time (well over a week straight), plus easily $5000–$10,000 in incentives. Now, what about if you needed 500 participants instead of 100 and they were in different cities? As you see, the costs quickly become unaffordable and the logistics become impractical. This doesn't even include time to set up the study or analyze the results. In contrast, you can run an online usability study for a small fraction, perhaps just a day to set up a study, $1000 in incentives, and another day to analyze and report the findings. It is even possible to go from start to finish in a single day, without spending anything on incentives.

Show off your data. You are most likely sitting on one of the richest data sets about the user experience your organization has ever collected. While you want to keep your message short and sweet, take full advantage of data. Don't simply focus on one set of metrics; bring together clickstreams, success, efficiency, satisfaction, usefulness, expectations, scorecards, verbatims, and demographic and psychographic variables. Use the whole data set to paint the complete picture of the user experience.

Similar to other user research methods, selling your results is a team effort. It's critical that you include your stakeholders in the project, such as the design team, business partners, technology, marketing, and user experience professionals. If the project is done largely in isolation, you will no doubt face many more challenges, most likely around tasks, metrics, participant recruiting, and conclusions you make about data. By including stakeholders, particularly early on in the study, you will have a much easier time selling your results.

10.9 TRUST DATA (WITHIN LIMITS)

If the results from an online usability study are not what you expected or you have some questions or concerns about the study, your sense of trust in data may be an issue. After a period of reflection and consideration, every researcher must trust his/her data and analysis. There is trust that data were collected properly, trust that the study is measuring what you intended, and trust that the participants were performing in an appropriate, engaged way.

We believe in having a healthy dose of skepticism in every study. Rarely is there a study in which all data make perfect sense. There are usually a couple of tasks that look unusual, a few metrics that don't make sense for some reason, or the responses from a group of participants that look odd. In any of these situations, we recommend you take steps to better understand why you got the data you did. The best way to do this is to replicate the tasks from the participant's perspectives to help understand data. If this is not sufficient, consider observing a group of participants go through the study or, if you have permission from the participants to contact them after the study, consider asking some follow-up questions about their experience. Once you go to this level of effort, you are likely to identify a plausible explanation for any "misbehaving" data. It's very unlikely that a large group of people would all behave the same way without any rhyme or reason.

Some people make the mistake of discounting some new results based on previously held expectations coming from past research, anecdotal evidence, or just a gut feeling. Because it is very hard to let go of expectations, there is a tendency to jump to the conclusion that some aspect of the study is flawed, and therefore the study results are not valid. This certainly could be the case. However, after performing due diligence exercises, it is best to accept and promulgate the results as valid. It is critical that you keep an open mind, and always remember that you are likely not representative of a larger user base and don't represent hundreds or thousands of users.

10.10 YOU DON'T HAVE TO BE AN EXPERT—JUST DIVE IN!

Online usability testing is simple enough for most people to run at least a basic study. It is not that much more difficult than using a basic Web application for building a generic online survey. It is getting simpler every day, with new technologies becoming available, greater choice in participant recruiting options, and more consultants and vendors with increasing expertise. It is hoped that this book has helped demystify online usability testing, making it accessible to all, regardless of background or budget. Just dive in!

We strongly encourage you to carry out your own research. Start small by planning a simple study, examining a core set of tasks and collecting a few key metrics. Work your way up over time to include more variables, perform deeper analyses, and make your findings more widely known within an organization. It's important to give yourself time and forgiveness for making mistakes. Learn by trial and error. Take advantage of people around you. Bring in subject matter experts who can help with survey design, quantitative analysis, or understanding different aspects of the design. If you need outside help, there are many consultants who will be able to assist you in any facet of an online usability study or even run the entire study for you.

Ultimately, the success of your online usability test is going to be based on the results it delivers. Online usability testing is fast becoming an indispensable tool to drive user experience strategy for many organizations. Individuals in many professions will soon start conducting their own online usability tests as demand continues to grow. Just as this research method grows in popularity, so will other user research methods. Our intention in writing this book was not just to provide you with a guide to conducting online usability tests, but, more importantly, to expand your research toolkit to help you better understand the entire user experience. We hope that you find as much value in this method as we do.

Albert, W., & Dixon, E. (2003). Is this what you expected? The use of expectation measures in usability testing. In *Proceedings of the Usability Professionals Association 2003 Conference.* Scottsdale, AZ.

Brazil, J., Jue, A., Mullins, C., & Plunkett, J. (2008, March 12). Variables that influence drop-out rates and data quality in web-based surveys. Retrieved August 24, 2009, from http://www.decipherinc.com/news/white_paper_01.pdf.

Burke Panel Quality R&D. (2008). Burke, Inc. http://www.burke.com/.

Buxton, B. (2007). *Sketching User Experiences: Getting the Design Right and the Right Design.* Burlington, MA: Morgan Kaufmann Publishers.

Chadwick-Dias, A., Tedesco, D., & Tullis, T. (2004). Older adults and Web usability: Is Web experience the same as Web expertise? In *Proceedings of ACM 2004 Conference on Computer-Human Interaction* (pp. 1391–1394).

Dillman, D. A., Smyth, J. D., & Christian, L. M. (2008). *Internet, Mail, and Mixed-Mode Surveys: The Tailored Design Method* (3rd ed). Hoboken, NJ: Wiley.

Dumas, J., & Redish, J. (1999). *A Practical Guide to Usability Testing.* Chicago, IL: Intellect.

Feldman, R., & Sanger, J. (2006). *The Text Mining Handbook: Advanced Approaches in Analyzing Unstructured Data.* Cambridge University Press.

Few, S. (2004). *Show Me the Numbers: Designing Tables and Graphs to Enlighten.* Oakland, CA: Analytics Press.

Few, S. (2006). *Information Dashboard Design: The Effective Visual Communication of Data.* Sebastopol, CA: O'Reilly Media, Inc.

Few, S. (2009). *Now You See It: Simple Visualization Techniques for Quantitative Analysis.* Analytics Press.

Fogg, B. J. (2002). *Persuasive Technology: Using Computers to Change What We Think and Do.* San Francisco, CA: Morgan Kaufmann.

Fowler, F. J. (1995). *Improving Survey Questions: Design and Evaluation (Applied Social Research Methods).* Thousand Oaks, CA: Sage Publications.

Grubbs, Frank. (1969, February). Procedures for detecting outlying observations in samples. *Technometrics, 11*(1), 1–21.

Hackos, J., & Redish, J. (1998). *User and Task Analysis for Interface Design.* New York, New York: John Wiley & Sons, Inc.

Hogg, A., & Miller, J. (2003). Study shows impact of online survey length on research findings. *Quirk's Marketing Research Review,* July/August 2003.

Holtzblatt, K., Wendell, J.B., & Wood, S. (2004). *Rapid Contextual Design: A How-to Guide to Key Techniques for User-Centered Design.* San Francisco, CA: Morgan Kaufmann.

Internet World Stats. (2009). http://www.internetworldstats.com/stats.htm. Accessed 7.24.09.

Jarrett, C. (2009, accessed). *Editing that works: Principles and resources for editing for the Web.* http://www.editingthatworks.com/.

Kaushik, A. (2007). *Web Analytics: An Hour a Day*. Indianapolis, IN: Wiley.

Krosnick, J. (1991). Response strategies for coping with the cognitive demands of attitude measures in surveys. *Applied Cognitive Psychology, 5*, 213–236.

Kuniavsky, M. (2003). *Observing the User Experience: A Practitioner's Guide to User Research*. San Francisco, CA: Morgan Kauffman.

Lewis, J. R. (1991). Psychometric evaluation of an after-scenario questionnaire for computer usability studies: The ASQ. *SIGCHI Bulletin, 23*(1), 78–81. Also see http://www.acm.org/~perlman/question.cgi?form=ASQ.

Lund, A. (2001). Measuring usability with the USE questionnaire. Usability and User Experience Newsletter of the STC Usability SIG. See http://www.stcsig.org/usability/newsletter/0110_measuring_with_use.html.

McBurney, D. H. (1994). *Research Methods*. Pacific Grove, CA: Brooks/Cole.

Millen, D. (2000). Rapid ethnography: Time deepening strategies for HCI field research. In *Proceedings of DIS '00*. (pp. 280–286). Brooklyn, New York.

Miller, J. (2006). Online marketing research. In R. Grover & M. Vriens (Eds.), *The Handbook of Marketing Research: Uses, Misuses, and Future Advances* (pp. 110–131). Thousand Oaks, CA: Sage Publications.

Nielsen, J. (1993). *Usability Engineering*. San Francisco, CA: Morgan Kaufmann.

Plain Language Action and Information Network. (2009, accessed). *Plain language: Improving communications from the federal government to the public*. http://www.plainlanguage.gov/.

Redish, J. (2007). *Letting Go of the Words: Writing Web Content That Works*. Boston, MA: Morgan Kaufmann.

Rubin, J., & Chisnell, D. (2008). *Handbook of Usability Testing: How to Plan, Design, and Conduct Effective Tests*. Indianapolis, IN: Wiley.

Satmetrix Systems. (2008). *Net Promoter Score® (NPS)*. http://www.netpromoter.com/site/.

Sauro, J., & Lewis, J. (2005). Estimating completion rates from small samples using binomial confidence intervals: Comparisons and recommendations. In *Proceedings of the Human Factors and Ergonomics Society Annual Meeting*. Orlando, FL.

Spangler, S., & Kreulen, J. (2007). *Mining the Talk: Unlocking the Business Value in Unstructured Information*. IBM Press.

Stat Trek: Teach Yourself Statistics. (2009, accessed). http://stattrek.com/Reading/Sampling.aspx.

Survey Sampling International. (2007). *Understanding Respondent Motivation*. Retrieved December 18, 2008 from http://www.surveysampling.com/files/imce/_paper_9_Understanding_respondent_motivation.pdf.

Tedesco, D., & Tullis, T. (2006). A comparison of methods for eliciting post-task subjective ratings in usability testing. In *Proceedings of the Usability Professionals Association Conference*. June 12–16, Broomfield, CO.

Tullis, T., & Albert, B. (2008). *Measuring the User Experience: Collecting, Analyzing, and Presenting Usability Metrics*. Burlington, MA: Morgan Kaufmann.

Tullis, T., & Stetson, J. (2004). A comparison of questionnaires for assessing Website usability. In *Usability Professionals Association Conference*. June 7–11, Minneapolis, MN.

Printed and bound by CPI Group (UK) Ltd, Croydon, CR0 4YY

03/10/2024

01040319-0009